▶ Time Is of the Essence:
Learning in Schools

Sarah H. Huyvaert
Eastern Michigan University

Allyn and Bacon
Boston • London • Toronto • Sydney • Tokyo • Singapore

AHE8333

Senior editor: Virginia Lanigan
Series editorial assistant: Kris Lamarre
Advertising manager: Anne Morrison
Manufacturing buyer: Suzanne Lareau

Copyright © 1998 by Allyn & Bacon
A Viacom Company
Needham Heights, MA 02194

Internet: www.abacon.com
America Online: keyword: College Online

Library of Congress Cataloging-in-Publication Data

Huyvaert, Sarah H., date
    Time is of the essence : learning in schools / Sarah H. Huyvaert.
      p.   cm.
    Includes bibliographical references and index.
    ISBN 0-205-17150-8
    1. Schedules, School—United States. 2. School year—United
States. 3. School day—United States. 4. Learning. I. Title.
  LB3032.H89 1997 *1998*
  371.2′4′0973—DC21   97-24730
                                                     CIP

Printed in the United States of America

10 9 8 7 6 5 4 3 2 1   01 00 99 98 97

Contents

▶

List of Tables and Figures

List of Figures

▶

Foreword

Since the 1984 publication of the landmark report *A Nation at Risk*, American public education has been under a microscope. The report spoke eloquently and disturbingly about "a rising tide of mediocrity" sweeping the nation's schools. It concluded that the quality of education and the quality of life in America were inextricably linked, and that both were in jeopardy.

Since the publication of *A Nation at Risk*, there have been many other reports, commissions and blue ribbon panels, and national conferences on the subject of education reform, providing a continuous supply of editorial fodder for the media and a sturdy platform for politicians to stand on. President George Bush launched America 2000, whose six national goals for education reform were so indisputable and bipartisan that they were adopted wholesale by his Democratic successor, Bill Clinton. Clinton's 1996 reelection to the Presidency was fueled in large part by his persistent effort to represent himself as "the education president."

Despite almost universal agreement on the need for education reform, there has been widespread disagreement over the nature of the problem. Some people argue that the trouble lies with the curriculum, which has been variously criticized as too comprehensive, too lax, too politically correct, or too narrow and doctrinaire. Others claim it is our teachers who are at fault—they need more solid academic training or they need more practical training in pedagogy. Still others point the finger of blame at superficial or slanted textbooks, or the obsession with TV and video games, or absent working parents, or inadequate salaries for teachers, or bloated class sizes and school populations, or inadequate school discipline.

The list of potential causes is nearly endless and reminds us of the story of the school board member whose daughter was failing algebra. The board member complained to the superintendent, demanding that something be done about the quality of instruction in his district. The superintendent explained that the problem lay with the principal, who was known to run a loose ship. "I'll have a talk with her," he promised.

When he confronted the principal, she explained that the girl's algebra teacher was ineffective in the classroom, but there was little she could do because the teacher enjoyed ironclad job security. But she would have a talk with him nevertheless.

The algebra teacher denied all responsibility, saying that the young woman simply would not do her homework. "In a case like this," he said, "it's the parents who are to blame. We can't force students to do their homework if their parents won't cooperate. But her mother is coming in tomorrow for a parent–teacher conference. I'll have a talk with her."

The next day he confronted the girl's mother, who defended herself. "I do the best I can with my daughter," she protested, "but you don't know what I'm up against. You should meet her father's side of the family."

The diagnosis of the malaise affecting K–12 education has been as various and complex as the solutions that have been proposed: We need less rote memorization and more critical thinking; we need active learning, cooperative learning, school uniforms, same-sex schools, charter schools, continuous quality improvement, community-centered management, alternative schools, less tracking and more mainstreaming, more mentoring, more parent involvement, more equitable funding formulas, and so on.

Having worked at all levels of education—as school teacher, principal, administrator in two-year and four-year colleges, and now as President of a large, comprehensive state university—I wonder if the problem is as complicated as we have made it seem. Over the course of almost 30 years spent in various educational institutions, I have observed many changes. But one of them has occurred so gradually and inexorably that we have scarcely noticed it.

The academic segment of the school day has become shorter and shorter. And, in some instances, the length of the school day and year have diminished. At the same time, the list of tasks we have given our teachers and school administrators has become longer and longer and the tasks that have to do with learning have become fewer and fewer.

Is it possible we have simply stretched the mandate of our schools beyond the breaking point? Have we made time the constant and learning the variable, instead of the reverse?

In 1991 Congress passed the Education Council Act, creating the National Education Commission on Time and Learning. I was honored to serve on this nine-member commission, which was charged with examining the relation between time and learning in America's schools and reporting our findings to Congress and the Secretary of Education. After two years of study, discussion, school visits, fact-finding missions to Japan and Germany, survey research, and national hearings, we arrived at a sobering but inescapable conclusion: Time is the missing element in our national debate about learning and higher standards for our nation's schools. We have been asking the impossible of our students—that they learn as much as their foreign peers despite spending only half as much time on core academic subjects. America's teachers and pupils, we concluded, have become Prisoners of Time.

Throughout the history of American public higher education, we have treated time as invariable and learning as the variable. In the nineteenth century, the American school year, with its summer hiatus and recesses at planting, harvesting, and hunting times, was designed around the reality of the heat of urban summers and agrarian life, long walks between village and farm, and the major Christian holidays. With the Industrial Revolution, the national calendar changed, but the school calendar did not. We have continued to rely on a "school year" that is really less than half a year (180 days) and a school day of five to six hours, despite the electronic revolution and the explosion of knowledge it has brought. As our report states, learning continues to be defined "by bells, buses, and vacations instead of standards for students and learning,"

Education reform has been an urgent priority for me. My own institution, Eastern Michigan University, was founded nearly 150 years ago as a "normal school," charged with establishing and ensuring "norms" for the preparation of teachers. Even though we have evolved over the years into a large, comprehensive state university, teacher preparation remains a major part of our mission. More education personnel graduate from Eastern Michigan than from any other institution in the United States, usually by a wide margin.

Accordingly, we call ourselves The Learning University. We want our students to graduate with a "learning edge." The measurements we value are not so much the learning students bring with them when they enter the university, but the added learning they have acquired by the time they graduate. We have launched a major initiative called Barriers to Learning in which we are systematically identifying those barriers of time, space, and process that prevent students from learning as much as they are able. Whether these barriers are a class schedule that is out of synch with the work schedule of an adult learner, or a registration process that robs students of time that might be spent at the library, or an instructional delivery system that requires students to drive sixty miles to campus instead of using distance-learning facilities in their home town, we try to identify the barrier and then lower it or remove it altogether.

Sarah Huyvaert, a distinguished member of Eastern's faculty, has been instrumental not only in our own efforts to identify and remove barriers to learning at Eastern Michigan University, but also in the work of the National Education Commission on Time and Learning. Her testimony at Commission hearings and the background research she conducted for the Commission had a profound and lasting influence on our work.

In *Time Is of the Essence: Learning in Schools* she provides a comprehensive study of the problem of time and learning. First, by reviewing the relevant research, she clears away the underbrush and debunks the myths that have obstructed our understanding of the issues surrounding time and learning. Yes, more time spent on a subject does result in more learning about that subject, and higher standards for academic performance will require more time for learning. Yes, some students do need more time to learn than others, more time is needed for some subjects than others, and some learning strategies are more time-consuming than others, and their value and permanence must be measured against the time they require. And yes, there is no such thing as a free school lunch: As our expectations of our schools increase, so must the length of the school day and school year increase accordingly along with the time available for our teachers to prepare.

Nonacademic activities, Huyvaert points out, are devouring the fixed amount of time available in our schools for learning. Our own commission discovered that nonacademic activities now account for nearly 50 percent of the time a students spends in school. Yet new nonacademic mandates continue to be imposed on our schools without any thought being given to compensatory time, just as federal mandates on the states are passed into law without any budget provisions to pay for them.

Professor Huyvaert, in *Time Is of the Essence: Learning in Schools*, provides an historical context for the issues, an extensive review of significant research on time and learning, disturbing depictions of the erosion of actual learning time, and possible approaches to addressing the challenge. She effectively makes the case for factoring time into educational reform.

Nevertheless, as Huyvaert is quick to point out, time itself "is not the culprit, the savior, or the foe." Simply adding time to the school calendar, like throwing money at our schools, is a simplistic solution to a difficult problem. Huyvaert makes the point that time is just one element, albeit an important one, in an equation complicated by personal concerns, site-specific problems, and conditions of the moment.

I am stealing her thunder now, but there is plenty more of it in Professor Huyvaert's book, and a good deal of lightning, too. I have read it from cover to cover, and I urge everyone concerned with the current state of American education to do the same. Education reform—it's about time!

William E. Shelton
President, Eastern Michigan University

▶ 1

The Issue of School Time

Time has always been of concern in education and, as anyone who has served on a negotiating team can tell you, it remains one of the most feverishly discussed issues in education today. "What time should the school day begin and end?" "How many days should children attend school and how many vacation days do they need?" "How many days should be scheduled for teacher planning and how much time should be dedicated to parent/teacher conferences?" "Should we adhere to the minimum number of days mandated by the state or do we schedule additional days?" "What do we do about the days schools have to be closed because of unforeseen problems such as bad weather, water pipes breaking, or fires?" "Do we go to school year-round or do we follow a more conventional calendar?" These, and other schedule-related questions, arise year after year.

Time-related questions reach far beyond those associated with the school schedule. Educators often find themselves asking questions such as "How can we find time for all of the material we are expected to cover?" "How do I find time to prepare for the school day?" "How can we reduce the interruptions in the classroom so that we spend more time on teaching and less on non-teaching activities?" "When should we introduce a particular topic?" "At what age should a child begin school?" "How do we make better use of the school day?"

Like many significant questions in education, finding answers to time-related questions is seldom easy, especially if disparate groups are doing the seeking. The questions, and their subsequent answers, are greatly influenced by curriculum theory, management needs, budget constraints, learning theory, educational philosophy, knowledge of human growth and development, special needs of the student population, community concerns, site-specific problems, and conditions of the moment. These last four elements—special needs of the student population, community concerns, site-specific problems, and conditions of the moment—dictate the need to reexamine the questions year-after-year and district-by-district.

Even though this reexamination may be frustrating and seem pointless at times, research, professional intuition, and common wisdom all validate the importance of questioning how time is being used in school. Both research and practice have confirmed that:

1. An increase in the amount of *time* spent on an academic subject can increase academic achievement in that subject area.
2. *Time* can be used more effectively and efficiently in almost every classroom.
3. Students vary in the amount of *time* they need for learning.
4. Different instructional strategies require different amounts of *time*.
5. More rigorous standards of achievement require that students spend more *time* in learning.
6. As the responsibilities of schools increase, more *time* is needed for schooling.
7. Restructuring of schools requires that teachers' *time* be spent differently.

TIME AS A BARRIER TO SCHOOL IMPROVEMENT

Recognizing the importance of time in school learning, the United States Congress established the National Education Commission on Time and Learning (NECTL) to examine the quality and adequacy of the time spent on study and learning by students in the United States. As a result of their intensive two-year study, the commissioners, in their final report, *Prisoners of Time*, concluded that "Time is the missing element in our great national debate about learning and the need for higher standards for all students" (NECTL, 1994, p. 4). They went on to identify five time-related characteristics of schools that create formidable barriers for those who wish to reform the school of today. These barriers include:

- the fixed nature of the school clock and calendar
- the large amount of school time spent on nonacademic activities
- the lack of sufficient academic time that is required for students if they are to meet world-class standards
- a schedule that is unresponsive to the needs of a changing society
- educators who have not been provided with enough time to do their jobs properly

The first barrier identified was the "fixed clock and calendar." According to the commission, the fixed school schedule is a fundamental design flaw that leads to the assumption that learning can be "doled out by the clock and defined by the calendar." Almost every teacher knows the frustration of being controlled by the clock. There is nothing more frustrating for a teacher than to be working with a student who is struggling with a concept and to have the bell ring just as the student begins to understand the concept. The type of instructional activities chosen, the length of the final exam, and the amount of time devoted to the adjustment of instruction to the needs of the individual are limited by the number of minutes available in the class period. In addition, instructional decisions are closely regulated by the calendar as well as the clock. It is not unusual for the amount of time left before an upcoming school vacation to influence the length of an instructional unit, the introduction of new concepts, and/or the type of instructional activities that a teacher assigns. Not only does the calendar influence instructional decisions, it often serves to undermine attempts at authentic educational assessments because it is used as a key indicator of educational progress. Statements such as "Tommy is reading at the second grade level" or "Sally is in second semester algebra" tell us little about what the students know or what they have learned, but rather how much material they have covered based on a time-defined criterion. Teachers know that students learn at different rates, and this professional knowledge is supported by research. Yet, in many classrooms, students are allotted a specific amount of time to master key concepts and this time is determined by the clock and calendar rather than by individual rates of learning. Even in classrooms where teachers attempt to make allowances for individual needs, the fixed nature of the clock and calendar serve to restrict what happens in the classroom. This is because typical class periods are still made up of 55-minute sessions, scheduled vacations interrupt the continuity of instruction, and student progress is evaluated, in part, by the time they have spent in school. Hence, the fundamental design flaw inherent in a fixed schedule leads to learning being "doled out by the clock and defined by the calendar."

The second barrier to school reform identified by the NECTL is the number of nonacademic activities that are incorporated into the "school day." The Commissioners found that nonacademic activities now account for up to 50 percent of the time a student spends in school. It is self-evident that time is a non-replenishable, finite resource, and any time spent on nonacademic activities is subtracted from time that could be spent on academic activities. If it is true that an increase in the amount of time spent on an academic subject can increase academic achievement in that subject, it follows that the time spent on nonacademic activities may have a negative impact on achievement. Many would argue that this is what is happening in our schools today.

Even though only 50 percent of the school day is spent on academic subjects, there is an increasing demand for higher academic standards for students. This leads to a third barrier to school reform that was identified by the commission—lack of sufficient time for students to meet world-class standards. The commissioners have stated unequivocally that, "The American people and their educators need to be very clear about the standards movement. *It is not time free* [emphasis added]." (NECTL, 1994, p. 21). According to professional organizations, the new standards that have been established in the areas of geography, foreign languages, and the arts can only be met if additional time is allocated for these areas. The new standards call for a more demanding curriculum in the traditional core academic areas of math, science, and language arts, and this more demanding curriculum necessitates that a greater emphasis be placed on cooperative learning, problem solving, experiential learning, and critical thinking. As Marvin Pasch, Department Head of Teacher Education at Eastern Michigan University, has noted:

> The greater the scope of learning, that is, the number of outcomes we hope to achieve, the more time that will be required to accomplish them. Furthermore, the more penetrating the depth of study into a particular topical area, the more learning time that will be required. The same is true in respect to the level of complexity we demand from students in their response to a topical area. A requirement that students recall information previously taught is less exhaustive of time than is a demand that students apply that information to solve unfamiliar, real-life problems. The latter requires practice activities that devour classroom time (Pasch, 1993, p. 1).

Overcoming the barrier of insufficient time to meet world-class standards might be as simple as adding minutes to the school day or days to the school year. However, the problem is much more complicated when considered in light of a fourth barrier to school reform—a school schedule that is unresponsive to the changing needs of society. The NECTL asserts that "students bring many more problems to school than children did a generation ago. Today's students receive less support outside school and increasingly exhibit destructive behavior ranging from drug and alcohol abuse to gang membership and precocious sexual activity" (NECTL, 1994, p. 16). The commission goes on to note that "It is clear that schools cannot be all things to all people—teachers cannot be parents, police officers, physicians, and addiction or employment counselors. But neither can they ignore massive problems" (p. 17). The implication is that it is becoming more and more critical for schools to consider and address the needs of the whole child. Linking this implication to an "unresponsive school schedule" suggests that school time must be allocated not only to meeting the intellectual needs of our students but to meeting their social, emotional, and physical needs as well. It can be argued that while this may not be a *new* responsibility for the schools, it certainly represents an increased responsibility and, as the responsibilities of schools increase, more time is needed for schooling. In recognition of this, the NECTL recommended that we "keep schools open longer to meet the needs of children and communities" (p. 34). This raises a number of questions: "What are the needs we are trying to meet?" "Are the needs related to providing additional support for children or are they related to achieving higher academic standards?" "If the needs are composed of a combination of the two, then how do we allocate the additional school time?"

These are difficult questions to answer, but one thing that does seem certain is that "we don't want more of the same"—we want our schools to be reformed or restructured. However, the NECTL is concerned that "Adding school reform to the list of things schools must accomplish, without recognizing that time in the current calendar is a limited resource, trivializes the effort" (NECTL, 1994, p. 19). Time is a limited resource for educators as well as students, and just as school time has been depleted for students, so also has it been depleted for teachers and other educators. The commission believes that the current school calendar does not provide educators with the time they need to do their job properly—especially in the area of school reform—and they recognize this lack of time as the fifth barrier to school reform. School reform demands, among other things, that educators have time to plan the reorganization of the school structure, time to design and develop curriculum and lesson plans that adhere to the new standards, and time to develop worthwhile partnerships with the community so that schools are responsive to societal needs.

Because time plays such a prominent role in school reform, it is easy to understand how the issues embodied in the concept of school time can become trivialized. It often appears that policy makers believe the issues can be resolved by simply providing for additional school time without ever confronting the complexity of the issues involved. The primary focus of the NECTL report, as is true of other reform reports and research studies that deal with time and learning, is on learning, and ways of *using time to improve learning*. It is important to realize that time is not the culprit, the savior, or the foe. Nonetheless, time can, and often does, become the catalyst for massive change and, for this reason, the NECTL has declared that "The reform movement of the last decade is destined to founder unless it is harnessed to more time for learning (NECTL, 1994, p. 4)

TIME AS A SOLUTION IN SCHOOL REFORM

The interest in "harnessing" school reform to "more time for learning" is not new. In 1967, for example, Holmes and Seawell observed that reforming schools by changing the school calendar was "one of the oldest 'new ideas' in education." Although this observation was made over a quarter of a century ago, it still rings true today. Throughout history, the arguments for changing the school schedule have revolved around the educational issue of the moment. Consider, for instance, these arguments.

At present we are permitting the great majority of American children to go out into the world as unskilled laborers . . . This is an evil that must be cured by a serious modification of the program at the elementary and secondary school. And this is not an impossibility, because Germany, France, Switzerland, and Belgium can all show this thing as actually done.

However, whoever advocates the introduction of more concrete work and the elements of industrial training into the public schools will meet with three objections: (1) there is no time for more subjects; (2) the present amount of instruction in the so-called academic subjects is inadequate and ought not to be reduced; (3) instruction in industrial subjects and in applied science is costly and there is not enough money for what is already being done.

To meet the first objection, the best way is to increase the school time per day and per year. . . . The increased time per day and per year would also remove any necessity for reducing the academic or cultural elements" (Garber, 1911, p. 345)

We talk of individual differences but smash human lives between the grindstones of our fixed times, terms, and grades. (Roe, 1930, p. 6)

The school day, week, and year must be extended if the school is to do its part in providing educational, vocational, cultural, and recreational opportunities for the community it serves. ... if the school is to serve its present clientele more adequately and extend its service to other groups, the school session must be lengthened. (Henry, 1945, p. 300)

Today, children have a greater need for a high quality and flexible educational program than at any time in history. Although the public demands more services from educational institutions, the necessary economic and financial support is severely limited by over-burdened governmental budgets and taxpayer resistance. (From a feasibility report prepared for the Freeland, MI Community Schools, 1969–70, p. 421)

The necessity for using all available educational resources to the best possible advantage and a concern for finding ways to teach more and to teach it better have stood out clearly in the recent nationwide discussion of educational problems. . . . If the signs of the time can be read with any degree of accuracy, they clearly indicate need in the years to come for more highly developed skills, more technical information, and a broader range of vision and understanding on the part of every citizen.

To the practical-minded citizen, the hardheaded businessman, or the anxious parent who desperately wants broader and better educational opportunities for his children, the year-round school makes a lot of sense (American Association of School Administrators, 1970, pgs. 7–8).

The arguments for altering time allocation as a way of increasing school efficiency and improving instructional programs have remained relatively stable. Close examination of these quotations demonstrates the persistency of the five time-related barriers that were identified by the NECTL. Four of the five barriers—the fixed school schedule, inadequate time for academic subjects, increased demands being placed on the schools, and the need for higher academic standards—are reflected within these quotations that span seven decades. One of the reasons for the intractable nature of time-related problems is that additional time has been seen as a solution to the problems rather than lack of time being seen as an indicator of the problems. Consider, for instance, that in 1911 the problem was an unskilled workforce, in 1930 the problem was meeting the needs of the individual, in 1945 and 1969 the problem was the public's demand for more services from educational institutions, and in 1970 the problem was the need to teach more and to teach it better. In each of these cases the lack of time was an indicator of the problem—there was inadequate time for academic subjects, the fixed schedule didn't allow for individualization, there was not enough time to meet the increased demands placed on educational institutions, and time was not being used to its best possible advantage. Time was also offered as a solution to the problems—increase school time (1911), extend of the school day, week, and year (1945), and adopt a plan for year-round school (1970). Education has often been accused of "throwing money" at problems. In these cases, it was time that was the weapon of choice. Educational literature is replete with instances in which time has been used as the solution to educational problems. Summer schools have been employed to address the increasing demands on public schools; the school year has been extended in an effort to increase the amount of instructional time required by an exploding curriculum; a four-day school week was employed in Colorado as a way of dealing with the energy crisis in the 1970s; and year-round schools have been used by numerous districts throughout the nation to reduce the impact of overcrowding in schools. In some instances these attempted solutions worked, and in other instances they did not. The reason for the inconsistent results is quite simple—schools are, by nature and design, complex systems. A *system* is composed of a set of interacting elements that operate together to achieve some goal or purpose. A *complex system* is one that is composed of a complicated or involved arrangement of elements that are interconnected over time and activity (Huyvaert, 1985). Because of this complicated arrangement of interconnected elements, including personal concerns, site-specific problems, and conditions of the moment, solutions work in some districts and not in others, or work one year and not the next.

The complexity of the interaction between time and activity is one reason why time use holds such a fascination for educational researchers and policy makers. Examining how time is used in education, combined with an examination of the arguments that are presented for how time should be used, provides us with insight into the critical educational issues of the day and helps us to evaluate the magnitude of the issues. The insight gained through this process aids in the understanding of the relationship between time and learning in school and serves to inform those who wish to improve the educational system.

RESEARCH FINDINGS

One of the first educational research studies was undertaken by Ebbinghaus to determine the relationship between the amount of time (number of trials) a subject would need to learn a list of nonsense syllables. He would repeat the experiment after a time delay to see how much time it would take to "relearn" the list (Schunk, 1991, p. 14). Subsequent to this very simplistic study conducted in the late 1800s, there have been a myriad of studies conducted on time and learning, and, over the last several decades, educators increasingly have directed their attention toward the use of time in education.

In 1963, John Carroll introduced his "Model of School Learning." This model is considered to be one of the definitive models in the study of time and learning. Carroll believed that achievement was directly influenced by the amount of time a student spent working on a learning task. He defined the learning task as the task of "going from ignorance of some specific fact or concept to knowledge or understanding of it, or of proceeding from incapability of performing some specified act to capability of performing it" (p. 723). In the model he postulated that "the learner will succeed in learning a given task to the extent that he (sic) spends the amount of time that he (sic) needs to learn the task" (p. 715). If the time available for learning (opportunity to learn) was less than the time a student needed or if the student was unwilling to spend the time needed to learn the task, learning would be less than complete. The model can be represented by the following formula:

Degree of learning = f (time spent ÷ time needed)

The amount of time a student needs for learning is affected by the learner's aptitude for the subject, his or her ability to understand the instruction, and the quality of the instruction received. The amount of time a student spends in learning is a function of the amount of time allowed for the learning task and the degree to which the student is willing to persevere with (stick to) the task. The implication that can be drawn from the Model of School Learning is that if a student is forced to adhere to certain time limits or blocks—which is the case in most classrooms—and if this time is less than the time the student needs, then the student will be unable to reach his or her learning potential.

Benjamin Bloom (1974b), building on the work of Carroll, developed the theory of Learning for Mastery. Bloom maintained that time spent, in and of itself, was not enough to explain the difference in student achievement (Bloom, 1974a) Research had demonstrated that variations in pupil engagement were highly predictive of student achievement and accounted for as much as 20 percent of the differentiation in achievement. Based on this research, Bloom postulated that several factors affected the amount of time a student is engaged with an activity, not the least of which is the quality of instruction. The quality of instruction is dependent upon four factors: (1) instructional cues, (2) reinforcement, (3) type of student participation, and (4) feedback and correction.

Bloom also believed that the timing of instruction was just as important as the amount and quality of time spent engaged with a learning task. Bloom concluded that the timing of initial instruction, the timing of testing and feedback, the timing of guided practice, and the timing of the progression to the next step all had an effect on how much time a student would need in order to reach mastery.

Both Carroll's Model for School Learning and Bloom's model of Learning for Mastery were supported by the Beginning Teachers Evaluation Study (BTES) conducted by the Far West Laboratory between 1972 and 1978. The original intent of the study was to identify ways in which the behaviors of first-year teachers differed from more experienced teachers in the teaching of second- and fifth-grade reading and math (Fisher et al. 1978). As the study progressed, however, the focus changed to behaviors that separated successful teachers from less successful teachers. The one characteristic of successful teachers that remained consistent throughout the multi-year study was what the researchers called *academic learning time* (ALT). ALT refers to the amount of time a student spends successfully working on an academically relevant task. ALT can be represented by the following formula:

ALT = f(allocated time, engaged rate, error rate, task relevance)

In this formula, *allocated time* is a function of school time and classroom management and is very similar to Carroll's "opportunity to learn." Allocated time is dependent not only on how much time is provided for a certain subject, such as reading, but also on how much of the reading time is lost due to the management functions such as discipline, attendance, resource management, and other non-instructional activities. *Engaged rate* is the proportion of time a student actually spends working on an activity. This is equivalent to the "time spent" in Carroll's model. *Error rate*, as the name implies, is the number of errors a student makes when working on an activity. In the original model, this was referred to as "success rate," but when placed into practice the term more commonly used was error rate. Error rate is assessed in three broad categories—low error rate, medium error rate, and high error rate. A low error rate means that most of the student's errors are due to carelessness. A high error rate means that most of the student's successes are due to chance. Medium error rate means that a student understands enough to make some correct responses but also commits errors because of lack of understanding. *Task relevance* is the degree to which the task in which a student is engaged contributes to meeting the learning objective. The researchers found that ALT was increased when (1) there were high levels of interactive teaching with frequent feedback, (2) the teacher's directions were clear and the students knew how to proceed when their work was finished, (3) the teacher accurately diagnosed student skill levels, and (4) the students were given learning experiences of the appropriate difficulty. Accordingly, the study concluded that teachers and administrators must be concerned with how much time is spent on learning, how much time is available for learning, the nature of the task, and the developmental learning level of the student.

Since the development of these three models—Model of School Learning, Learning for Mastery and Academic Learning Time—numerous studies have been conducted on the relationship between time and learning. (See for instance Wiley & Harnischfeger, 1974; Anderson, 1984; Karweit, 1988; Gettinger, 1990). An overwhelming majority of the studies have found a direct and positive relationship between time and learning, and, as Borg and Gall have noted, "The consistency of results indicates that amount of instructional time reliably increases student learning: the more instructional time, the more students learn. The effect has been found by many researchers in many school systems" (Borg & Gall, 1983, pgs. 5 & 9).

CLASSIFICATIONS OF SCHOOL TIME

In spite of the seemingly conclusive nature of the time and learning research, some will argue that the results of the research are confusing and even contradictory at times. The conflict, and hence the debate, over the effects of time to learn arises in part because those who review the literature on time and learning often treat "time" as a single variable. However, *four different* "time" variables are identified in the research, and it is seldom that any one research study will address all four variables. Frequently, the findings from one study are generalized and compared to the findings of another study without verifying that the two studies examined the same time variable(s). Therefore, the confusion arises from the interpretation of the research rather than from the research itself.

When reviewing literature or interpreting research findings, it is important to understand the different time classifications (levels) and the relationships between the classifications. The diagram shown in Figure 1–1, and corresponding discussion, should serve as an aid in comparing and contrasting the different levels of time usage.

The first level is *scheduled time*. This is the time represented by the school calendar and includes the number of hours in the day and the number of days in the year (e.g., 180 6-hour days). Increasing scheduled time will not necessarily increase academic achievement.

The second level, *allocated time*, is the time that is assigned to a specific subject (e.g., Algebra I meets 5 days a week for 55-minutes). Allocated time may be affected by such things as a school-wide assembly or a snow day. Increasing allocated time in a particular content area tends to result in some increase in academic achievement in that area, but the amount of the increase is difficult, if not impossible, to predict. In addition, allocating time to one subject will reduce the amount of time that can be allocated to the other subjects.

The third level of time usage is *engaged rate*. This is the amount of time that a student spends working on a task assigned by the teacher. Engaged rate is also referred to as time-on-task. If the first ten minutes of a 55-minute class period are devoted to attendance taking and announcements and the last five minutes to cleaning up, the student engaged rate is 40 minutes. Engaged rate will vary from student to student and can be affected by such things as a fire drill, a disruptive student, an announcement over the public address system,

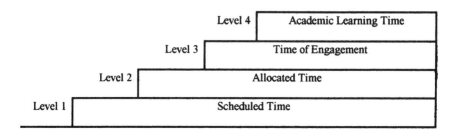

FIGURE 1–1   Levels of school time

or a wandering mind. Typically, an increase in engaged rate results in some increase in academic achievement, but this is not always true. If a student is involved with an inappropriate learning task, we can be almost certain that academic achievement will either be unaffected or negatively affected.

The fourth level of time usage is *academic learning time*. Academic learning time is the amount of time a student spends engaged in an academically relevant task in which he or she experiences a high degree of success. There is a direct, positive relationship between academic learning time and academic achievement. Notice that academic learning time differs from engaged rate. At the engaged-rate level, the task may or may not be relevant and the student may or may not be successful at the task, whereas with academic learning time the student is successful with a relevant learning task. If a student spends more time on a relevant learning task and is successful at that task, achievement increases.

Being able to distinguish between scheduled time and allocated time is especially important when making decisions about school schedules and time allocation. If a school district were to lengthen the school day to seven hours and extend the school year to 220 days, as recommended by the Commission on Excellence in Education, for instance, it is quite possible that there would be no change in the academic achievement of the students within the district. The conclusion could be drawn that time has little or no effect on learning. The same could hold true if math scores did not go up after a district chose to follow the National Council of Teachers of Mathematics' recommendation and increased the amount of time students spent on mathematics. However, both conclusions may be inaccurate. What is true is that scheduled time alone has little or no effect on learning and allocated time may not have as dramatic an impact as would be desired. Decisions to change the school schedule and/or the way time is allocated within the school schedule often prove to be "political hotcakes." It is imperative, therefore, that decision makers understand the limited degree to which each of these strategies can affect achievement before any decision is made to change the school schedule or the time allocation.

Likewise, it is important to separate academic learning time from engaged rate when evaluating the quality of instructional time in the classroom. Distinguishing between engaged rate and academic learning time is a more difficult task than distinguishing between scheduled time and allocated time. To the casual observer, the activities of the students who have a high engagement rate will look very similar to activities of the students who are involved in academic learning time. To an experienced observer, however, it soon will become apparent that there is a difference in the relevance of the learning tasks and the degrees of success that the students are experiencing with these tasks. Working with teachers to ensure that the majority of classroom time is at the academic learning time level is one of the surest ways to increase the academic achievement levels of the students within a building.

But remember, academic learning time can only increase to the level of engaged rate, engaged rate can only increase to the level of allocated time, and allocated time can only be increased to the level of scheduled time. If time is already being used at, or near, its highest level of efficiency, an increase in scheduled time and/or allocated time will be required in order to increase the academic learning time of our students.

MYTHS ASSOCIATED WITH TIME AND LEARNING

Just as educational decision makers will need to become more astute at differentiating between the different levels of time use, they also will need to be able to separate fact from fiction regarding school time. In 1974b, Benjamin Bloom, reflecting on the fact that time had just recently become a central variable in the study of schooling, noted that:

> While on the surface this does not seem to be a drastic change, I regard it as one of the most fundamental shifts in our attempt to study school learning. It forces us to look again more directly at aspects of learning that have long been buried under a mass of publications and dogma about education in the schools. It once again raises questions for which we thought we had most of the answers, but for which we had developed a mythology that served to dull our perceptions of phenomena taking place before us (Bloom, 1974b, p. 684)

Unfortunately, over the last twenty years a new mythology related to school time and learning has begun to develop. Following are seven of the more common myths associated with time and learning.

1. The current school calendar that sets aside June, July, and August for summer vacation grew out of the needs of an agricultural society.
2. The traditional school schedule is composed of 180, six-hour days.
3. Worldwide, those countries that have more than 180 school days do better academically than do students in the United States.
4. Concerns, issues, and conditions of education and schooling are different today, giving rise to the need for change in the schools.
5. Year-round education means that children spend more time in school than they would with a nine or ten month schedule.
6. Children actually spend less time on academic subjects today because of all of the nonacademic subjects that are included in the schedule.
7. All of the research, talk, and general hype about time and learning has had no real effect in the classroom.

So that these myths do not "dull our perceptions of phenomena taking place before us," it is important that we examine each myth and the misconceptions that are associated with it.

Myth: *The current school calendar that sets aside June, July, and August for summer vacation grew out of the needs of an agricultural society.*

This is probably the most widely accepted of the myths. In 1917, J. Wilmer Kennedy, assistant city superintendent for Newark, New Jersey public schools, noted that the three-month summer vacation was "a modern growth." In 1866 students in New York had one month of summer vacation. Students in Newark had three weeks of vacation in April and another three in October. In the early 1900s schools in Buffalo, Baltimore, Cincinnati, and Chicago operated for at least eleven months per year while many rural schools operated on a shorter four- to-five-month calendar (Alam, 1970).

Early educational writing indicated that for children in the country, spring was the time they returned to school, not the beginning of an extended vacation as many now assume. In an early edition of *Primary Education*, A. C. Scammell wrote: "By the calendar of country children, spring begins the first or second Monday in April, according to the conditions of the roads. For schools re-open after two months or possibly the entire winter's vacation" (March 1896 p. 99) In the Thirty-Fifth Annual Report of the Superintendent of Public Instruction of the State of Michigan (1872), it was noted that ". . . being chained in the schoolroom . . . during those hot, sultry, scorching summer months, is anything but pleasant." (p. 9–10) and it was recommended that the school vacation be changed from September and October to July and August. There was no mention of the need for students to be available to help with planting, harvesting, or any of the other chores associated with the agricultural society.

One of the major reasons for the establishment of the nine-month calendar was the growth of state Departments of Education. In an attempt to standardize education throughout their state, many Departments of Education commenced to mandate the minimum number of days in the school year and, as a result, city schools gradually began operating for shorter periods of time while rural areas increased the length of the school year. It wasn't until 1915 that, with some variations, the present nine-month school was established in both urban and rural areas throughout the nation (Alam, 1970).

Myth: *The traditional school schedule is composed of 180, six-hour days.*

There is no such thing as a traditional schedule. In 1980, according to the Education Commission of the States, the number of mandated days varied from 150 in Arkansas to 190 in New York. In 1990 the number of days varied from 174 in Missouri to 182 in Ohio. According to data compiled by the Council of Chief State School Officers, there was even wider variation in the number of hours that students were required to be in school during the day. For instance, at the ninth grade, the New Jersey mandate calls for students to be in school four hours a day while Texas requires students to attend for seven hours.

Myth: *Worldwide, those countries that have more than 180 school days do better academically than do students in the United States.*

The International Association for the Evaluation of Education Achievement (IEA, 1987) ranked the academic achievement and the length of the school year for 20 nations. The rankings (see Table 1–1) demonstrate that the number of school days alone cannot account for the differences in levels of

TABLE 1–1   International comparison of academic rank of students by time allocated

Country	Length of school year	Rank in academic achievement	Number of hours of math instruction per year	Rank In math achievement
Japan	243	1	101	1
Israel	216	15	130	15
Luxembourg	216	18	144	18
Scotland	200	10	147	10
Thailand	200	16	100	16
Netherlands	200	2	112	2
Canada (B. C.)	195	6	120	6
Hong Kong	195	8	120	8
England/Wales	192	11	115	11
Hungary	192	3	96	3
Swaziland	191	20	140	20
Finland	190	12	84	12
New Zealand	190	13	130	13
Nigeria	190	19	158	19
Canada (Ont.)	186	9	132	9
France	185	5	130	5
Sweden	180	17	96	17
United States	180	14	144	14
Belgium (Flemish)	160	4	140	4
Belgium (French)	175	7	150	7

Based on data reported by International Association for the Evaluation of Education Achievement (IEA). (1987). *The underachieving curriculum: Assessing U.S. school mathematics from an international perspective.* Urbana, IL: University of Illinois, Author. Used with permission.

school achievement. For instance, Flemish Belgium has an average of only 160 scheduled days and ranks fourth in academic achievement while Luxembourg averages 216 school days and ranks 18th out of 20 on academic achievement. All but one of the nations that were ranked lower than the United States had more than 180 days. The one exception was Sweden which averages 180 days.

The association also compared the number of hours per year spent in mathematics instruction to the mathematics achievement of the students in the twenty nations. The United States ranked 15 out of 20, but students in only two of the nations, Scotland and French Belgium, spent, on the average, more time in math than did students in the United States.

Myth: *Concerns, issues, and conditions of education and schooling are different today. Therefore, the arguments for changes in the school schedule are also different.*

Contrary to this myth, it is surprising how consistent the arguments for schedule changes have remained throughout history, as was noted in an earlier section of this chapter and supported by this statement made in 1953:

> There is an increasing awareness on the part of laymen and educators that if we are to do an adequate job of educating our youth, we are justified in examining the possibilities of a twelve-month school year.
>
> The needs of our youth today are quite different from those which existed even as short a time ago as 1925—only twenty-five or thirty years ago. The curriculum in our modern school is vastly different from that which was found in the secondary school of twenty-five years ago. This is not so, however, with the calendar under which and around which we operate (Johnson, 1953, p. 326).

Myth: *Year-round education means that children spend more time in school than they would with a nine- or ten-month schedule.*

Contrary to popular belief, most year-round plans do not increase the number of days that students are in school but merely repackage the existing days so that the buildings are used twelve months out of the year rather than the traditional nine or ten months. In many year-round programs, students are actually in school fewer days, but the days are longer, and as a result, students spend the same amount of time in school as they would in a nine- or ten-month schedule.

Myth: *Children actually spend less time on academic subjects.*

In order to dispel this myth, consider the following factors:

- Before World War II, there were more students who didn't complete eighth grade than who did. The average student today spends four more years in schools than did the student of the 1940s.
- Prior to the 1970s, the lunch period was usually an hour to an hour and a half because most students, especially at the elementary level, went home for lunch.
- In the late 1800s, the first three hours of school were spent on academic subjects, the last three hours on nonacademic subjects.
- Although additional subjects have been added to the curriculum, subjects have also been dropped from the curriculum.
- School attendance has gradually increased over the years.

These are just a few of the examples than can be used to dispel the myth that students today spend less time on academic subjects than students in the past.

Myth: *All of the research, talk, and general hype about time and learning have had no effect in the classroom.*

Based upon classroom observations, discussions with school administrators, and a review of the literature, it is obvious that educators have taken steps to improve time usage in the classroom. For instance:

- Principals and other school staff are making concerted efforts to reduce classroom interruptions.
- Teachers have implemented strategies for class start-up and closing that reduce students' time-off-task.
- Some schools are experimenting with longer class periods, longer days, and/or changes in school schedules.
- District-wide policies are being implemented related to time usage.
- Teacher evaluations often include a section on classroom management, especially as it relates to time usage (Huyvaert, 1992).

Many of the myths, and their associated misconceptions, have become "common wisdom" among both the educational community and the general public. The common acceptance of the myths has helped to make issues related to time and learning a perplexing problem for educational policy makers, school administrators, historians, researchers, and the general public.

RECOMMENDATIONS OF THE NECTL

Perhaps no group of individuals understands the complex and perplexing nature of the relationship between time and learning as do the members of the National Education commission on Time and Learning. The charge presented to the Commission, the list of questions they were expected to address, and the diversity of the testimony of the many witnesses that appeared before them all attest to this fact. In their capacity as commissioners, they attempted to gain an understanding of both the depth and breadth of the issues related to time and learning. As they strove to understand the depth of an issue, they looked at one variable at a time (e.g., year-round schools, motivation and time spent, academic learning time). As they looked at the breadth of the subject, they no longer sought to isolate the variable but rather strove to develop a broader understanding of the interactions of the variables and their effects on one another. The commissioners identified the problems associated with time and learning, considered the relevant aspects of the interdependencies of the various components of the educational system, and studied the effects of these component interdependencies on time and learning.

Based on this in-depth study of the issues, the NECTL made eight recommendations that, if and when implemented, will "put time at the top of the nation's reform agenda." The recommendations are:

- Schools be reinvented around learning, not time.
- Education be redesigned so that time becomes a factor supporting learning, not a boundary marking its limits.
- Schools provide additional academic time by reclaiming the school day for academic instruction.
- Schools remain open longer during the day and that some schools in every district remain open throughout the year.
- Teachers be provided with the professional time and opportunities they need to do their jobs.
- Schools seize on the promise of new technologies to increase productivity, enhance student achievement, and expand learning time.
- Every district convene local leaders to develop action plans that offer different school options and encourage parents, students, and teachers to choose among them.
- All people shoulder their individual responsibilities to transform learning in America.

Although it is difficult to evaluate the ultimate impact the NECTL's recommendations will have on state and local districts, it can be said with utmost certainty that educational decision makers at all levels will find an increase in the demand to address many of the issues related to time and learning. Anyone who hopes to improve the quality of learning through the manipulation of time must recognize the interdependencies of the various components related to time and learning, must acknowledge that no one right solution exists but rather that some solutions are better than others, and must challenge the political leaders and educational professionals to work hand-in-hand with the general public to revitalize and reaffirm the power of education for our students.

REFERENCES

Alam, S. (1970, January). *The four quarter plan and its feasibility for the Port Huron area school district: A research study presented to the Michigan State Department of Education.* Port Huron, MI.: Port Huron School District.

American Association of School Administrators. (1970). *9+: The year-round school.* Washington, DC: Author.

Anderson, L. W. (Ed.). (1984). *Time and school learning: Theory, research and practice.* New York: St. Martin's Press.

Bloom, B. S. (1974a). An introduction to mastery learning theory. In J. H. Block, (Ed.), *Schools, Society, and Mastery Learning* (pp. 4–14). New York: Holt, Rinehart and Winston, Inc.

Bloom, B. S. (1974b). Time and learning. *American Psychologist, 29*(9), 682–688.

Borg, W. R., & Gall, M. D. (1983). *Educational research* (4th ed.) (pp. 5 & 9). New York: Longman.

Carroll, J. B. (1963). A model of school learning. *Teachers College Record, 64*(8), 723–733.

Education Commission of the States Clearinghouse. (1992, February). *Minimum school calendar 1980 and 1990.* Denver, CO: Clearinghouse Notes.

Fisher, C., et al. (1978, June). *Teaching behaviors, academic learning time and student achievement: Final report of phase III-B, beginning teacher evaluation study.* (Technical Report V-1). San Francisco, CA: Far West Laboratory for Educational Research and Development.

Freeland Community Schools. (1969–70). *In-depth study for Freeland Community Schools.* Freeland, MI: Author.

Garber, J. P. (1911). *Annals of educational progress in 1910: A report upon current educational activities throughout the world.* Philadelphia: J. B. Lippincott Company.

Gettinger, M. (1990). Best practices in increasing academic learning time. In Thomas, A., & Grimes, J. (Eds.), *Best Practices in School Psychology – II* (pp. 393–405). Washington, DC: The National Association of School Psychologists.

Henry, N. B. (1945). *The forty-fourth yearbook of the national study of education: American education in the postwar period: Part II structural reorganization.* Chicago: The University of Chicago Press.

Holmes, G. W., & Seawell, W. H. (1968, January). Summer school reappraised. *American School Board Journal,* 10–12.

Huyvaert, S. (1985). *Queueing theory and education: A theoretical study of the feasibility of applying queueing theory as a research method in education.* Unpublished doctoral dissertation, Indiana University, Bloomington, IN.

Huyvaert, S. (1992). *Refinement of a computer simulation model developed to student time-on-task in the educational environment.* Unpublished sabbatical report, Eastern Michigan University, Ypsilanti, MI.

International Association for the Evaluation of Education Achievement (IEA). (1987). *The underachieving curriculum: Assessing U.S. school mathematics from an international perspective.* Urbana, IL: University of Illinois, Author.

Johnson, R. D. (1953). What are the evidences of a need for a year-round educational program? *National Association of Secondary School Principals: Proceedings of the Thirty-Seventh Annual Convention, 37*(192), 325–327.

Karweit, N. (1988 February). Time-on-task: The second time around. *NASSP Bulletin,* 31–39.

Kennedy, J. W. (1917). The all year school! Developed from the summer school. *American Education, 21*(2), 78–84.

National Education Commission on Time and Learning. (1994). *Prisoners of time.* Washington, DC: Office of Educational Research and Improvement.

Pasch, M. (1993). *Another view of time and learning.* Paper presented to the National Education Commission on Time and Learning. Ypsilanti, MI: Eastern Michigan University.

Roe, W. A. (1930). All-year schools—A potential progressive educational improvement. *Educational Methods, X*(1), 3–6.

Schammell, A. C. (1896, March). Early spring in the country school-room. *Primary Education,* 99–100.

Schunk, D. H. (1991). *Learning theories: An educational perspective.* New York: Merrill.

State of Michigan. (1872). *Thirty-fifth annual report of the superintendent of public instruction of the state of Michigan.* Lansing, MI: W.S. George & Company.

Wiley, D. E., & Harnischfeger, A. (1974). Explosion of a myth: Quantity of schooling and exposure to instruction, major educational vehicles. *Educational Researcher, 3*(4), 7–1.

▶ 2

History of the School Calendar

How would you respond if someone were to ask, "Why do schools have such long summer vacations?" You would be in the majority if you mentioned that in the past children were needed to help with the crops in the summer and from this need grew the tradition of a long summer vacation. However, historical documents and the writings of educational leaders of the 1800s and early 1900s contradict this belief. A review of the documents and writings reveals that:

1. During the 1800s, the school calendars of many rural areas were almost the exact opposite of today's school calendar. Roads were often impassable in the winter and children were needed at home to help with planting in the spring and harvesting in the fall, so often rural schools were opened only in June, July, and August and closed the other nine months (see, for instance, Mann, 1843, and *The Thirty-fifth Annual Report of the Superintendent of Public Instruction of the State of Michigan*, 1872).

2. By 1870, in city schools from Massachusetts to California, the school calendar closely resembled the school calendar of today. Children were in school nine to ten months and were allowed a long vacation in July and August (Barnard, 1870).

3. Even as late as 1921 the agricultural sections of the country were not always following a three-month summer vacation pattern. For instance, in Kentucky and Oklahoma, rural students were in school during July and August and the extended vacation ran from February to the end of June. Michigan schools provided for a "beet" vacation of two to four weeks during October, and in Napa County, California the fall term began August 1 and five weeks later provided an extended vacation so that students could help with the picking of plums (Ayer, 1921).

If the current school calendar didn't grow out of the needs of an agrarian society, where did it come from? Turning to historical documents and writings, we find that a number of factors had an impact on the design of the school calendar. Among these factors were issues related to social, political, economic, and yes, even educational concerns. The emergence of state departments of education, basic changes in life style, and an increasing need for standardization of public schools all contributed to creation of the school calendar. By studying the history of the school calendar, not only is our intellectual curiosity satisfied but we begin to understand how truly pervasive are the factors that influence the development of the school calendar. If we understand that the issues related to the school calendar go beyond the simple altering of a tradition to a plethora of intrinsic factors that habitually emerge and are fundamentally intractable and unyielding, this can serve to help those who wish to reform, improve, or restructure our schools.

STATE DEPARTMENTS OF EDUCATION

At the beginning of the nineteenth century, there were sixteen states—the original thirteen plus Vermont, Kentucky, and Tennessee. Each of these states had made some provision for public education and it became a requirement that any territory that applied for statehood had to include within its enabling acts a plan for the development of a state system of education. By the end of the century, there were forty-five states, each of which had a department of education.

In its early days, a state department of education served as a support unit for the chief state school officer, whose primary duty was to collect data and report the findings to the state legislature. Schools were under the control of the local community and each community had complete autonomy to decide for itself when and how long schools would be open. Occasionally, the state superintendent would act as an educational advisor to a local district, but this was not a routine part of the job and state governments exerted little influence on community schools. The basic function of the state department of education, in its support role, was to gather, compile, and publish statistics related to public education within a given state.

By the middle of the nineteenth century, educational programs throughout the nation were expanding and with this expansion new functions and responsibilities were assigned to the departments of education. The departments entered what has been called the Inspectoral Stage. According to Knezevich:

The inspector's functions were defined during the period when the legislature hoped to improve the quality of education through the establishment of regulatory controls over local school units. It was believed that local school improvement would be achieved if the state enacted standards and sent inspectors to determine if the standards were observed (Knezevich, 1975, p. 263).

Mandating of School Days

Among the data collected was information on the number of days that schools were open. The inspectors found that there was great variation from district to district. States tried to rectify the discrepancies by mandating the minimum number of days that schools within each state should be in session. This practice holds historical significance because it represents one of the earliest initiatives of state governments to regulate and control public education and it demonstrates the persistence of using time as a component in school improvement and reform.

Compulsory Education

Massachusetts was one of the first states to require that schools be open for a given number of days and it was also one of the first states to utilize local tax monies for the support of public schools. However, as Massachusetts quickly found out, simply opening schools and providing funding was not enough to guarantee that children would attend school. Horace Mann, who served as secretary to the Massachusetts' State Board of Education from 1837 to 1848, was troubled because many children never attended school, and many who did attend did so in an irregular pattern. Although Mann was basically concerned about the welfare of the children and the quality of their education, as secretary of the board he was also a political man who understood the subtleties of taxing citizens for services that were underutilized. In his report of 1847, Mann strongly condemns the practice of leaving school attendance to the discretion of parents, stating that:

> Men of wealth, who have no children to send to school, or who for any reason send none, complain of it {poor attendance}, because, though they may be willing to be taxed for the education of all, yet they are not willing to be taxed to have their money taken and thrown away. They think it, and with good reason too, to be an intolerable hardship, to be first confronted with the argument that they are bound to secure the general intelligence and morality of the people, through the instrumentality of schools, and when they have acknowledged the validity

of this argument and cheerfully paid their money, to have the very men who so argued and so claimed, turn upon them and say, 'We are still at liberty to throw your money away by keeping our children at home; and though you must keep the school regularly for us, we have a right to use it irregularly, or not at all, as we please' (Mann, 1847, pp. 108–109)

By 1852, Massachusetts had enacted the first compulsory school attendance law. The law required that children between the ages of eight and fourteen attend school for at least three months each year. Exceptions to the rule included those children who had already mastered the curriculum, those children whose physical or mental health precluded their attendance at school, and those children who lived in poverty. Children of poverty were excused from school attendance so that they could go to work because their income was often essential for the family's survival.

Other states followed Massachusetts' lead. By the end of the nineteenth century, 31 of the 45 states had compulsory attendance laws and by 1918 all states made school attendance mandatory. The compulsory laws changed the emphasis from the number of days that schools should be in operation to the number of days that children should be in school. However, because there were seldom any consequences associated with the compulsory education laws, the laws did little to solve the problem of children not attending school or attending irregularly. In 1884, Michigan's state superintendent of public instruction echoed the feelings of many state school administrators when he stated that:

Compulsory school laws are generally inoperative on account of a prevalent indifference to their enforcement, and from the fact that no particular person or persons are held responsible for their faithful execution. To make such laws effective certain persons should be designated to see that they are strictly enforced, and the officers so designated should be held accountable for a nonperformance of their duties.

A most efficient *aid* in the enforcement of any compulsory school law, would be the apportionment of the primary school interest fund to the different districts on the basis of the daily attendance of resident children (State of Michigan, 1884, p. li).

The superintendent then goes on to say:

The money received from the State would be in direct proportion to the amount of school taught and the percentage of attendance.

It would be for the interest of each district, under such a law, to have the maximum number of months of school each year, and to secure a full enrollment and a regular attendance (p. lii).

Educational leaders from other states, experiencing the same frustration as the superintendent from Michigan, urged their state legislatures to initiate policies that would tie the amount of monies received by a school to both the length of the school year and to average daily attendance. This practice added "clout" to the law that mandated the minimum number of school days and was so successful that most states continue this practice to some degree even today.

In addition to tying monies to attendance, states also demanded that local districts hire truant officers to uphold the law. By law, parents could now be fined or even imprisoned if their children did not attend school on a regular basis.

Minimum Number of Days

The length of the school year, the average daily attendance of students, and the average number of days that individual students attended increased across the nation as compulsory education laws were enacted and enforced (see Table 2–1).

The figures in Table 2–1 are based on national averages that can be somewhat misleading. However, the trend itself is consistent throughout historical state documents. Within the individual states, data on the length of the school year are more readily accessible than are data on average daily attendance. The primary reason for this is that different reporting techniques were used to establish averages. Extensive calculations were often needed before the data from year-to-year or state-to-state could be compared. Data on the average length of the school year were more straightforward and easily compared. Data from New York, Pennsylvania, Ohio, Michigan, and North Car-

TABLE 2–1   Student attendance data

School Year	1869–70	1899–1900	1919–20
Average length of school term in days	132.2	144.3	161.9
Percent of enrolled pupils attending	59.3	68.6	74.8
Average number of days attended by each pupil	78.4	99	121.2

Snyder, T. D., & Hoffman, C. M. (1994). *Digest of educational statistics.* (DHEW Publication No. (OE) 72–75). Washington, DC: U.S. Government Printing Office.

olina all confirm that there was indeed a trend toward lengthening the school year. In New York, the Compulsory Education Act of 1874 required that children attend school at least fourteen weeks (70 days) each year, but by 1893 the minimum number of days was fixed at 160 (Crooker & Sandford, 1893–94) and by 1916 the law required that they attend 36 weeks or 180 days (Finegan, 1916). In 1854, schools in Pennsylvania were required to be open a minimum of four months and this did not change until 1872, at which time schools were required to be in session for five months. However, a law drafted in 1878 provided additional funds for districts that kept their schools open at least seven and a half months (Wickersham, 1886).

In Ohio, the length of the school year increased from three months in 1829 to six months by 1850 (Miller, 1920, p. 43). Michigan achieved statehood in 1837 and at that time fixed the school year at three months, but by 1883 Michigan law required seven months of attendance and by 1900 the length of the average school year was 8.2 months (State of Michigan, 1872, 1884, 1900).

In the South, the length of the school term increased, but not as rapidly or as dramatically as in the North. In 1891, North Carolina's state superintendent bemoaned the fact that average school term for the nation was 135 days but the average term in the South was only 101 days. However, little was done to correct the situation and as late as 1900 the mandated school term in North Carolina still stood at just 70 days (Knight, 1916, pp. 315–316).

CHANGING LIFESTYLES

The actions taken by state departments of education regarding mandated days and compulsory attendance certainly helped to shape the school calendar, but it must be recognized that much of the impetus for the increasing school attendance came from the general public. Francis Adams noted in 1875 that, "The period of school attendance is being gradually lengthened throughout the Union. In this respect the laws are behind the spirit of the people. The school terms in many states are considerably longer than the periods required by law" (Adams, p. 240). One of the reasons for this was that there were a number of lifestyle changes taking place during the 1800s and these changes often provided the catalyst for expanding and standardizing the school calendar.

Immigration

During the later half of the 1800s, immigrants flooded to the United States, bringing with them their hopes, desires, problems, and afflictions. In 1862, 72,183 immigrants settled in the United States. This number increased every year until 1900 when 1,100,735 immigrants entered the country. The immigrants had come to America seeking a better way of life and believed that the school would open the door into the privileges of American society, especially for their children. Many urban schools remained open all year to help meet the needs of this population.

Nationalism

The nation experienced two major wars during the nineteenth century—the War of 1812 and the Civil War. With each of these major conflicts came a renewed spirit of nationalism. The school was seen as the institution that was most likely to impart the goals and values of a nation united. An address by J. R. Preston, Mississippi State Superintendent of Public Instruction, to the National Education Association in 1891, reflects the essence of this view:

> We have half the railways of the world to exchange our products for us and to facilitate the intermingling of our people. This is a strong mechanical bond, but it appeals to no higher motive than self-interest, and therefore cannot be relied upon to produce a true spirit of nationality. The press, except in rare cases, speaks only to the section in which it is printed. Sectional interests and prejudice once parted our nation in two; and there is danger ahead that this same spirit, if not counteracted, may sever us again. This time not the North and South; but the East, the West, the South, the Centre (sic). We need the force of a dominant national patriotism to counterwork the perilous tendencies of this sectional spirit (Preston, 1891, p. 102).

Superintendent Preston goes on to say:

> . . . I assert that the public school is the agency we must rely upon. Its army of half a million teachers, sustained by popular devotion to the cause, must in times of peace and through peaceful measures fight this continuous battle for the perpetuity of national life. This army stands to-day *(sic)* holding the hands and hearts of to-morrow's *(sic)* nation. To make a citizenship whose intelligence, moral rectitude, and steadfast virtues will counteract these disintegrating forces and social disorders is the function and the mission of our public schools (p. 103).

Although the direct impact of this new sense of nationalism had only a limited effect on the school calendar, it did introduce a new component to the calendar—the right of schools to dismiss schools on patriotic days such as state and national fasting days, artillery election, and George Washington's birthday.

Urbanization

In 1820, the population of the United States was just a little over 9.6 million, only 7 percent of whom lived in urban areas. By 1849, the population had more than doubled and was close to 22.5 million, 15 percent of whom lived in the city, and by the end of the century the population had increased to 76 million, a third of whom were living in urban areas. Cities grew rapidly and haphazardly, and life in the city was anything but pleasant. Tenements sprang up and quickly became fire hazards. Often there was not enough food and in many cities the water supply was insufficient. Disease spread rapidly. Parents worked long hours and children were left on their own. Gangs of older teenagers roamed the streets and violent crimes became commonplace. Horace Mann lamented the conditions in the cities, acknowledging that:

> . . . children are the sufferers; where moral distempers are inflicted upon them by parents, . . .; where they are born into atmosphere saturated with the infection of crime; where vice obtrudes itself upon every sense, and presses inward, through every pore, to be imbibed and copied, just as the common air forces itself into the nostrils, to be breathed; and where, in their early imitative transgressions, they are no more consciously guilty, than in the heaving of their lungs in an act of respiration (Mann, 1848, p. 114).

Mann saw schooling as the way out of the atrocious conditions that most children were confronted with daily. He believed that:

> . . . if all our children were to be brought under the benignant influences of such teachers as the State can supply, from the age of four years to that of sixteen, and for *ten months in each year* (emphasis added), then ninety-nine in every hundred of them can be rescued from uncharitableness, from falsehood, from intemperance, from cupidity, licentiousness, violence, and fraud, and reared to the performance of all the duties, and to the practice of all the kindnesses and courtesies of domestic and social life (Mann, 1848, p. 113).

Many shared Mann's concern and saw education as:

- a way out of poverty
- a way to control violence in the streets
- a way to instill youth with moral values
- a way to provide a healthy environment for children

To accomplish these objectives, city schools were kept open as long as possible. In 1840, schools were open 259 days per year in Detroit and 252 days in Philadelphia. Schools in Chicago were open for 48 weeks, 43 weeks in Cleveland, and 49 weeks in New York (Lovell, 1927).

Industrialization

The first textile factory built in the United States was erected in the 1790s. Gradually, more factories were built, but it wasn't until the War of 1812 that the factories became a common sight in New England. Prior to the War of 1812, commodities generally were either manufactured in the home or imported from Europe. However, as a consequence of the war, restrictions were placed on imports from England and this created a shortage of goods and a growing need for mass production.

Factories quickly sprang up across New England causing an acute labor shortage. Children were used to alleviate the problem because they were a source of cheap labor. Although many parents believed that the way out of poverty was through education, they saw education as a luxury they could not afford because it was necessary for their children to earn the few dollars that might mean the difference between survival and starvation. And so, even though parents valued education, they were forced to choose survival over schooling.

Conditions in the factories became so bad that, by the mid-1800s, hiring of children younger than 14 years of age came to be seen as an abusive practice. Child labor laws, restricting the number of hours a child could work, were implemented. The laws often made it illegal for children to work unless they attended school for a minimum number of days per year. For instance, Connecticut enacted a child labor law in 1842 that made it illegal for a company to employ a child under the age of 15 unless the child had attended school for at least three of the last twelve months. Any business that violated the law was fined $25.

Many companies chose to ignore the child-labor laws when they were first enacted, but came to embrace the laws as new technologies required that employees be trained in the "scientific" methods of work. Horace Mann tells of discussing the effects of education with an employer;

> I have been told, by one of our most careful and successful manufactures, that, on substituting, in one of his cotton mills, a better for a poorer educated class of operatives, he was enabled to add twelve or fifteen per cent, to the speed of his machinery, without any increase of damage or danger from the acceleration. Here there was a direct gain of twelve or fifteen per cent,—a larger percentage *(sic)* than that

of the supposed whole number of children under sixteen years of age, in all our factories. And this gain was effected, too, without any additional investment of capital, or any increased expense for board (Mann, 1848, p. 117).

Educated employees came to be seen as an important asset and the need for the "educated worker" continued to grow as the number of new inventions increased rapidly. From 1850 to 1860 at least 2,000 new patents were awarded *each year* and by the end of the century these innovations were helping to mechanize much of the work being done in both the factory and on the farm. The length of the work day and week was reduced, making it easier for children who were working to attend school for longer periods of time. Parents' attitudes toward sending children to school began to change when workers in the factory became aware that "the more education you had, the more money you could make." Where earlier many parents found it almost impossible to send their children to school for any amount of time, they were now starting to demand that their children have access to higher levels of training. Leonard Koos, writing about the history of secondary education in the United States, accredited the growth of the high school to American individualism and to the "partly selfish desire of parents to secure for their children the social and economic benefits accruing from higher training" (Koos, 1927, p. 13).

Continuing industrialization made education essential and hence increased the demand for free education among the general public. The net result was that the number of days and years that children were required to be in school steadily increased.

Rural Life

During the early part of the 1800s public schools in the rural areas served to supplement the teachings of the home and the church. In the South, children of the wealthy plantation owners often had a private tutor, while those who worked for the owner were usually denied the right to an education. Children who did not live on a plantation were most frequently taught in private schools. If the parents of the child were unable to pay for the child's education, most states provided some form of aid. Even farms in the North tended to be self-supporting and most of what children needed to know in order to be successful could be learned at home. The curriculum of the school was basically determined by the teacher or by the local community and, in most cases, consisted of some form of reading, writing, and arithmetic (Morrison, 1917).

The period following the Civil War brought a number of changes to rural areas of the country. New methods of farming were introduced and technology found its way to the farm. Factories that had been built in the city eliminated the need for many of the old trades and small industries that previously had been located in the villages. New machinery also decreased the need for farm labor and many rural families were forced to move to the city in order to make a living. Changes in living conditions in rural communities obviously called for a change in the educational system. According to Cubberley:

> . . . the old educative influence of the home, the church, and the farm began rapidly to decline. New methods of procedure were introduced so rapidly that the old father-to-son form of instruction, which had for so long prevailed, gradually became inadequate. New methods of farming, calling now for the application of scientific knowledge, began to be introduced. All of these changes naturally tended to make the instruction offered in the rural school less vital than it had previously been (Cubberley, 1914, p. 90).

The rural schools, however, were slow to adapt to the changing needs of their students. Rural communities had designed, developed, and controlled their entire educational process for well over a century. Historically, there had been little influence exerted over the schools by anyone outside of the local community and this contributed to the reluctance to change. Communities often felt that the school had proven itself to be effective and there was no reason to change it. "The rural school has become endeared by age and by sentiment, and those who experienced its benefits have been most vigorous in opposing any changes in organization. Regardless of the fact that practically all of the life conditions surrounding the rural school have since materially changed, these members of the older generation are hardest to convince that there is any need of a change in the school" (Cubberley, 1914, p. 89).

By the end of the nineteenth century and into the twentieth century, there was a great discrepancy between the quality of education being provided by city schools and that being provided by rural schools. Concerns about the inequities in education reached far beyond the state governments and could be found throughout the educational community. Committees were formed, conferences held, and articles written in an effort to delineate the causes of, and possible solutions to, the problem. And, as is so often the case, both the educators and the policy makers looked for obvious or easy answers. What they found was that one of the biggest discrepancies between the two types of school districts was the number of days that children were required to attend school. The following quote from the Committee of Twelve's report on rural schools is reflective of the typical solutions that were recommended:

> Only a single point remains to be pressed, but it must be pressed strongly. This is the necessity of lengthening materially the time that the country schools, on the average, are in session each year, and the

securing of a more regular attendance of the pupils. The legal years now vary widely in different states, and the practical or real, years still more widely. . . . In the thickly settled states of the East the rural schools are in session eight, nine, or ten months in the year; but often in the South, and sometimes in the West, one-half the shortest of these terms is not reached. The legal year is frequently absurdly short. . . . It is as wasteful method of education to send children to school seventy or eighty days in the year as it is to send them two or three hours in the day. Persons interested in popular education, and particularly in rural education, should not rest, therefore, in their efforts until they have made the legal school year in every state at least 160 or 180 days (NEA, 1897, p. 51).

As lifestyles changed, citizens looked to the schools for guidance and answers to their problems. The schools were seen as a way to reduce violence, improve child welfare, escape poverty, prepare for employment, improve the moral fiber of society, and decrease the class inequalities among children. In order to accomplish all of these goals, there was a constant movement toward increasing the number of days that children were required to be in school. The ideal number of days that all seemed to be reaching for was 180 days, or the equivalent of eight to ten months per year.

STANDARDIZATION OF PUBLIC SCHOOLS

The latter half of the nineteenth century has been called the Age of Education Awakening in America. The amount of schooling that children received increased steadily throughout the century. During the first half of the century, the emphasis and concern was on primary or basic education. By the second half of the century, institutions of higher education—academies, high schools, and colleges—were cropping up across the nation, shifting the emphasis from basic education to advanced education. One of the troubling aspects of this growth was that the term "higher education" was used extensively but it meant different things to different people. Newly formed professional organizations and associations, such as the National Education Association, the North Central Association, and the Association of Colleges and Secondary Schools of the Southern States (now the Southern Association of Colleges and Secondary Schools), wrestled with the problems created by this lack of standardization. Several of the organizations, working with state departments of education and established universities, formed committees to try to institute some kind of standard that could be used to evaluate the quality and level of education being offered by institutions of higher education. Recommendations were made and attempts to implement the recommendations were undertaken. Because school districts suffered only minor consequences from not following the suggestions, however, they often chose to ignore them.

Carnegie Unit

The Andrew Carnegie Foundation helped to remedy this situation in 1905 when it established a retirement fund for professors in institutions of higher education. The guidelines for application stipulated that:

> The purpose of this fund is the strengthening of the profession of the teacher and the dignifying of that profession. To this end it is essential that the endowment should be used to found a system of retiring allowances which should come to the professor as a matter of right, not as a matter of charity. To this end, therefore, it is essential that so far as possible the retiring allowances should be conferred thru *(sic)* an institution and in accordance with fixed rules.
>
> Secondly, the gift is also one to higher education and such institutions must therefore be selected with some regard to their academic standing (NEA, 1907, p. 505).

The fund was quickly inundated by an overwhelming number of applications. It seemed that any school that went beyond basic or elementary education considered itself an institution of higher education. Knowing that Mr. Carnegie had established the endowment for college professors rather than high school teachers, the trustees found it necessary to develop their own criteria for judging an institution. After preliminary research, the commission discovered that the state of New York had established what it called a "standard unit of work" for secondary education. The commission adapted the unit and used it as a criterion for judging the status of an institution and its eligibility to apply for the retirement fund. The commissioners decided that in order for an institution to be considered a college, its students must have completed fourteen standard units of school work prior to entering that institution. A standard unit consisted of "regular attendance in a course that met one class period per day, five days per week, thirty-six weeks per year" (Besvinick, 1961, p. 365). This standard became known as the Carnegie Unit.

By 1909, these standards had been adopted by several high school and college accrediting associations, including the North Central Association (NCA). NCA outlined eleven standards that secondary schools had to meet before they could be accredited by the association. The first of these standards was as follows:

No school shall be accredited which does not require fifteen units for graduation. More than twenty periods per week should be discouraged.

(A unit course of study in a secondary school is defined as a course covering an academic year that shall include in the aggregate not less than the equivalent of one hundred and twenty sixty-minute hours of classroom work, two hours of manual training or laboratory work being equivalent to one hour of classroom work.) (Brown, 1916, p. 61).

At the 1916 annual meeting, the association went on to append these additional guidelines to the standard:

A unit is a series of recitations or exercises in a given subject pursued continuously throughout the school year.

The school year must be at least thirty-six weeks in length, each week to be made up of five school days. In computing the number of weeks and days, single holidays may be disregarded, but not suspensions of schools, which involve the loss of three days in a week.

The number of class exercises required in a week for each unit shall, in general, be five (Brown, 1916, p. 196).

The guidelines also stipulated that class periods should not be less than forty minutes and recommended longer periods be provided for purposes of supervised study. The thirty-six, five-day weeks and the equivalent of 180 school days—the ideal that many were reaching for during the latter part of the 1800s. This is also the number of days most frequently mandated by state departments of education today.

SUMMER VACATION

Early laws mandated that schools be open only three months out of the year, but by 1870 schools were in session an average of 132.2 days and students attended an average of 78.4 of those days. By 1900, schools were in session an average of 143.7 days and students attended an average of 98 days. This trend has continued on through the twentieth century to the point that in many areas of the country the current school calendar is defined as 180 days—the ideal session length identified throughout the latter half of the 19th century (see Table 2–1).

A number of factors help to explain this gradual lengthening of the school year—lifestyle changes demanded that children receive more education; state governments, following the will of the people and under the guidance of educational leaders, legislated increasingly more school days; and professional organizations and associations adopted the Carnegie standard of thirty-six weeks as a basis for determining level of accreditation. Taken together, these factors help to account for the current length of the school calendar.

The question that remains to be answered is, "Why the long break in the summer?" It should come as no surprise that one of the major reasons that schools originally set aside June, July, and August for vacation was the intense summer heat. In 1820, teachers in New York requested three weeks off in August, citing the insufferable conditions in the classroom created by the intolerable heat (Boese, 1869). In 1872 the Michigan Superintendent of Public instruction recommended that the school vacation be changed from September and October to July and August because of the "hot, sultry, scorching" summer weather.

Even when schools were in session during the summer months, enrollments tended to be low and so public sentiment, presented in the form of public action, played a role in determining that an extended vacation was needed during the summer. Even Horace Mann was swayed by public opinion. In his 1843 report to the state board of education, Mann noted that "there are certain seasons of the year when the average of attendance falls to a low ebb. Would it not be better, in all such cases, to prolong the vacation, and thus to avoid an evil which cannot be successfully combated?" (Mann, 1843, p. 24). He goes on to identify summer as the season in which attendance was lowest. One factor that appears to have contributed to the low enrollment was that families, if they could afford it, often left the city and went to the country for at least some part of the hot summer months. Children were taken out of school so that they could go with their parents. Summer session interfered with family vacations and vacations took priority because family life was valued so highly.

Thomas Finegan, Deputy Commissioner of Education and Assistant Commissioner for Elementary Education for the State of New York in 1916, identified two additional reasons for the long summer vacation—"One is for the purpose of giving the teachers a needed rest and the other is to reduce the expense of the maintenance of schools" (p. 155).

In the vernacular of the time, the term "school maintenance" referred to more than repair and upkeep of the school. Functions and tasks of school operations and management, including school funding, were included under maintenance. States mandated the number of days that children were required to be in school and they tied state funding to the average daily attendance. Local districts found that they could get more for their money if schools remained open during the winter when attendance was high and closed during the summer when attendance was low.

Another justification for closing the school during the summer months was, in the words of Horace Mann, "The well-known passion for novelty inherent in the young, and their love of change in their occupations, as well as observations and experience, teach us that children return to their studies with greater zest and vigor after a temporary suspension." Mann argued that summer vacation was needed because:

> On the whole, from the testimony of the most judicious and experienced of teachers and friends of Common Schools, as well as from my own observations, I am strongly inclined to the opinion that, for all our annual schools, a vacation of at least two weeks should be allowed at the end of each quarterly term; and for those schools which are composed of children under eight years of age, an additional week should be granted, either at the close or in the middle of each quarter. Probably it would be still better to have a long vacation of three weeks, or an intermediate one of one week, during the hottest season of the year, for all Public Schools without exception" (Mann, 1843, p. 26).

The argument that schools were closed during the summer so that children could work on the farm did not appear in the educational literature until the early part of the 1900s. The interesting thing about this argument is that it was used by advocates of year-round schools to infer that this was the main reason that schools were in session for nine months rather than twelve months. However, as we have already seen, many rural schools still were not on a "nine-month school/three-month vacation" calendar even as late as 1921. The beginning of the twentieth century found schools in session ten months or less. By 1904, however, Bluffton, Indiana had gone to a four-quarter year-round school calendar to help alleviate overcrowding in the schools. The concept of year-round school excited many school administrators because they too were faced with crowded schools and no money to build new ones. Year-round schools seemed like a feasible solution to their problem, but before it could be implemented the general public needed to be convinced. Blaming the summer vacation on the needs of an antiquated past was a successful strategy, especially for a society that was entering a new millennium. At the same time, it was also an easy explanation for a phenomenon whose roots were complex and hard to extract.

CONSTRUCTION OF THE FIXED SCHEDULE BARRIER

The National Education Commission on Time and Learning in their report, *Prisoners of Time*, identified one of the barriers to school learning as the fixed schedule. As we have just seen, the barrier of the fixed schedule, as it currently exists, took almost a century to build and was built in response to a number of concerns. Among these concerns were the need to:

- control and regulate public schools
- develop a way of overcoming poverty
- expand the curriculum to include science principles and technological skills
- combat the constraints imposed by limited funding
- help society adjust to changing life styles
- make schools more equitable by standardizing school practices
- protect children from overwhelming social problems
- provide an educated work force
- meet the needs of a diverse society

In many cases the fixed schedule, combined with other such remedies, reduced the concern but didn't eliminate the problem that created the concern in the first place. The social, political, economic, legal, and educational issues that influenced the development of the school calendar remain with us even today. This is not to diminish the need for debate on the reevaluation of the school calendar, but it does focus our attention on the difference between the form of the calendar and the substance of the school day.

REFERENCES

Adams, F. (1875). *The free school system of the United States.* London: Chapman and Hall.

Ayer, A. M. (1921). A study of rural school attendance. *The Journal of Rural Education,* 4(9–10), 396.

Barnard, H. (Ed.). (1870). Digest of the rules and regulations of public schools in the principal cities of the United States. *The American Journal of Education,* 6(3), 418–463.

Besvinick, S. L. (1961). The expendable Carnegie unit. *Phi Delta Kappan,* 42(8), 365–366.

Boese, T. (1869). *Public education in the city of New York: Its history, condition, and statistics: An official report to the board of education.* New York: Harper & Brothers, Publishers.

Brown, H. E. (1916, March 24–25). *Proceedings of the twenty-first annual meeting of the North Central Association of colleges and secondary schools:* Chicago, IL: North Central Association.

Crooker, J. F., & Sandford, J. (1893–94). *Department register: Department of Public Instruction.* Albany: State of New York.

Cubberley, E. P. (1914). *Rural life and education: A study of the rural-school problem as a phase of the rural-life problem.* Boston: Houghton Mifflin.

Finegan, T. E. (1916). *Elementary Education: Report for the school year ending July 31, 1916.* Albany: The University of the State of New York.

Knezevich, S. J. (1975). *Administration of public education* (3rd ed.). New York: Harper & Row.

Knight, E. W. (1916). *Public school education in North Carolina.* Boston: Houghton Mifflin.

Koos, L. V. (1927). *The American secondary school.* Boston: Ginn and Company.

Lovell, L. E. (1927, April). All-year school. *Educational Review, 196–202.*

Mann, H. (1843). *Sixth annual report of the Board of Education together with the sixth annual report of the secretary of the board.* Boston: Dutton and Wentwork.

Mann, H. (1847). *Tenth annual report of the Board of Education together with the tenth annual report of the secretary of the board.* Boston: Dutton and Wentwork.

Mann, H. (1848). *Eleventh annual report of the Board of Education together with the eleventh annual report of the secretary of the board.* Boston: Dutton and Wentwork.

Miller, E. A. (1920). *The history of educational legislation in Ohio from 1803 to 1850.* Chicago: The University of Chicago Press.

Morrison, A. J. (1917). *The beginnings of public education in Virginia, 1776–1860.* Richmond, VA: Davis Bottom, Superintendent of Public Printing.

National Education Association. (1897). *Report of the committee of twelve on rural schools.* Chicago: The University of Chicago Press.

National Education Association. (1907). *Fiftieth anniversary volume: 1857–1905.* Winona, MN: Author.

National Education Commission on Time and Learning. (1994). *Prisoners of time.* Washington, DC: Office of Educational Research and Improvement.

Preston, J. R. (1891). *Journal of proceedings and addresses.* NY: National Education Association, 102–105, 115.

Snyder, T. D., & Hoffman, C. M. (1994). *Digest of educational statistics.* (DHEW Publication No. (OE) 72–75). Washington, DC: U. S. Government Printing Office.

State of Michigan. (1872). *Thirty-fifth annual report of the superintendent of public instruction of the state of Michigan.* Lansing, MI: W. S. George & Company.

State of Michigan. (1884). *Forty-seventh annual report of the superintendent of public instruction of the state of Michigan.* Lansing, MI: W. S. George & Company.

State of Michigan. (1900). *Sixty-fourth annual report of the superintendent of public instruction of the state of Michigan.* Lansing, MI: Wynkoop Hallenbeck Crawford Co.

Wickersham, J. P. (1886). *A history of education in Pennsylvania.* Lancaster, PA: Inquirer Publishing Co.

▶ 3

Extending Time in School

The school calendar has been viewed as an instrument of school improvement and reform throughout the history of American education. The length of the school term was gradually increased throughout the 1800s with the belief that the longer school year could aid the nation in meeting its national goals and ease many of the social problems that seemed almost overwhelming at the time. In the early part of the 1900s the school calendar was seen as an instrument that could ease the problem associated with overcrowded schools. Advocates for year-round schools found their voice in 1904 when schools in Bluffton, Indiana designed their calendar around a four-quarter plan. Other districts quickly became interested in the concept of year-round schools, speculating that if an alteration in the calendar could ease overcrowding, the same process could be used to ease other problems, such as an expanding curriculum that was impossible to teach within the confines of the limited calendar.

Today, the curriculum continues to expand, academic achievement is reported to be on the decline, and schools are accepting responsibilities that were once the purview of the home and the church. Policy makers, the general public, and educational leaders are united in their demand for school reform, and once more the school calendar is being called upon to serve as a change agent.

Because the school calendar is the "box" within which all school time must fit, it seems logical that any attempt to increase academic achievement through the manipulation of time will require an alteration in the school calendar. The same holds true if we hope to extend the services provided by the school so that the school comes closer to meeting the needs of the whole child. This "logic" often makes the school calendar the target of school reform. But regardless of however logical it may be, changing the school calendar can be, and often is, an arduous task. Districts that attempt to make a substantial change in the school schedule often find themselves in the middle of an uproar that is unpleasant at best and disastrous at worst.

In most cases, the community, especially parents within the community, will support a change in the school calendar if it believes the change is for the good of the children and that the change will have little, if any, impact on the living patterns of the community. On the other hand, if it is perceived that a recommended alteration in the school schedule will have some impact on community life and make only a small difference in the children's education, the community typically won't support the change. The key here is community perception. The American Association of School Administrators has noted that:

> People's acceptance of an idea and the amount of support they are willing to give it are influenced by their perceptions of benefits. These perceptions are crucial because they constitute the reasons why people have cause to support development of a . . . school program. So before initiating widespread discussion with your board, staff, students, or the public, carefully prepare a very clear statement of the benefits involved (AASA, 1973, p. 33).

Before a clear statement of the benefit of any plan to change the school schedule can be formulated, one must be knowledgeable about alternative scheduling approaches, understand the pros and cons associated with the different approaches, be cognizant of the concerns of the vested parties as they relate to school scheduling alternatives, and be aware of how and when the various scheduling alternatives have been implemented in other districts. The next sections are designed to help you to understand each of these elements as they are associated with various types of school calendars. This chapter will examine typical school schedules that provide for a prolonged summer vacation and then look at extended school year (ESY) and extended school day programs that increase the amount of time students spend in school beyond state mandates. Chapter 4 will look at alternatives to the current calendar, including flexible scheduling that allows for variation among students and year-round schools (YRS) programs in which schools are open twelve months of the year.

THE CURRENT SCHOOL CALENDAR

The most popular school calendar currently in use calls for students to be in school approximately nine months a year and on vacation the other three months. This is often referred to as the traditional school calendar. Although this calendar is widely accepted, many believe that there is no reason for schools to be closed 2-1/2 to 3 months a year, especially when children today need more education than the schools are currently providing. The argument for changing the school calendar is often built on the misguided premise that the current school schedule grew out of the nation's agrarian past, a time when children were needed to help on the farm during the long summer months. Educational researcher and historian John McLain believed such oversimplification had led many educators "to commit basic blunders that have caused their plans to be rejected by the people" (McLain, 1973, p. 59). The blunders that McLain spoke of resulted from a lack of understanding of just how complex the issues related to the school calendar really are. In the last chapter we saw that the school calendar was used to address many different types of problems, concerns, and issues. Forces that helped to shape the calendar often had a political, economic, or social bias and these biases were reflected in the structure of the calendar. In spite of the volatile nature of the school calendar, by the end of the nineteenth century the basic structure of the calendar had become so well established that changes to the calendar became more and more difficult.

STATE MANDATES

The calendar structure was "legitimatized" through the use of state mandates and these mandates are now one of the major factors contributing to the intractable nature of the school calendar. Today, state imposed mandates continue to influence the structure of the calendar and to restrain what otherwise might be considered valid and beneficial changes.

State Mandated Days

Table 3–1 presents the minimum number of days required by each state in 1996 as compiled by the Education Commission of the States.. The number of mandated days varied from 174 in Missouri to 186 in Kansas. In spite of this variation, there is remarkable consistency among the states with approximately half of the states requiring a minimum of 180 days per school year.

When comparing the data in Table 3–1, it is important to note that in some states minimum number of days refers to the number of student days and in other states the number reflects teacher days. In addition, six states— Colorado, Idaho, Kentucky, Nebraska, New Mexico, and Oregon—mandate the minimum number of hours rather than number of days that schools are open during a year. In eight states—Connecticut, Delaware, Maryland, Missouri, Pennsylvania, Utah, Virginia, and Wisconsin—the minimum time is

TABLE 3–1 Length of school year—state policies, 1996

State	Minimum number of pupil/teacher contact days	Teacher in-service training/staff development requirements (unless otherwise indicated, days/hours are in addition to minimum pupil/teacher contact days/hours)
Alabama	175[1]	5 days
Alaska	180	Up to 10 days (included in 180 instructional days)
Arizona	175	LEA option
Arkansas	178	5-7 days
California	175	Up to 8 days (included in 175 instructional days)
Colorado	450 hrs.—Kindergarten 990 hrs.—Elementary 1080 hrs.—Middle & Secondary	Up to 24 hrs. (included in minimum instructional hours)
Connecticut	180 (900 hrs.)	18 hrs.
Delaware	180 (1070 hrs.)	5 days
DC	180	3 days (included in 180 instructional days)
Florida	180	LEA option
Georgia	180	Up to 10 days
Hawaii	176	Up to 5 days
Idaho	450 hrs.—Kindergarten 810 hrs.—Grades 1–3 900 hrs.—Grades 4–8 990 hrs.—Grades 9–12	Up to 11 hrs.—Kindergarten Up to 22 hrs.—Grades 1–12 (included in minimum instructional hours)
Illinois	176	Up to 4 days[2]

TABLE 3–1 *Continued*

Indiana	180	LEA option[3]
Iowa	180	1 day
Kansas	186 days (465 hrs.)—Kindergarten 186 days (1116 hrs.)—Grades 1–11 181 days (1086 hrs.)—Grade 12	LEA option
Kentucky	1,050 hrs.	4 days
Louisiana	175	Up to 5 days
Maine	175	Up to 5 days
Maryland	180 (1080 hrs.—Elementary 1170 hrs.—Secondary)	LEA option
Massachusetts	180[4]	LEA option
Michigan	180—96–97 school year One day added each succeeding year until 190 is reached in 2006–07 (990 hrs.—96–97 1,041 hrs.—97–98 1,047—98–99 1,098—99–00 an and additional 6 hours each year until 1140 hours are reached in 2006–07)[5]	1 day, 97–98; 2 days, 98–99; 3 days, 99–00; 4 days, 00–01; 5 days, 01–02 and each succeeding year
Minnesota	LEA option as of 96–97 school year. Districts are expected to set school year length necessary for students to meet state and local graduation requirements.	No non-instructional day or hour requirements as of 96–97 school year
Mississippi	180	Up to 7 days
Missouri	174 (1,044 hrs.)	LEA option
Montana	180	3-7 days

Continued

TABLE 3-1 *Continued*

State	Minimum number of pupil/teacher contact days	Teacher in-service training/staff development requirements (unless otherwise indicated, days/hours are in addition to minimum pupil/teacher contact days/hours)
Nebraska	400 hrs.—Kindergarten 1,032 hrs. —Grades 1–8 1,080 hrs.—Secondary	10 hrs.
Nevada	180[7]	Up to 5 days (included in 180 instructional days)
New Hampshire	180	Up to 10 days
New Jersey	180	LEA option
New Mexico	450 hrs.—Kindergarten 990 hrs.—Grades 1–6 1,080 hrs.—Grades 7–12	Up to 3 days
New York	180	Up to 4 days (included in 180 instructional days)
North Carolina	180	Up to 20 days
North Dakota	175	2 days[8]
Ohio	182	Up to 2 days (included in 182 instructional days)
Oklahoma	175	Up to 5 days
Oregon	405 hrs.—Kindergarten 810 hrs.—Grades 1–3 900 hrs.—Grades 4–8 990 hrs.—Grades 9–12	Up to 30 hrs. (included in minimum instructional hours)

TABLE 3–1 *Continued*

Pennsylvania	180[9] (450 hrs.—Kindergarten 900 hrs.—Grades 1–6 990 hrs.—Grades 7–12)	Up to 5 days
Rhode Island	180	LEA option
South Carolina	180	Up to 10 days
South Dakota	175	LEA option
Tennessee	180	5 days
Texas	180	5 days—96–97[10]
Utah	180 (450 hrs.—Kindergarten 810 hrs.—Grade 1 990 hrs.—Grade 2–12)	LEA options
Vermont	175	5 days
Virginia	180 (540 hrs.—Kindergarten 990 hrs.—Grades 1–12)	Up to 20 days
Washington	180	LEA option
West Virginia	180	3–5 days (2 days must be scheduled prior to January 1)
Wisconsin	180 (437 hrs.—Kindergarten 1,050 hrs.—Grades 1–6 1,137 hrs.—Grades 7–12)	LEA option
Wyoming	175	Up to 5 days

Continued

TABLE 3-1 *Continued*

[1] In 1995, Alabama repealed legislation enacted in 1994 which would have phased in 180 days of instruction and 10 professional development days by the 2004–2005 school year.

[2] In Illinois, days not used for staff development must be added to the 176 instructional days.

[3] In Indiana, upon approval of the Indiana Department of Education, schools may accumulate student release time to use for staff development, performance-based accreditation, or program development activities. Schools must have a base 105% of the required minimum instructional time before they can accumulate release time (at least 945 hrs. per year for elementary, 1134 hrs. per year for secondary). Students must be released on 6 occasions for a minimum of 30 minutes and a maximum of 2.5 hours a day. Release time may not exceed 15 hours per school year, even if a school accumulates more than 15 hours.

[4] In Massachusetts, effective in the 1997–98 school year, elementary school students must receive a minimum of 900 hours, secondary students 990 hours, and kindergarten students 425 hours of "structured learning time."

[5] In Michigan, the scheduled increase in days/hours will not go into effect if the percentage growth in the basic foundation allowance in a state fiscal year, as compared to the preceding year, is less than the percentage increase in the average consumer price index. MICH. COMP. LAWS ANN. (380.1284 (West 1996 Supp.).

[6] In Missouri, the length of the school day may vary for 3–7 hours, giving districts the flexibility to schedule release time for in-service training.

[7] The Nevada State Superintendent of Public Instruction may authorize a reduction in the required minimum number of days per year up to 15 days. The reduction may be allowed only if the new schedule provides for an equivalent or greater number of minutes of instructional time than is provided in the 180-day school year.

[8] North Dakota schedules two days for a teachers' convention. According to the state's Department of Public Instruction, Department policies promote in-service training by acknowledging schools that have extended their school year for in-service training and by recommending that some time be set aside for in-service training, which may require the shortening of some days.

[9] In Pennsylvania, school districts wishing to fulfill minimum instructional requirements using hours instead of days must obtain approval from the Secretary of Education.

[10] In Texas, for the 1997–98 school year, the teacher in-service training days will be determined by a formula. The results will be at least 5 days of in-service training. TEX. EDUCATION CODE ANN (21.401 (b) (West 1996 Special Pamphlet)

Source: Used with permission of the Education Commission of the States, 1996.

represented in both days and hours, thus providing for some flexibility within the schedule.

Most school districts adhere closely to state guidelines even though there may be compelling reasons for changing the school calendar. For example, some districts go so far as to schedule "snow days." They begin by calculating the average number of school days that are typically missed due to inclement weather and then add that number to the minimum number of days mandated by the state. The "snow" days are included as part of the school calendar that is distributed to the parents in the fall. If the winter is mild, the students are given the unused "snow" days as vacation days during the spring or they are released early for summer vacation. For the teachers, the days that were scheduled as "snow days" are used for planning time or professional development. In other districts, "snow days" are made up by adding them to the end of the year or subtracting them from spring break.

Such care is taken because the amount of state funding a school district receives is calculated, in part, by the number of days that school is in session. In 1990, the mandates in all but 7 states—Alaska, Colorado, Delaware, Hawaii, New Hampshire, New Mexico, and Ohio—provided for some type of sanction against those districts that did not meet the minimum standard (CCSSO, 1990). Sanctions are not always enforced, but when they are they typically result in a reduction or loss of financial aid from the state. In an extreme case, a sanction may result in a school losing its accreditation.

State Mandated Hours

In addition to mandating the minimum number of days that schools must be open, most states also mandate the minimum number of hours that schools are to be in operation. Data compiled by the Council of Chief State School Officers (CCSSO) in 1995 demonstrate that there is more variation in the number of hours mandated by the states than there is in the number of days (see Table 3–2). High school students in Texas attend school seven hours a day while the school day may be as short as two hours for high school students in Illinois and as short as three hours for students in Missouri. According the data compiled by the CCSSOs, five states—Colorado, Michigan, New Hampshire, Nebraska, and Oregon—have no state policy regarding the minimum number of hours students are to be in school during the school year.

EXTENDED SCHOOL YEAR

From the mid-1800s until the mid-1900s there was a steady increase in the amount of school time mandated by departments of education throughout the nation. The average length of the mandated school terms increased from

TABLE 3–2 Length of school day in minimum hours by grade level: 1994

	Pre-Kindergarten	Half-day Kindergarten	Full-day Kindergarten	Grades 1-6	Grades 7–8	Grade 9–12
Alabama	—	—	6	6	6	6
Alaska	—	—	—	4-5	5	5
Arizona	1.2	2	6	4-5	6	—
Arkansas	—	3.3	—	6	6	6
California	—	—	—	5	5	6
Colorado	—	—	—	—	—	—
Connecticut	2.5	2.5	—	4	4	4
Delaware	—	2.5-3	—	6	6	6
District of Columbia	6.5	—	6.5	6.5	6.5	6.5
Florida	—	—	—	5	5	5
Georgia	4.5	—	4.5	4.5	5	5
Hawaii	6	6	6	6	6	6
Idaho	—	2.5	4	4	4	4
Illinois	—	2	4	2	2	2
Indiana	—	2.5	—	5	6	6
Iowa	—	—	—	5.5	5.5	5.5
Kansas	—	2.5	—	6	6	6
Kentucky	3	3	—	6	6	6
Louisiana	N/A	N/A	N/A	N/A	N/A	N/A
Maine	—	2.5	2.5	5	5	5
Maryland	—	—	—	3	3	3
Massachusetts	2.5	2.5	5	5	5.5	5.5
Michigan	—	—	—	—	—	—
Minnesota	—	2.5	—	(1)	(1)	(1)
Mississippi	5.5	—	5.5	5.5	5.5	5.5
Missouri	—	1.5	3-7	3-7	3-7	3-7
Montana	2	2	—	(2)	(2)	(2)
Nebraska	—	—	—	—	—	—
Nevada	—	—	2	4	5	5.5

Continued

State					
New Hampshire	—	—	—	—	—
New Jersey	2.5	2.5	2.5	—	—
New Mexico	2.5	5	5.5	6	6
New York	2.5	5	5	5.5	5.5
North Carolina	5.5	5.5	5.5	5.5	5.5
North Dakota	2.5	5	5.5	5.5	6
Ohio	2.5	2.5	5	5.5	5.5
Oklahoma	2.5	6	6	6	6
Oregon	—	—	—	—	—
Pennsylvania	2.5	5	5	5.5	5.5
Rhode Island	2.5	5	5	5-5.5	5.5
South Carolina	2.5	5	6	6	6
South Dakota	2.5	5(3)	(4)	(4)	—
Tennessee	—	—	—	—	—
Texas	—	7	7	7	7
Utah	2.5	—	(5)	5.5	5.5
Vermont	—	(6)	(6)	(6)	(6)
Virginia	3	5.5	5.5	5.5	5.5
Washington	(7)	(7)	(7)	(7)	(7)
West Virginia	2.6	5.25	—	—	—
Wisconsin	2.5	5	6	6.5	6.5
Wyoming	2.5	5	5	6	6

N/A = no answer to question

"—" Indicates that a state does not have a requirement in this category.

(1) Grades 1–3 policy is 5, grade 4 policy is 5.5, grades 5–12 policy is 6 hours.
(2) Grades 1–3 policy is 4 hours, grades 4–12 policy is 6 hours.
(3) Kindergarten policy is every other day.
(4) Grades 1–3 policy is 5 hours, grades 4–8 policy is 5.5 hours.
(5) Grade 1 policy is 4.5 hours, grades 1–6 policy is 5.5 hours.
(6) Kindergarten policy is 2 hours per day (not full day), grades 1–2 policy is 4 hours, grades 2–10 is 5.5 hours.
(7) Half-day kindergarten policy is 450 hours per year, full-day is 900 hours, grades 1–3 policy is 900 hours, grades 9–12 is 1,080 hours.

Source: State Departments of Education, CCSSO Policies and Practices Survey, January 1994. Council of Chief State School Officers, State Education Assessment Center, Washington, DC, 1995.

144 days in 1900 to 178 days by 1950, but the last half of the twentieth century has brought little change to the length of the school year—from 178 in 1950 to 180 in 1997 (Synder, 1994). In 1950 schools were required to be open an average of 177.9 days while in 1990 the average was 180 days (see Table 3–3).

Many believe that the time has come to once again increase the amount of school time. Denis Doyle of the American Enterprise Institute and Chester Finn of the Vanderbilt Institute for Public Policy Studies represented the position well when they declared that:

> A longer school year could help school reformers achieve many of their objectives: higher pay for teachers, opportunities for disadvantaged and slow-learning youngsters to catch up, enrichment programs for the gifted, and simplification of the child-care problems encountered by working parents during the long summer holiday (Doyle & Finn, 1984, p. C1).

Like Doyle and Finn, many believe that Extended School Year (ESY) programs, programs that extend the school year beyond the "normal", "traditional" or "customary" school year, could and should be used to address these problems. For instance, Michael Barrett, a Massachusetts state legislator, one of the nine NECTL commissioners, and a fervent advocate for ESY programs, has declared that, "The United States faces a time-in-school deficit every bit as serious as the trade deficit and the balance-of-payments problem: Each year, American children receive hundreds of hours less schooling than many of their European or Asian mates, and the resulting harm promises to be cumulative and lasting" (Barrett, 1990, p. 87).

Stevenson and Stigler acknowledge that there is a basis for assertions such as those made by Barrett but claim that the underlying assumptions are false. It is true, according to Stevenson and Stigler, that during their elementary years, Chinese children spend 1,500 to 3,000 more hours at school than

TABLE 3–3   Historical comparison of average annual time in school

	1869-70	1879-80	1889-90	1899-00	1909-10
Average length of school term in days	132.2	130.3	134.7	144.3	157.5
Percent of enrolled pupils attending	59.3	62.3	64.1	68.6	72.1
Average number of days attended by each pupil	78.4	81.1	86.3	99.0	113

Snyder, T. D., & Hoffman, C. M. (1994). *Digest of educational statistics*. (DHEW Publication No. (OE) 72-75). Washington, DC: U.S. Government Printing Office.

do American children. This is the equivalent of one to two years of school life. However, the researchers believe that the numbers are deceiving because they do not take into consideration *how* the time in school is spent. For instance, children in Beijing have a recess of approximately fifty minutes while students in Chicago receive only ten minutes for recess. An hour and a half is allocated for lunch in Beijing while in many American schools the lunch period is only thirty minutes. Many of the activities that American children participate in after school are included as part of the school day in Beijing. These activities can take up as much as an hour or two of the Chinese school day. These data have led Stevenson and Stigler to conclude that, "Although Asian children spend more time at school than American children, the difference in amount of academic instruction is not so profound as the more general statistics imply" (Stevenson and Stigler, 1992, p. 143).

Nevertheless, there is an element of common sense in the argument that the longer children spend in school the better their chances are of achieving a higher level of academic success. Wiley and Harnischfeger have noted that:

It is obvious that if a child does not go to school at all, he [she] will not directly benefit from schooling. If a child goes to school every day for a full year, he [she] will achieve his [her] maximum benefit from that schooling, other circumstances being equal. It would also seem clear that if he [she] attends school less than the full year, but more than not at all, the benefits he [she] derives from school should be in between. That is, the quantity of schooling should be a major determinant of school outcome (Wiley and Harnischfeger, 1974, p. 8).

Many school administrators and educational policy makers agree with Wiley and Harnischfeger that the quantity of time spent in school is a "major determinant of school outcome" and that the school year is too short to accomplish the many additional tasks that have been set before the schools.

TABLE 3–3 *Continued*

1919-20	1929-30	1939-40	1949-50	1959-60	1969-70	1979-80	1990-91
161.9	172.7	175.0	177.9	178.0	178.9	178.5	178.9
74.8	82.8	86.7	88.7	90.0	90.4.	90.1	—
121.2	143	151.7	157.9	160.2	161.7	168.0	—

Therefore, more and more school districts are exploring the possibility of extending the school year.

Extension of the school year can be accomplished by adding days to the school year or by adding programs during the summer months. When days are added to the school year, the ESY is mandatory for all students. When programs are added during the summer months, ESY programs are usually voluntary. If taken to the extreme, an ESY program may extend the educational year to the point where children are in school 240 days per year.

Full-Year Attendance

Programs that require students be in school 220 to 240 days per year are called full-year attendance programs. Under a typical 240 day schedule, students are in school forty-eight weeks per year and on vacation four weeks out of the year—one week in the winter, one week in the spring, and two weeks during the summer. With a 220-day schedule, the students are in school forty-five weeks and on vacation two weeks in the winter, one week in the spring, and four weeks in the summer. The extra five days of vacation are spread out among national, state, and local holidays.

Warren Roe, who served as secretary of the National Education Association during the mid-1920s, was an early, strong proponent of full-year attendance. In 1927, Roe wrote a rather colorful article in which he criticized the practice of long summer vacations, declaring that they were based on the concept of an ideal rural life and not the reality of the urban child. In the article he observed that those who defended closing the schools for the summer often did so by conjuring up images of a whimsical past and erroneously assuming the majority of children lived in such a summer wonderland.

> For the little ones there were the minnows in the brook, the woodchuck on the hill, the birch and sassafras in the thicket, make-believe houses with imaginary walls laid in stony outline, mud pies on the bank, and toes wriggling in the mud. . . .
>
> Such recollections cause strenuous defense of closing of our city schools that these delights may come to our city children. What a travesty of reasoning! For a small per cent, yes! For a few score at summer camp; for a couple of hundred, perhaps, a few days in a city seaside camp.
>
> For the other thousands asphalt streets, concrete playgrounds with swings and slides if they are fortunate. Steel and iron! The pitiless noise of the city! The rumble of the truck with its warning horn, and for the children, be they Pietro, or Wladyslaus, Moe or Mike, nothing to do. So our American streets educate for hospital and asylum, for jail and penitentiary, while the great school building provides a job for a janitor or

two and eats, like a moth, its hole of fixed charges that the taxpayer must ultimately meet; and the school shops and gymnasiums, the cool classrooms with their beautiful pictures, motion picture machines and lanterns, books and blackboards, windows that might be filled with growing plants, all stand idle, or at best are used for only an hour or two (Roe, 1927, pp. 5–6).

Since the time Roe made this statement, educational reformers have routinely and consistently called for a change in the school calendar that would require students to be in school a full year. And like Roe, many of those who favor such a calendar are frustrated by the romantic sentiment that the idea of summer vacation often elicits. Consider, for instance, the following observation by Barrett:

> Many parents would insist that their reservations are immediate and practical. They see summer as special, as a time for young people to be with their families, to do something that helps them grow—even if it is only attending summer camp—or to earn some money. Push these parents a little, and the objections become more emotional: kids need a chance to play, darn it, and they're under a lot of pressure as it is. What happened to the idyllic side of childhood? Is life to be all work? When will there be time for young people to explore the quirky and personal magic of their own creativity?
>
> These questions are hard, and those of us who believe in the necessity of more schooling must not answer them glibly. But these questions are also rhetorical, and loaded. They rely for their effect on an idealized image of childhood which does not correspond to the down-to-earth, day-to-day summer experience of even middle-class kids. A school environment can be humane and true to the curiosity of children, and learning to read and write and compute and analyze is the key to unlocking the creative urge, not squelching it. For that matter, extended schooling can allow time not only for more instruction but also more play. And surely summer is special for many families. But a school year that is stretched into the last week of July would still leave more than a month for a family vacation, a stint at camp, or both (Barrett, 1990, p. 87).

Advocates for full-year attendance have been consistent in their contention that the conventional school calendar fails to be responsive to societal needs. Today, as in the past, they argue that knowledge is expanding at an exponential rate and schools are struggling to keep up with the changes. This is occurring at the same time that schools are being asked to take on the responsibilities that once belonged to the family, the church, and the community as a whole. Under these circumstances, say the advocates for full-year atten-dance, it is ridiculous to enforce a school calendar that relegates teaching and learning to part-time occupations. They believe that schools need to be open 220 to 240 days per year and that whenever the school is open, attendance should be mandatory.

Even though the arguments for adopting a full-year attendance program appear to be logical, school districts have been slow to adopt this approach. According to the National Association for All-Year Schools, there are very few schools within the United States that require their students to be in ses-sion the full year, and most of these schools are private.

Increased Number of School Days

Many who would otherwise support full-year attendance often shy away from suggesting such a calendar because they believe it would be impossible to get the public support that is needed. Instead they are inclined to recom-mend the more conservative approach of gradually adding days to the school year. Although it would appear to be easier to get approval for increasing the school year in this way, those who attempt to increase the amount of time stu-dents spend in school by adding days to the school year are often thwarted by two additional barriers—economic restraints and social impediments.

Economic Restraints

For many school districts, the cost of increasing the length of the school year is simply too formidable to consider. It has been estimated that to add twenty days to the school year would increase a school district's budget by 9.9 percent (Segal, 1992). In Louisiana, a bill to lengthen the school year from 175 to 180 days was defeated because it was estimated that it would cost the state an ad-ditional $30 million a year. The Michigan legislature has mandated that the length of the school year be increased from 180 days in 1996–97 to 190 days by the 2006–07, but included the caveat that the "scheduled increase in days/hours will not go into effect if the percentage growth in the basic foun-dation allowance in a state fiscal year, as compared to the preceding year, is less than the percentage increase in the average consumer price index" (reported in a 1992 clearinghouse note for the Education Commission of the States).

Using figures compiled by the NEA, the National Association for Year-Round Education (NAYRE) calculated how much it would cost each state to add one day to the school year. The results of the NAYRE calculations are presented in Table 3–4. Because averages are being used in the calculations, one must be careful of the degree of significance assigned to the figures. Ac-cording to Charles Ballinger, executive director of NAYRE, "While the figures for 'expenditures per day statewide' correctly reflect the daily cost of already-existing school programs in a given state, it would be incorrect to extrapolate an exact calculation for an additional five days, for example" (C. Ballinger, personal communication, December 20, 1996). Ballinger goes on to explain that the primary reason for the lack of a one-to-one correspondence is that the cost of health benefits would be unchanged whether the teachers and staff worked all year or just a portion of the year. However, the figures presented in Table 3–4 do provide us with at least some idea of just how costly it would be to extend the school year to 220 days.

TABLE 3–4   Cost per day for lengthening the school year (compiled by the National Association for Year-Round Education, January 1995)

State	Daily expenditure per pupil*	Number of pupils statewide	Expenditure per day statewide*
Alabama	$23.21	728,533	$16,909,251.00
Alaska	$54.51	122,291	$6,666,082.00
Arizona	$24.49	695,682	$17,037,252.00
Arkansas	$21.94	443,023	$9,719,925.00
California	$25.67	5,285,000	$135,665,950.00
Colorado	$26.05	625,062	$16,282,865.00
Connecticut	$46.83	497,328	$23,289,870.00
Delaware	$36.59	105,547	$3,861,965.00
DC	$47.96	80,678	$3,869,317.00
Florida	$29.64	2,040,763	$60,488,215.00
Georgia	$24.85	1,235,304	$30,697,304.00
Hawaii	$32.98	179,876	$5,932,310.00
Idaho	$23.38	236,774	$5,535,776.00
Illinois	$31.36	1,886,947	$59,174,658.00
Indiana	$32.72	961,413	$31,457,433.00
Iowa	$31.30	497,882	$15,583,707.00
Kansas	$31.41	458,538	$14,402,679.00
Kentucky	$29.57	639,200	$18,901,144.00
Louisiana	$26.71	780,346	$20,843,042.00
Maine	$34.55	212,245	$7,333,065.00
Maryland	$36.12	772,638	$27,907,685.00
Massachusetts	$36.73	865,618	$31,794,149.00
Michigan	$36.52	1,609,304	$58,771,782.00
Minnesota	$32.97	811,295	$26,748,396.00
Mississippi	$19.06	503,374	$9,594,308.00
Missouri	$26.68	851,086	$22,706,974.00

Continued

TABLE 3–4   *Continued*

State	Daily expenditure per pupil*	Number of pupils statewide	Expenditure per day statewide*
Montana	$29.31	164,891	$4,832,955.00
Nebraska	$28.86	283,935	$8,194,364.00
Nevada	$27.55	235,800	$6,496,290.00
New Hampshire	$33.30	184,916	$6,157,703.00
New Jersey	$55.90	1,152,205	$64,408,260.00
New Mexico	$27.59	299,343	$8,258,873.00
New York	$47.78	2,746,200	$131,213,436.00
North Carolina	$27.62	1,123,636	$31,034,826.00
North Dakota	$24.72	119,115	$2,944,523.00
Ohio	$34.45	1,812,300	$62,433,735.00
Oklahoma	$23.12	603,600	$13,955,232.00
Oregon	$33.71	515,774	$17,386,742.00
Pennsylvania	$45.67	1,745,230	$79,704,654.00
Rhode Island	$37.58	144,932	$5,446,545.00
South Carolina	$25.26	635,883	$16,062,405.00
South Dakota	$27.05	135,267	$3,658,972.00
Tennessee	$23.33	857,051	$19,995,000.00
Texas	$28.97	3,606,457	$104,479,059.00
Utah	$18.99	468,675	$8,900,138.00
Vermont	$44.12	99,717	$4,399,514.00
Virginia	$30.87	1,045,472	$32,273,721.00
Washington	$31.99	921,337	$29,473,571.00
West Virginia	$32.17	313,750	$10,093,338.00
Wisconsin	$38.89	841,856	$32,739,780.00
Wyoming	$32.91	100,899	$3,320,586.00
United States	$31.99	43,283,988	$1,384,654,766.00

*Data Source: National Education Association, *Estimates of School Statistics* 1993–94, and Education Commission of the States. Figures calculated by the National Association for year-round education. Used with permission from NAYRE.

Social Impediments

A second obstacle to adding days to the school year is that many families, communities, and even businesses have an established lifestyle that revolves around the school calendar. Any change to the school calendar, no matter how minor, will be met with opposition if it threatens to alter this life style.

Consider, for instance, the obstacle presented by the Labor Day holiday. Throughout much of the country, Labor Day serves to mark the end of the "lazy days of summer" and any attempt to send children back to school before the "official end of summer" is a psychological barrier that is almost as real as any physical barrier. As a case in point, consider this story told by William Shelton, president of Eastern Michigan University and one of the NECTL commissioners. On his way to a news conference in May 1994, Shelton happened to pick up a copy of the *Washington Post* and was delighted to see an article about Prisoners of Time, the NECTL report that had just been released the previous month. The article was very complimentary of the work of the commission and strongly supported the need to consider time as an essential element in the equation for quality education. Then he happened to notice an article about a local school board meeting. The topic of the board meeting was the school calendar and, of course, it piqued Shelton's curiosity. According to the article, approximately two hundred parents had attended the board meeting and were in an uproar because the board was recommending a calendar change that would require students to attend school the week before Labor Day. According to Shelton, the juxtaposition of the two articles served to remind him that, regardless of how important the issues are or how strong the need for change, there will always be constraints and restraints that must be confronted.

This anecdote helps to demonstrate how public opinion can act as a critical restraint to educational change and reform. But before becoming too discouraged, remember that a growing number of districts do start classes before Labor Day and many, if not the majority, have found that by the second and third year there is little, if any, grumbling or even discussion about the "early start." Also remember that starting school before Labor Day is just one example of how a minor change in the school calendar can be perceived as having a major effect on a community's lifestyle. For instance, when schools in Collier County, Florida were scheduled to reopen after a two-week winter break in 1995, absenteeism ran higher than normal. According to an article in the Naples Daily News entitled "A football holiday? Something kept Collier kids, teachers home Monday" (Freeman, 1995, pp. 1a, 3a) "The absenteeism rate at Collier County schools averaged about 20 percent Monday for students, nearly 4 times the normal rate, but school officials don't blame it *all* (emphasis added) on the resumption of classes on Jan. 2, a day much of the nation observed as a holiday and the occasion of most college football's major bowl game." The article goes on to state that, "In December some teacher-grumbling about classes resuming Jan. 2 when the rest of the country would have the day off, led Superintendent Robert Munz to consider, then reject, a change in the schedule." Dan White, executive director of administrative services for western Collier County, referring to the higher than normal level of absenteeism commented that "It's not all related to the national holiday, but in general, the majority is because of the national holiday." This demonstrates, once again, that any time it is perceived that a change in the calendar will affect the community lifestyle, no matter how minor the change, a challenge to the change can be expected.

Summer School

It would seem that if the general public objects to children starting school before Labor Day, they would resist even more ardently children being in school during the summer. The quotes by both Roe and Barrett support this contention. Except for individual cases, however, there seems to be little resistance to summer school programs. Three factors contribute to this lack of resistance. First, summer school is almost always voluntary. Children and parents are able to make their own decisions about whether the child should attend school during the vacation time. Second, summer school programs have been around since 1885 and therefore do not represent a true change in the calendar. Finally, summer school programs usually are structured to provide different types of educational experiences than those provided in the regular school year.

Summer programs commonly are established for the purposes of remediation, acceleration, and/or enrichment and are beneficial in helping to overcome many of the problems associated with a lock-step program. Some students are unable to handle the normal academic work load successfully simply because it takes them longer to complete the learning tasks. Summer school provides an opportunity for these children to "catch-up."

At the high school level, summer programs are designed to allow students to retake courses, to take additional courses in their regular program, and/or to take enrichment courses. Students often choose to take difficult courses during the summer when their course load is light rather than during the regular year when their load is heavier. Some students find that the only way they will be able to graduate on time is if they are able to take or retake a course during the summer just prior to their graduation. Other students choose to take enrichment courses such as band, drivers education, and computers during the summer. In addition, there are a number of universities that offer special credit and non-credit bearing courses to high school students during the summer months.

For elementary students, the motivation for attending summer school is most often provided by the parent, principal, or teacher. Frequently, low-achieving students are required to take summer school in the hope that the extra time spent in instruction will help to overcome their learning deficiencies. The curriculum is designed to meet very specific needs, classes tend to be smaller, teachers are more relaxed, and students are more motivated.

Effectiveness of Summer School Programs

If it is true that there is a direct, positive relationship between time and learning, then it would be expected that attendance at summer school would result in an increase in a student's academic performance. The research on the relationship between summer school and cognitive development is inconclusive, however.

A number of studies have been conducted on the effectiveness of summer school at the elementary level and are consistent in demonstrating that summer school is effective in stemming *summer loss among disadvantaged children* (Heyns, 1987). After an extended summer vacation, teachers often find it necessary to spend several weeks reviewing material that the students have forgotten. This is referred to as "summer loss" and is measured in terms of the amount of time that is spent on material that was previously learned. The general findings from the research on summer loss are far from conclusive, but do support the contention that the amount of time that disadvantaged students must spend in review is substantially reduced when they attend summer school. The same may hold true for other children as well but research has failed to support this contention of summer loss because the majority of the studies have focused on the disadvantaged. Therefore, it would be unwise to draw conclusions about other populations of children. The research does suggest, however, that intensive remediation can help to bridge the gap between abled and less abled students at all levels and that summer school can be an effective way to provide this remediation (Branch, Milliner, & Bumbaugh, 1986; Zubik, 1991).

The summer school organizational pattern allows high school students educational opportunities that otherwise would not be available to them. These opportunities, in and of themselves, provide a strong rationale for offering at least some summer courses at the high school level. Summer programs also provide social services for underprivileged children and supply recreational activities for children who have little to do over the summer. Evaluation of the effectiveness of any summer school program must be made in light of the purpose of the program, the priority of goals within a district, and the practicality of using this intervention strategy rather than one of the others such as extended year, year-round school, or extended day programs.

EXTENDED SCHOOL DAY

Rather than lengthening the school *year*, some districts prefer to extend the school *day*. Extended school day programs increase the length of the day, usually by an hour or more. The day may be extended by adding a before or after school program or by adding an additional period to the day. Like ESY programs, extended-day programs may be mandatory or voluntary but, under normal circumstances, meet with less resistance. Also, extending the day normally proves to be less costly than extending the year because transportation, food services, and other auxiliary costs remain virtually the same.

Extended High School Day

At the high school level, the length of the school day is often regulated by accrediting associations that use the Carnegie unit as one of their standards for evaluation. When the North Central Association (NCA) first implemented the Carnegie Unit as the standard for high school accreditation in 1904, it strongly recommended that a student be allowed to take no more than three units per year. A unit was awarded for regular attendance in a recitation (academic) class that met for forty-five to fifty minutes, five days a week, 36 weeks per year. A half unit was awarded for shop and laboratory classes. As the curriculum expanded, the number of classes students took increased to four and sometimes five. The increase in the number of subjects concerned many educators and, in 1915, the NCA acknowledged the concern. In the introduction to its annual report, the committee on the Revision of the Definition of the Unit stated that:

> The Committee believes that the great increase in the number of subjects taught in the schools has, in various ways, led to a dissipation of effort and a consequent superficiality in results. The demand that the student prepare lessons in four subjects daily rather than in three is likely to lower the standard of work. More intensive work on fewer subjects is, therefore, desirable, if a student is to attain the habits of concentrated and persistent effort leading to success. We therefore recommend that the daily number of recitations of the Upper Secondary be placed at three, recognizing that students of superior ability may increase the number to four (Clark, 1915, p. 29).

Today the *average* high school student takes between five and six classes per semester and many districts have recently implemented, or are proposing to implement, a seventh period. With the addition of a seventh period, the number of academic classes a student takes often increases. However, the warning provided by NCA in 1915 still rings true. This is true especially in light of the more demanding standards being endorsed by national organizations such as the National Council of Teachers of Mathematics, the National Council for the Social Studies (NCSS), the Consortium of National Arts Education, the National Council of Teachers of English, the National Geographic Society, and the National Academy of Sciences. Cognizant of these rising standards, many educators question the logic of adding a seventh period. Students today have many other obligations—such as work, sports, and community service—so many educators fear that adding a seventh period will take away from the limited time that students spend on homework. They also worry that adding a seventh period may decrease the academic achievement in the classes that the students are already taking. They ask, "If students are having difficulty mastering five classes, how is adding another class to their load going to help them?" Although the concerns are indeed valid, it must be remembered that a seventh period is not always assigned to an additional class. The time may be, and often is, used to provide more time to existing classes. The seventh period can also be used to provide services and activities—such as counseling, tutoring, and mentoring—that are not provided in the traditional day. Therefore, any decision to add more time to the school day must go hand in hand with determining how that time will be used. It is imperative that this determination be made with regard to student needs and aspirations, district goals, and community responsibilities.

Extended Day—Elementary Programs

At the elementary level, justification for extending school time often revolves around the need to augment services provided to the young child. Current efforts to extend the elementary day began in the late 1950s when many schools implemented a "closed-lunch period." Prior to this time, the majority of students attended neighborhood schools and were sent home for a lunch period that lasted anywhere from 45 minutes to 1 and 1/2 hours. Beginning in the late 1950s and continuing through the 60s and 70s, an increasingly larger number of children were bused to schools outside of their neighborhoods, so that it was no longer feasible to send the children home during the school day. As a result, schools began serving lunch, the lunch hour was shortened, and the "closed lunch hour" became the norm.

Other schools quickly became interested in the closed lunch hour even though the majority of their children could easily go home for lunch. There is some indication that the impetus for the change in these schools developed as a result of the growing number of mothers who were entering the workforce. Working mothers often found it inconvenient, if not impossible, to be home during the lunch hour and many of them felt that it was unfair for the school to assume that they could rearrange their day to meet the needs of the school schedule. They knew that the closed lunch period was working in other schools and they asked, and in some cases demanded, that their school adopt a similar schedule.

Educators who favored the closed lunch saw it as a way to increase the instructional time of students because the minutes that had been shaved off the lunch hour could easily be added to the instructional day. There were some who argued against the program, however, because they felt that children needed a break during the day to keep them from becoming overly fatigued in the afternoon. It was argued further that, under the closed lunch program, teachers would lose their longer lunch hour and as a result would be required to work longer for the same amount of pay. Although some schools did attempt to adjust the teachers' schedule so that this did not happen, in reality many teachers were required to work during the time that had once been their lunch hour and they received no additional compensation.

Before and After-School Programs
More recently, the push to increase the length of the elementary school day is emanating from the need for parents to seek alternatives to more traditional forms of child care. The 1970s saw an increase in the number of women entering the workforce and this trend continues. The 1980s brought with them an increase in the number of single-parent families and this trend is also continuing. As a result, more and more children are being labeled "latchkey" or "self-care kids." These children are left home alone before and/or after school and are expected to care for themselves and, just as the children who came home for lunch created a problem for their working mothers, self-care children create a problem for their working parents. Self-care children are, to a great degree, responsible for what has become known as the "3 o'clock syndrome" in which, "the quality of parents' performance at work suffers from giving long-distance attention to children at home alone" (Powell, 1987, p. 64). In addition, research has shown that self-care children tend to experience a higher degree of fear and are subject to more peer pressure when they are home alone.

One solution to the problems associated with children caring for themselves is before- and after-school child care programs. Such programs provide a sense of security to both parent and child. Many believe that schools should offer before- and after-school programs not only because they provide a safe place for children but because they furnish an opportunity to provide remedial instruction to children who need it most. Although more and more schools appear to agree with this position, only 18 percent of the approximately 1.7 million students in grades kindergarten through eight who attended before-and/or after-school child care programs attended one offered by a public school. In addition, less than half of the program directors stated that one of the roles of their program was to provide remedial help to students who are having difficulty in schools. By comparison, more than 75 percent of them indicated that the supervision of children was the primary purpose of their program (Seppanen, deVries, & Seligson, 1992).

While most before and after school programs require some financial support from parents, few programs are self-supporting. Many who oppose public schools offering before- and after-school programs argue that such programs make it easy for parents to neglect their parental duties, expecting schools to pick up the slack and taxpayers to pick up the bill. They go on to argue that the programs are "anti-family" because they are unfair to the mother who stays home to "raise her kids." The mother who works may increase the material worth of her family but, in order for this to occur, society has to accept more of the childrearing responsibilities. Therefore, the argument goes, our public institutions are supporting materialism over family life. A growing number of senior citizens feel it is unfair for them to pick up child care expenses so that families can live in expensive homes, drive luxury cars, and indulge themselves in extravagant vacations, especially considering that so many of the senior citizens had to do without all of these luxuries while raising their own children.

Perhaps of even greater concern are the issues that revolve around the quality of before- and after-school programs. Quality programs involve nurturing, mentoring, free-play, structured and unstructured learning activities, and a level of spontaneity that encourages the development of creativity. (Seligson, Gannett, Cotlin, 1992; Powell, 1987; Nietig, 1983; Mills & Cooke, 1983). There is a delicate balance among the nurturing, custodial, and educational roles played by child-care programs. This is especially true when the programs are offered by public schools that have, if not a stated, at least an implied purpose of enhancing academic performance. A report submitted to the U.S. Department's Office of Policy and Planning expressed the concern in the following manner:

We see a danger in the schools extending their role into the after school time of the child that has traditionally involved activities in the home, neighborhood, and community. As the schools move into the provision of before- and after-school care, will program planners emphasize academic learning, when many parents and children may instead desire safe and reliable child care with informal learning in an enriching environment that emphasizes social and emotional growth? If academic work and remedial assistance is to be one function of a before- and after-school program, will such programs be available only to those children whose parents can afford the fees or children whose families qualify for government subsidies? (Seppanen, deVries, & Seligson, 1992, p. 16).

Like all extended-time programs, the worthiness of the program must be tested against valid evaluation criteria. Unfortunately, before- and after-school programs often fail to meet the established criteria. This failure, as often as not, results from the wrong criteria being used rather than from an inherent weakness in the program. If, for instance, the standards are based on improved academic performance, but the program's purpose and design focus on child supervision and nurturing, the program will fail. The program also may be subject to failure if the stated purpose is different from the perceived purpose. This occurs most frequently when parents and teachers perceive the purpose of the program to be child supervision while the program may have been "sold" to funding agencies as a way to improve the academic achievement of elementary-aged children. The caution here is quite simple: Before establishing a program or when conducting an evaluation of a program, make certain that the evaluation criteria that are to be, or are being, used match the implied and stated purposes of the program.

Full-Day Kindergarten

One extended-day program that has grown significantly in the last thirty years is the full-day kindergarten. In a survey conducted by the National Education Association (NEA) in 1961, only 3.5 percent of the administrators who responded indicated that they offered a full-day session for kindergarten children. A similar survey conducted in 1989 by Education Research Services (ERS) found that 27 percent of the programs surveyed had full-day programs (Bickers, 1989).

A renewed interest in full-day kindergarten has grown out of a 1991 report written by Ernest Boyer for the Carnegie Foundation. The report, entitled "Ready to Learn: A Mandate for the Nation" asserts that approximately 35 percent of all kindergarten children do not have the language skills necessary to be successful in school. In support of this finding, Boyer quotes from an assessment done by the Southern Regional Education Board in which it was noted that, "Today not all children are ready to begin the first grade. Too many never catch up. Unless additional steps are taken, possibly one-third of the approximately one million children projected to be entering the first grade will not be ready to do so in the year 2000" (Boyer, 1991, p. 6). Boyer then goes on to identify a number of factors that contribute to this lack of readiness. The factors that were identified included overworked parents who don't have time to spend quality time with their children, children who suffer from poor nutrition, inadequate health care for young children, the limited number of child care alternatives available for poor families, the number of hours that children spend watching television, and the unsafe neighborhoods in which many of these children live.

If these factors sound familiar, it may be because they have a rich historical foundation. You may recall that many of these same factors played an important role in the establishment of the "traditional" school calendar. In the past, the time that children spent in school was often extended to allow the school to augment the services it provided to the children, and the full-day kindergarten falls into this paradigm.

Resistance to the full-day program embodies many of the same arguments that have been offered in opposition to other extended-day programs. Economic, social, and educational issues are threaded throughout the arguments. For instance, opponents contend that full-day programs are more expensive that half-day programs (an argument heard against every extended-day program), that taking the young child away from his or her parents for a full day implies that the institution does not value family life (an argument that is also raised against before- and after-school programs), and that the curriculum that is implemented in the full-day kindergarten is often developmentally inappropriate for the young child (an argument that is echoed in phrases such as "curriculum expects too much from high school students").

Although the economic and social issues do have some impact on the acceptance of the full-day kindergarten, the argument that most concerns educators is the last one—that the curriculum used in many full-day kindergartens is inappropriate. It has been observed that "overall those who implement extended-day programs appear to share the overriding belief that more intensive diagnostic procedures, longer periods of instructional time, and a more diverse academic curriculum are essential to ensuring a future school achievement" (Olsen & Zigler, 1989, p. 167). However, the National Association for the Education of Young Children (NAECY) has expressed concern about this trend in its 1990 position statement on school readiness:

> Today not only do many kindergartens and primary grades focus on skill acquisition in the absence of meaningful context, but the expectations that are placed on children are often not age-appropriate. Whether the result of parental pressures or the push to improve student performance or standardized tests, the curriculum has shifted. Children entering kindergarten are now typically expected to be ready for what previously constituted the first-grade curriculum. As a result, more children are struggling and failing.
>
> Even those children who have received every advantage prior to school entry find the inappropriate demands difficult to meet, often experiencing great stress and having their confidence as successful learners undermined (NAEYC, 1990, p. 22).

The problem for those who do try to implement an age-appropriate curriculum is that educators are still trying to determine what "age-appropriate" curriculum really means. Kindergarten children vary greatly in interest, ability, intelligence, psychomotor skills and attention span. (For this reason, many educators prefer the term "developmentally appropriate" over "age-appropriate"). Trying to find the perfect blend of academic, social, and physical activities is difficult, at best.

Research on Full-Day Kindergarten

In spite of the concerns about, and arguments against, full-day kindergarten, research findings tend to favor full-day over half-day kindergartens. In 1989 the Educational Research Service did a review of research studies conducted that compared full-day and half-day kindergarten schedules. (Bickers, 1989) The researchers reviewed thirty-seven studies conducted from 1970 through 1988. The studies examined one or more of the following: the effect of the kindergarten schedule on the childrens' academic achievement; the effect of the kindergarten schedule on the childrens' social skills development; and/or the attitudes of parents, teachers, and principals with regard to the two different scheduling approaches. Table 3–5 provides a summary of these research findings.

It is interesting to note that the majority of the research studies reviewed by ERS focused on academic achievement. This is especially interesting in light of Boyer's conclusion regarding school readiness and the concerns expressed by NAYEC relating to age-appropriate curriculum. However, seven of the studies examined the effects of the full-day schedule on educationally disadvantaged students and all seven reported a significant difference in favor of the full day over half day. Does this mean that NAYEC is overly concerned or that, in spite of what Boyer suggests, full-day kindergartens are most successful when they focus on academics? No! We simply can't answer the question based on the information given, because over 80 percent of the studies failed to look at the other areas of interest. It may very well be that the limited nature of the research studies has led us to what Caldwell (1989) has labeled a false dichotomy—erroneously distinguishing between *educating* and *caring* for the young child. Anyone who is in any way responsible for implementing or evaluating a full-day kindergarten should be aware of this tendency.

TABLE 3–5   Summary of research findings on the length of the kindergarten day

	Favored full-day	Favored half-day	Mixed results	No difference	Wasn't addressed
Academic achievement	18	1	5	8	5
Social skills	6	1	2	0	28
Parents' attitudes	10	1	3	0	23
Teachers' attitudes	10	0	3	0	24
Principals' attitudes	5	1	0	0	31

Source: Bickers, P. M. (1989). *Effects of kindergarten scheduling:* A summary research. Arlington, VA: Educational Research Service. Used with permission.

COMPARISON OF EXTENDED TIME PROGRAMS

This chapter has reviewed a number of ways to extend the amount of time students spend in school, including extended year programs, full-year attendance, summer school, before- and after-school programs, and full-day kindergartens. When comparing the ways used to increase the length of time students spend in school, it is important to consider the reason for increasing the amount of time. If it is believed that there is just too much material to cover in the limited time available, adding days to the school year probably makes the most sense. If the concern is that some children need remedial work, some would benefit from advanced work, and others need enrichment, then summer school or before- and after-school programs may be the best alternative. If the concern is the low academic achievement of a majority of the students, then a move to a full-year, 220 to 240 day, calendar is probably best.

Summer school programs will probably meet with the least resistance, as long as they are voluntary. Adding a day or two to the school year does not represent a major change, and therefore it is unlikely this strategy will meet with much opposition and what resistance is met will be short-lived. Going to full-year attendance, on the other hand, is likely to meet with resistance, because it not only affects family lifestyle but it also increases the cost of schooling.

Extended programs need to be considered in light of the arguments most frequently presented against them. The two most common arguments against extending the school year are, first, "If what we have now isn't working, then why give us more of the same?" and second, "We simply can't afford to spend more money on schools and extending the amount of time that children spend in school will certainly cost us more money." For these reasons, the National Education Association recommends that "before committing to this type of investment, policy makers should insist on concrete proof that they could expect to get something for their money, or that of all the possible uses of available educational funds, buying more instructional time is the best option" (NEA, Oct. 1987, p. 20).

REFERENCES

American Association of School Administrators. (1973). *Year-round community schools: A framework for administrative leadership.* Washington, DC: Author.

Barrett, M. J. (1990, November). The case for more school days. The Atlantic Monthly. pp. 78, 80–106.

Bickers, P. M. (1989). *Effects of kindergarten scheduling: A summary research.* Arlington, VA: Educational Research Service.

Boyer, E. L. (1991). *Ready to learn: A mandate for the nation.* Princeton, NJ: The Carnegie Foundation.

Branch, A. Y., Milliner, J., & Bumbaugh, J. (1986). *Summer training and education program (STEP): Report on the 1985 summer experience.* Philadelphia: Public/Private Ventures.

Caldwell, B. M. (1989). All-day kindergarten—Assumptions, precautions, and over-generalizations. *Early Childhood Research Quarterly, 4,* 261–266.

Clark, T. A. (Ed.). (1915, March 19–20) *Proceedings of the Twentieth Annual Meeting of the North Central Association of Colleges and Secondary Schools:* Chicago, IL: North Central Association.

Council of Chief State School Officers (CCSSO). (1995). *State education indicators: 1995.* Washington, DC: Author.

Council of Chief State School Officers (CCSSO). (1990). *State education indicators: 1990.* Washington, DC: Author.

Doyle, D., & Finn, C. (1984, December 30). Huck Finn is dead: Long live year-round school. *The Washington Post,* pp. C1, C4.

Education Commission of the States Clearinghouse. (1992, February). *Minimum school calendar 1980 and 1990.* Denver, CO: Clearinghouse Notes.

Freeman, L. (1995, January 3). A football holiday? Something kept Collier kids, teachers home Monday. *Naples Daily News.*

Heyns, B. (1987). Schooling and cognitive development: Is there a season for learning? *Child Development, 58,* 1151–1160.

McLain, J. D. (1973). *Year-round education, economic, educational, and sociological factors.* Berkeley, CA: McCutchan Publishing Corporation.

Mills, B. C., & Cooke, E. (1983). Extended day programs—a place for the latchkey child. *Early Child Development and Care, 12*(2), 143–151.

National Association for the Education of Young Children (NAEYC). (1990). NAEYC position statement on school readiness. *Young Children, 45*(5), 21–23.

National Education Association. (1987). *What research says about: Year-round school.* No. 8. Washington, DC: Author.

Nietig, P. L. (1983). School-age child care: In support of development and learning. *Childhood Education, 60*(1), 6–11.

Olsen, D., & Zigler, E. (1989). An assessment of the all-day kindergarten movement. *Early Childhood Research Quarterly, 4,* 167–186.

Powell, D. R. (1987). After-school child care. *Young Children, 42*(3), 62-66.

Roe, W. A. (1927). The all-year school. *American Childhood, 1*(10), 5–6, 57–58.

Segal, T. (1992, March 30). Better schools, not just more school. *Business Week,* p. 93.

Seligson, M., Gannett, E., & Cotlin, L. (1992). Before- and after-school child care for elementary school children. *Childhood Education, 3,* 125–142.

Seppanen, P. S., deVries, D. K., & Seligson, M. (1992). *National study of before- and after-school programs: Executive summary.* Washington, DC: U.S. Department of Education, Office of Policy and Planning.

Stevenson, H. W., & Stigler, J. W. (1992). *The learning gap.* New York: Summit Books.

Synder, T. D. (1994). *10 Years of American education: A statistical portrait.* Washington, DC: U.S. Department of Education, National Center for Education Statistics.

Wiley, D. E., & Harnischfeger, A. (1974). Explosion of a myth: Quantity of schooling and exposure to instruction, major educational vehicles. *Educational Researcher, 3*(4), 7–12.

Zubik, D. L. (1991). *High school students' motivation for attending summer school.* Field study report. Unpublished master's thesis, Eastern Michigan University, Ypsilanti, MI.

▶ 4

School Time
Restructured

In the last chapter we looked at programs that extended the amount of time that students spend in school. Many believe, however, that it is not more school time that is needed but rather that school time needs to be reorganized. As evidence of where the school calendar is less than effective, those who favor the restructuring school time point to (1) the lack of continuity in learning brought on by the long summer vacation, (2) the fixed schedule that forces all courses into the same time frame, and (3) the stagnant viewing of school time that holds time as a constant and learning as a variable. They share many of these arguments with those who favor extending the school year. Advocates for the restructuring of school time believe, however, that these problems can be eased by reorganizing the time that children now spend in school rather than by adding more time to the school day or year. Among the scheduling devices that are often recommend as ways of restructuring school time are year-round schools and flexible scheduling of the school day and year. A few of the more innovative approaches include going to a shorter week, having kindergartners come to school all-day every other day, and reducing the number of years that students spend in school while increasing the amount of time they spend in school each year.

YEAR-ROUND SCHOOLS

One of the most frequently suggested reforms in the school calendar is year-round school (YRS). Policy makers, along with members of the education community, have spent the better part of a century toying with the idea of

YRS. The educational literature contains occasional references to all-year schools (or year-round schools) from about 1895 forward, but it wasn't until the schools in Bluffton, Indiana went to a four-quarter plan in 1904 that these early murmurings gave way to a strong voice. Bluffton implemented a year-round program because the school district was faced with overcrowding and the district could not afford to build new schools. By using the school year-round, the district was able to increase the school's capacity by 25 percent. Other districts quickly became interested in the concept of year-round schools, speculating that if an alteration in the calendar could ease over-crowding, the same process could be used to ease other problems (Schoenfeld & Schmitz, 1964). With each new decade came a petition to at least examine YRS as an option. In the early part of the twentieth century, YRS was seen as a way of easing the problems associated with overcrowding, improving the skills of non-English speaking immigrants, and removing delinquents from the streets. During the 1930s, YRS was used to accelerate the graduation of students who would otherwise leave school before completing requirements necessary for graduation. After World War II, overcrowding became a prob-lem once again and schools went to double sessions and YRS programs were looked to for the answer. In the late 1950s, Sputnik orbited the earth and pol-icy makers and educational leaders offered YRS as a way of dealing with in-ternational competition. In the 1970s, school funding seemed to "dry up" and with decreasing funds came the cry that we must make better use of school facilities, and once again the call for YRS was rolling off the tongues of those in power.

The petition for year-round schools is upon us once again. Consider the following quote taken from a financial analysis of year-round education com-piled by Arthur Anderson and Co. for the Cypress-Fairbanks Independent School District.

> The public is making increasing demands on schools to raise the aca-demic achievement of students in order for our children to possess the skills needed to compete globally, but wants to minimize the tax burden needed to finance construction of new facilities. School lead-ers are faced with the question of how to control costs without re-ducing the quality of educational programs and services to children. One answer which is being used by some districts is year-round ed-ucation (Arthur Anderson, 1993, p. 1).

The number of schools that have gone to a year-round program has in-creased by 600 percent since 1986–87. (McGregor, 1996, p. B1). During the 1996–97 school year, a total of 2,460 schools in 38 states were on year-round calendars. Of this number, 2,400 were public schools and the majority of these were elementary schools (82% or 1,962). Only 175 public high schools and 235 middle/junior high schools were on a year-round program during the 1996–97 school year. The remaining 28 schools were special or atypical schools (National Association for Year-Round Education, 1996).

Even though the number of schools on year-round programs has increased dramatically in the last ten years, it would be a mistake to assume that the YRS is now here to stay. Many school districts that have investigated the possibility of going to year-round school have decided not to adopt the program, and there are still others that have adopted YRS only to drop the program after an initial trial period.

The Structure of Year-Round Programs

Contrary to popular belief, most year-round plans do not increase the number of days that students are in school but merely repackage the existing days. As a result, school buildings are used twelve months out of the year rather than the traditional nine or ten months, although most students are in school approximately 180 days out of the year. In many year-round programs, students are actually in school fewer days, but the days are longer so that the children spend the same amount of time in school as they did under the former schedule.

Over 60 different approaches to year-round school have been identified in the educational literature. Most of these approaches are spin-offs of five very basic plans: the 45-15 plan, Concept 6, the four quarter plan, the trimester, and the flexible school year.

The 45-15 Plan

One of the most popular of the year-round school plans, especially at the elementary level, is the 45-15 plan. The typical 45-15 plan is composed of 180 school days—the same as most conventional school calendars. However, rather than attending school from August or September to May or June, students go to school 9 weeks (45 days) and then get a three week vacation (15 days). An additional four weeks are allocated to winter breaks, spring vacation, and to selected national, state, and local holidays.

A typical layout for a 45/15 calendar is depicted in Figure 4–1. This particular calendar is the one that was used by Fairfield Elementary School in Fort Wayne, Indiana during the 1994–95 school year. Like most 45-15 calendars, the plan presented in Figure 4–1 has been modified to accommodate holidays.

The 45-15 plan can be organized as either a single-track or multi-track program. In the single-track plan, all students and teachers within a given building go to school at the same time and share a common vacation. In the multi-track plan, students within a building are divided into four groups and each group follows the same schedule. The groups share some common

1997-98 SCHOOL-YEAR CALENDAR

🖐 First day of school   ◯ Holiday   ⬜ Intersession   ▨ Professional day-NO SCHOOL

◇ Parent-teacher conferences   ◯ End of grading period

Make-up days *(in this order)*: 1/30, 7/3, 5/22

Fairfield Elementary Year-Round Education

AUGUST 1997
S M T W T F S
1 2
3 4 5 6 7 8 9
10 11 12 13 14 15 16
17 18 19 20 21 ▨ 23
24 (25) 26 27 28 29 30
31

SEPTEMBER 1997
S M T W T F S
(1) 2 3 4 5 6
7 8 9 10 11 12 13
14 15 16 17 18 19 20
21 22 23 24 25 26 27
28 29 30

OCTOBER 1997
S M T W T F S
1 2 3 4
5 6 7 8 9 10 11
12 13 14 15 16 17 18
19 20 21 22 23 (24) 25
26 27 28 29 30 31

NOVEMBER 1997
S M T W T F S
1
2 3 4 5 6 7 8
9 10 (11) 12 ⟨13⟩⟨14⟩ 15
16 17 18 19 20 21 22
23 24 25 26 (27)(28) 29
30

DECEMBER 1997
S M T W T F S
1 2 3 4 5 6
7 8 9 10 11 12 13
14 15 16 17 18 19 20
21 (22)(23)(24)(25)(26) 27
28 (29)(30)(31)

JANUARY 1998
S M T W T F S
(1)(2) 3
4 5 6 7 8 9 10
11 12 13 14 15 16 17
18 (19) 20 21 22 23 24
25 26 27 28 (29) ▨ 31

FEBRUARY 1998
S M T W T F S
1 2 3 4 5 6 7
8 9 10 11 12 13 14
15 16 17 18 19 20 21
22 23 24 25 26 27 28

MARCH 1998
S M T W T F S
1 2 3 4 5 6 7
8 9 10 11 12 13 14
15 16 17 18 19 20 21
22 23 24 25 26 27 28
29 (30)(31)

APRIL 1998
S M T W T F S
(1)(2)(3) 4
5 6 7 8 9 (10) 11
12 13 14 15 16 17 18
19 20 21 22 23 (24) 25
26 27 28 29 30

MAY 1998
S M T W T F S
1 2
3 4 5 6 ⟨7⟩◇⟨8⟩ 9
10 11 12 13 14 15 16
17 18 19 20 21 (22) 23
24 (25) 26 27 28 29 30
31

JUNE 1998
S M T W T F S
1 2 3 4 5 6
7 8 9 10 11 12 13
14 15 16 17 18 19 20
21 22 23 24 25 26 27
28 29 30

JULY 1998
S M T W T F S
1 (2) ▨ 4
5 6 7 8 9 10 11
12 13 14 15 16 17 18
19 20 21 22 23 24 25
26 27 28 29 30 31

FIGURE 4–1   Fairfield Elementary School Calendar, Fort Wayne, Indiana, 1997–98

Source: Fairfield Elementary School. Reprinted by permission.

holidays (such as Thanksgiving and Labor Day) and often share a one-to-two week break around the Christmas and New Year holidays and a three-to-four week break in the summer.

Approximately 75 percent of the students attend school at any one time on a multi-track plan. The remaining 25 percent of the students are on vacation. Teachers usually have the option of teaching year-round or sharing vacation times with one group of students. However, teachers who teach year-round are forced to move from classroom to classroom during their off-track time (time when they are not tracked with a group of students). This requires a greater amount of storage space for teaching materials, and scheduling of students and classes is much more difficult under the multi-track program than it is under the single-track program.

Those who support the 45-15 plan or one of its modifications note that it calls for consistent instructional pacing and thus helps to reduce "summer loss" by breaking up the long summer period of no formal learning. One of the most frequently cited disadvantages of the 45-15 plan is that it requires more "beginnings" and "endings" than any of the other year-round programs, and experience has demonstrated that more instructional time is lost in the days right before or right after vacation than at any other time during the school year.

Concept 6
The year-round plan that many high schools prefer is Concept 6. Under this plan, the school year is divided into six equal segments and the curriculum is redesigned to fit into 42-day units. Students are assigned to one of three groups. Each group attends the same four sessions, although students can be assigned to a new group at the end of each nine weeks. Sessions can be scheduled so that there are an equal number of students in school during each session with approximately one-third of the students on vacation at any one time.

Under Concept 6, the school term is made up of 168 to 172 days. This can cause a problem because of the minimum number of required school days that have been mandated by the various states. Some districts overcome this problem by shortening each vacation and by scheduling special activities during these additional days. Other districts choose to lengthen the school day so that students are required to be in school the same number of hours that they would be under the more traditional calendars.

Concept 6 is often used to ease problems associated with overcrowding because, theoretically, it can free one classroom for every two that is used. Many schools that have tried the plan have found that it does free some classrooms but not at the ratio of one to two (see, for example, Schoenfeld & Schmitz, 1964).

Four-Quarter Plan
In a four-quarter plan, the school year is divided into four 12-week sessions. The students are required to attend three out of four quarters so that 75 percent

of the students are in school while the other 25 percent on vacation. In some school districts, students are given the option of attending all four quarters so that they can complete four years of work in three years. The fourth quarter can also be used for remedial or "make-up" work for those students who need additional time with the subject matter.

Trimester

The trimester divides the school year into three equal sessions. The number of days in a session may vary from 60 to 78 days. In plans where sessions are 60 days, students must attend all three sessions for a total of 180 days. The benefit of the this type of plan is that it allows for more flexibility in scheduling students. In plans where sessions consist of 78 days, students attend school two of three sessions and are on vacation during the third session. Because there are only 156 days in the two sessions, the length of the school day is increased to seven hours. The school operates 234 days a year so that all students will have a common two-week vacation.

Flexible Year

Under a flexible year plan, schools are open 240 days a year. Students are *required* to attend the minimum days mandated by the state, but *may* attend all 240 days. The pattern of attendance is determined by the student and his or her parents. For students who attend 180 days continuously, the school calendar looks very similar to the 9-month/3-month calendar. Students may, however, decide to spread the 180 days over the entire year and so attend school half-days only.

Many feel that the flexible year program is the most innovative of all programs and the one that will help us achieve our educational objectives in the most efficient way. It allows for parental choice, provides extra days for remediation or acceleration, and can be managed through the use of technology. Others feel that it is a pipe dream that will never come to be because it is just too difficult to manage even with the help of the computer. The truth is that the flexible school year is actually a very old idea. If you will recall, urban schools used a flexible calendar during the early 1800s. However, implementing the plan is much more difficult today because of state regulations, college entry requirements, and scheduling difficulties that result from the greater variety in courses taught and the large number of students involved. Technology can help with the management and control of such a calendar, but even with technology, it is difficult to implement a flexible plan because of administrative concerns such as, "How do you plan your budget?" "How do you schedule classes?" "What do you do with the student who transfers into your system?" "What do you do with the students who transfer out of your system?" "When do you schedule graduation?" It is also difficult to communicate the details of the plan to the general public, and this can become a public relations nightmare. At the same time, many of the school restructuring proposals call for programs that would be enhanced by a flexible school calendar.

Other Alternatives

As was noted earlier, there are at least 60 different YRS designs, each of which has been modified numerous times so that there are almost as many YRS plans as there are school districts implementing YRS. In addition to the patterns that have already been discussed, other arrangements used are the 60-20 (school in session 12 weeks and then off 4 weeks), the 60-15 (12 weeks on and 4 weeks off providing for a common summer vacation of 3 to 4 weeks for all students and teachers) and the 90-30 plan (18 weeks on and 6 weeks off).

Popularity of the Various Year-Round School Programs

Data compiled on schools that were on a year-round calendar during the 1996-97 school year reveal that the most popular plan was the 60-20. (See Table 4–1) Of the 808 schools who used the plan, approximately 69% were on some form of a multi-track plan and the other 31% were on a single-track plan. The next most popular plan is the 45-15. Of the schools 760 schools using a 45-15 plan, approximately 76 percent used a single-track approach.

Advantages and Disadvantages of YRS

One of the most frequent arguments put forth in favor of YRS programs is that a continuous, year-round learning program can stem the regression, or forgetting, that occurs over extended vacations. The argument maintains that teachers tend to spend 2 to 4 weeks of any new school year reviewing material that was covered the year before simply because students have forgotten what they learned. This is very costly in terms of time because it represents between 5 and 10 percent of the total time allocated to formal education. If this is repeated year after year, from the time the students enter the second grade until they graduate, it means that they have lost between one-half and one grade level. If schools were year-round, the loss would be much less and students would be spending more time in learning than in reviewing

Another benefit that relates specifically to multi-track YRS is that the construction cost of new buildings can be delayed. For districts that are experiencing a great influx of students, being able to increase building capacity by 25 or 30 percent is a great short-term savings. Likewise, in districts that are experiencing a decline in enrollments, the move to YRS can be used to increase the use of expensive, well-equipped schools while closing those buildings that are in greatest need of repair. It is important to note, however, that YRS does not save costs in the long run. The costs for transportation, food services, and specialized professional services all increase when the school is

TABLE 4–1   Number of schools operating under various year-round calendars during the 1996–97 school year (figures compiled by the National Association for Year-Round Education).

Number of schools with year-round calendars*		2,502
Number of single track schools	1,380 (55%)	
Number of multi-track schools	1,122 (45%)	
Kinds of calendars in use		
A. 25-5		1
25-5 modified 1-track	1	
B. 30-5		28
30-5 1-track	17	
30-5 modified 1-track	11	
C. 30-10		17
30-10 1-track	15	
30-10 modified 1-track	2	
D. 35-10		2
35-10 1-track	2	
E. 40-10		4
40-10 1-track	4	
F. 45-10		55
45-10 1-track	41	
45-10 modified 1 track	14	
G. 45-15		760
45-15 1-track	467	
45-15 modified 1-track	113	
45-15 2-track	12	
45-15 3-track	2	
45-15 modified 3-track	2	
45-15 4-track	73	
45-15 modified 4-track	70	
45-15 5-track	1	
H. 50-10		3
50-10 1-track	2	
50-10 custom 1-track	1	
I. 50-15		2
50-15 1-track	2	
J. 55-18		2
55-18 4-track	2	
K. 60-10		2
60-10 modified 1-track	2	
L. 60-15		153
60-15 1-track	30	

TABLE 4–1 *Continued*

60-15 modified 1-track	9	
60-15 2-track	4	
60-15-3-track	2	
60-15 4-track	2	
60-15 5-track	99	
60-15 modified 5-track	2	
60-15 5-track (orchard plan)	5	
M. 60-20		808
60-20 1-track	182	
60-20 modified 1-track	71	
60-20 2-track	3	
60-20 modified 2-track	2	
60-20 3-track	11	
60-20 4-track	521	
60-20 modified 4-track	14	
60-20 5-track	4	
N. 65-20		1
65-20 1-track	1	
O. 90-30		109
90-30 1-track	9	
90-30 modified 1-track	2	
90-30 2-track	1	
90-30 4-track	94	
90-30 modified 4-track	3	
P. Concept 6		188
Concept 6 modified 1-track	1	
Concept 6 modified 2-track	2	
Concept 6 3-track	110	
Concept 6 modified 3-track	75	
Q. Other		367
Alternative	40	
Continuous/flexible all-year 1 track	37	
Continuous/flexible all-year 4-track	4	
Custom 1-track	84	
Custom 4-track	1	
Extended year	110	
Modified 1-track	84	
Modified mountain 1-track	3	
Personalized year	3	
Quarter 55 4-track	1	

*Includes data from American, Canadian, and Pacific Region Public and Private Schools

Data Source: National Association for Year-Round Education. *Twenty-third reference directory of year-round education programs for the 1996–97 school year.* San Diego, CA. Used with permission.

open year-round rather than nine months. The additional costs for the typical school tends to range from 10 to 15 percent of the original budget. Some schools, however, have experienced increases of up to 25 percent.

One of the biggest disadvantages to YRS is that it disrupts the lifestyle of the community. For instance, it is not unusual for the elementary and high school students from the same family to be on different schedules. When this happens, baby-sitting becomes a problem because high school students are no longer available to care for the younger children before and after school. Also, YRS may affect businesses and industries that hire part-time summer help because they will not have access to as many students as they would if all of the students were on vacation during the same months.

The advantages and disadvantages of a year-round school calendar have been under debate since the early 1900s. Table 4–2 presents a summary of the most frequently cited advantages and disadvantages of YRS. In some cases, an item appears as an "advantage" and then, with only a slight change, reappears as a "disadvantage." This reflects actual situations, because individual circumstances and the conditions of the moment will affect how the items are evaluated, which in turn will affect whether each is seen as advantage or disadvantage.

Some items on the list may seem trivial. This will only be true as long as the items are ones that your district doesn't have to deal with or are ones that are solved relatively easily within your district. The important thing to remember is that, no matter how great the advantages of the YRS, there will always be disadvantages. The more informed the decision-making team is, the better able the members will be to weigh the advantages and disadvantages. One organization that can be helpful to districts considering YRS is the National Association of Year Round Education (NAYRE). Although the organization is biased toward YRS and actively supports movement in this direction, it admits to its bias and the materials they provide are both practical and informative.

THE RESTRUCTURED SCHOOL DAY

Just as some call for a restructured school *year*, others call for a restructured school *day*. Those who argue in favor of a restructured day claim that the structure of the current daily schedules is designed to meet the needs of the organization while the restructured day is designed to meet the needs of the students. Most daily schedules are based on some abstract formula that neatly calculates the school timetable, taking into consideration teachers, resources, facilities, subjects, graduation requirements, and state mandates. The formulas allow for some wiggle room so that the extraordinary needs of individuals within the system (teachers, students, parents) can be met. However, if there

TABLE 4–2   Advantages and disadvantages of YRS

Advantages	Disadvantages
Allows students to enter school closer to legal age.	Entrance problems for students leaving or entering the school system.
Capable students may complete elementary and secondary school programs in fewer calendar years and thus cost taxpayers less money and become productive earlier than would be the case otherwise.	Students who graduate at some time other than the traditional June graduation often find that they do not get the introduction into college that their peers do.
Will add flexibility and a wider choice of courses to the curriculum.	Usually requires a complete revision of the existing curriculum.
Continuous learning year programs will lead to curriculum upgrading and modification of teaching and administrative practices.	
	Teachers are worn out by June and need the long summer to recuperate and prepare for the next year.
Can provide year-round employment for teachers who so desire.	Non-teaching summer jobs often pay more than summer teaching jobs.
	Large enrollments usually needed to make multi-tracking concept work. In small schools, classrooms will not be used to capacity.
Class size can be reduced.	Often requires teachers to work with split sections (4th/5th grade).
Expenditures for new construction can be reduced when multi-track programs are used.	Faster depreciation of building and equipment.
Year-round school plans assure taxpayers of a better return on their dollars because facilities used year-round.	All schools will have to be air conditioned.
	Operating and maintenance costs will increase because the new program will require extra staff or overtime wages.
Makes better use of resources (including teachers).	Multi-track YRS makes it difficult to hold workshops and in-service training programs.

Continued

TABLE 4–2   *Continued*

Advantages	Disadvantages
Fewer textbooks and expensive equipment (such as computers) will be required.	Increased use of textbooks, instructional material, and equipment leads to more frequent replacement.
Savings in transportation become possible if fewer students are in school.	Would lend itself to somewhat less efficient bus loads and possible increase in transportation costs.
New school vacation patterns will allow students to work during periods when jobs are available and not everyone is competing for them.	High school students will no longer be free to earn money to go to college because YRS puts an end to summer-long jobs.

A large segment of the school population has little to do over an extended summer vacation. Year-round school plan will keep children off the streets for long periods of time and thus juvenile delinquency will be reduced.	Lack of adequate supervision for students who are out of school during the regular school year.
	    Children will be denied an opportunity to participate in summer recreational activities provided by camps and other resorts.
	    New recreation programs and community supervision projects will be required to protect children not in school.
	    Winter is no time for vacation.
	    Children need to be with parents in the summer. It is the only time they can be together.
	    If parents elect which sessions the children attend, there will be uneven distribution of students. School officials will then be forced to assign children to classes arbitrarily, with resulting public relations difficulties.
	    Sports programs and extracurricular activities will be difficult to provide.

Students who fail would repeat only part of the work instead of semester or year.	Students and teachers object to the constant change of classrooms caused by the multi-tracking approach.
Capacity to offer remedial work for students during the intersession.	Makes for a much more complex scheduling process, especially at the secondary level.

TABLE 4–2 *Continued*

Advantages	Disadvantages
Students who are likely to become dropouts can reach higher rungs on the educational ladder before they terminate their formal education.	
A continuous learning year program can stem the regression or forgetting that occurs over extended vacations.	
	The general public will not accept the radical change in living patterns that will be necessary with adoption of a continuous learning calendar.

is an inordinate number of individual requests, the system quickly becomes overwhelmed and unable to accommodate the requests no matter how worthy they may be. The result is an universal headache for those involved. As a result, a number of alternative schedules have been designed in an attempt to anticipate the individual needs and preferences and to respond appropriately.

Alternative Scheduling at the High School and Junior High

Block scheduling, rotating periods, and the flexible modular schedule are among the most popular alternatives used at the junior and senior high level. Figure 4–2 presents examples of the more typical of these scheduling patterns.

The examples presented in Figure 4–2 are just that, examples. There are almost as many different ways of scheduling the junior high and high school day as there are junior and senior high schools. However, the principles and guidelines involved in implementing the various schedules remain constant, regardless of their many different formats.

Five-Day Pattern

Under the five-day pattern, students attend the same class at the same time throughout the semester. For instance, those students who have advanced algebra from 8:30 to 9:25 on Monday, will have advanced algebra at 8:30 on Tuesday, Wednesday, Thursday, and Friday as well. The only flexibility that is offered under this schedule is some individual choice of classes. Time periods are extremely inflexible and all courses are "treated equally under the clock." Consequently, physical education receives the same number of

A. The 5-Day Week Schedule

Time Period	MONDAY	TUESDAY	WEDNESDAY	THURSDAY	FRIDAY
1	Class A	Class A	Class A	Class A	Class A
2	Class B	Class B	Class B	Class B	Class B
3	Class C	Class C	Class C	Class C	Class C
4	Class D	Class D	Class D	Class D	Class D
5	Class E	Class E	Class E	Class E	Class E
6	Class F	Class F	Class F	Class F	Class F

B. Rotating Period

Time Period	MONDAY	TUESDAY	WEDNESDAY	THURSDAY	FRIDAY
1	Class A	Class B	Class C	Class D	Class E
2	Class B	Class C	Class D	Class E	Class F
3	Class C	Class D	Class E	Class F	Class A
4	Class D	Class E	Class F	Class A	Class B
5	Class E	Class F	Class A	Class B	Class C
6	Class F	Class A	Class B	Class C	Class D

C. Block Schedule

Time Period	MONDAY	TUESDAY	WEDNESDAY	THURSDAY	FRIDAY
1	Class A	Class E	Class A	Class E	Class A
2					Class E
3	Class B	Class B	Class B	Class B	Class B
4	Class C	Class F	Class C	Class F	Class C
5					Class F
6	Class D	Class D	Class D	Class D	Class D

D. Flexible Modular Schedule

30 Minutes	Large Group Instruction		
30 Minutes	Small Group Instruction	Small Group Instruction	Small Group Instruction
30 Minutes			
30 Minutes		<< Individualized Activities >>	

FIGURE 4–2   Alternative ways of scheduling the Junior High and Senior High School day

minutes as advanced algebra. An underlying assumption of the five-day scheduling pattern is that all of the students within a given group should be able to master the subject matter within a fixed amount of instructional time. In the example, it is assumed that, provided with approximately 4,000 minutes of instruction, all of the students who have been assigned to the 8:30 advanced algebra class are capable of mastering the concepts presented.

Rotating Period

The rotating period, as the name implies, rotates the time that each class meets. One rationale for this scheduling pattern is that some students are more alert in the morning, while others are more alert in the afternoon. Therefore, it is unfair for students to be assigned to their more academically rigorous classes by "luck of the draw." Rotating the periods means that the students will have at least some portion of each course in the morning and a nearly equal portion in the afternoon, which in turn means that they will have at least some segment of each course during the part of the day when they are most alert.

With the exception of the five-day pattern, the rotating period is the least flexible of the scheduling patterns. Like the five-day schedule, it contains the underlying assumption that all students assigned to the class require the same amount of instruction in order to master the objectives of the course. Teacher reaction to this plan varies, as one might expect. Although the research in this area is weak, there is anecdotal evidence that the schedule is effective for students who might otherwise be considered "borderline" in a given subject. Teachers do see a difference in the way students perform at different times of the day. Correspondingly, the ability to deal with student needs varies from class period to class period. These differences are clearly noted in the differences between the first and last periods of the day.

Block Scheduling

With block scheduling, classes are grouped so that students spend more time in some classes than they do in others. For instance, they may spend 55 minutes in gym and 120 in math. Educators have long felt that treating all subjects as "equal under the clock" is an extremely unsound instructional policy. The sentiment is echoed in the following comment made by Wiley and Bishop:

> Whence came the notion that all subjects are equally important in terms of time? If offered a choice in importance would schoolmen and parents equate music with mathematics? Art with English? Physical education with United States History? Creative writing with science? What hierarchy of values can and should be applied to the various subjects found in today's high schools? The conventional schedule assumes no hierarchy. It claims all subjects offered not only

of equal value, but it also assumes that the learning process involved in each subject is identical (Wiley & Bishop, 1968, p. 11).

Educators understand that varying degrees of time are needed for the different subjects and instructional techniques. Therefore, they may choose a block schedule because it allows for additional time to be devoted to those subjects that are more academically rigorous or that incorporate a hands-on approach to learning.

A block schedule may call for teachers to share some of the teaching responsibilities in a team teaching approach. Rather than assigning 30 students to one teacher for one class period, 60 to 90 students may be assigned to two or three teachers for two class periods. The teachers decide the best way to use the time allocated to them. For instance, one teacher may show a film to a large portion of the group, while the second teacher works interactively with the smaller group. The team may be composed of teachers who teach the same subject area (e.g., math) or it may be composed of teachers who teach in different subject areas (e.g., math, science, and language arts).

In order for this type of block scheduling to work, the teachers involved must understand and embrace the concept of team teaching. Not only are they sharing students, they are also sharing subject matter time. It is not unusual for the teachers to disagree on how the time is best spent, so turf issues can quickly arise. The more time the teachers have to plan together, however, the more likely it is that block scheduling will be successful.

A number of advantages have been associated with block scheduling. Among these are:

- It permits variation in length of time allotted to individual subjects based on teacher and student need.
- It provides options for scheduling special activities such as assemblies, team meetings, or field trips and still permits each student to meet with each teacher during the day.
- It provides opportunities to group and regroup students without totally reorganizing classes or tracking.
- It provides options for team teachers to correlate subject matter and engage in interdisciplinary instruction.
- It permits instructional staff to organize students to provide both large and small-group instruction (Williamson, 1993, p. 11).

Flexible Modular Scheduling
The phrase "flexible scheduling" is used to describe a wide variety of scheduling patterns used in the junior and senior high school. As Heathman and Nafzinger have noted:

Flexible scheduling in an operation framework characterized by classes of unequal length which meet at differing periods throughout the week and which are geared to the individual needs of students. Flexible scheduling may vary from merely rearranging time allotments and sequences of established courses to a complex modular approach in which schedules for each student are generated daily and picked up by the student each morning (Heathman and Nafzinger, 1971, p. 95).

In its purest form, a flexible schedule is one that changes as the needs of the student change. When a truly flexible schedule is implemented it must, by definition, become an individualized program.

Flexible modular scheduling builds on the concept of blocking. Under a typical plan, the school schedules a combination of 55 and 110 minute blocks (allowing five minutes in each clock hour to allow the students to pass to another class or to take a break) but calls for the curriculum to be divided into modular units. The basic module is usually 15 to 20 minutes, and time blocks are established so that each block is large enough to incorporate at least two modules. Students are assigned to small groups of between 10 and 15 students and groups can be assigned to a different module at the end of each 15 or 20 minute time period.

There are three types of modules. The first type involves instructional activities that can be implemented easily in a large-group format. Lectures, videotapes, and paper and pencil tests are some examples of large-group activities. Large-group activities call for little direct student interaction and only one teacher is needed to administer the instructional task.

The second type of module encompasses those activities that are best used in a small-group format. These are activities that call for a great deal of student-to-student and student-to-teacher interaction. The activities are designed in such a way as to require the students to apply their newly learned skills and knowledge. Small-group activities can include lab work, class discussions, role playing, and debates.

The third type of module is comprised of individualized activities. Most activities in this group require the students to work by themselves, although there may be some one-to-one interactions. The interactions may be between teacher and student in a mentoring or coaching type activity, between student and student in a peer tutoring session, or between student and counselor in an advising situation. However, the majority of module three activities call for students to work independently on personalized exercises that involve some type of problem solving. The various types of activities may occur daily, weekly, or on an occasional basis.

Teachers work together to diagnose the needs of the students and, based on the diagnosis, determine the most appropriate instructional modules for each student. Alexander Swaab identified a number of reasons for adopting the FMS approach to program planning:

1. The desire to arrange for *variable time blocks* for different classes and on separate days
2. The creation (of) *variable instructional patterns* such as large group, labs, regular class, small groups, or individualized instruction
3. The *weighting of courses* on a varying basis using the amount of time allocated to each course as a determining factor
4. Permitting students greater selection of courses
5. Making available unstructured time in the school day for a student to engage in independent study
6. Increasing the program alternatives and options for the school
7. Breaking the monotony of the traditional schedule (Swaab, 1974, p. 20)

FMS provides time for teachers to interact with students during the day. Not only are the teachers able to diagnose student needs on a more individual level, they are able to personalize the instruction so that it meets the needs of the student.

Restrictive Element—The Carnegie Unit

Those who favor altering the high school day often cite the intractable nature of the Carnegie Unit as one of the greatest barriers to change. As Besvinick noted in 1961:

> The unit is inadequate and inaccurate as a measure of scholastic attainment. It is essentially a year-long record of quantitative exposure to a given discipline and reflects nothing of quality. It becomes a Procrustean bed for the curriculum—some courses have to be "padded" to cover one year while others have to be pared to the bone to fit within the prescribed thirty-six week limit.

Besvinick goes on to acknowledge that elimination of the unit would create a number of problems and then offers a solution that looks suspiciously similar to the unit.

> High-school principals and college registrars, however, will still need a measure for graduation and admission if the Carnegie unit is abandoned. Why not use the term "hour"? An accurate account of the number of hours of contact a student has with a given subject might be more meaningful than one standard unit. In this manner a student might complete a year with the following:

American History—180 hours
American Literature—100 hours
Grammar and Vocabulary—80 hours
Conversational French—220 hours
Chemistry—250 hours
Typing—70 hours
Driver Training—60 hours
Physical Education—60 hours
Supervised Reading—60 hours

This plan would still permit high schools to compute class rankings, students to see where they stand, and colleges to set minimal entrance requirements (Besvinick, 1961, p. 365).

As you can see, Besvinick also missed the point. Changing "units" to "hours" does not address the issues of quality of instruction, scholastic attainment, or padded courses. Although this seems self-evident and leads one to question why Besvinick would even make such a suggestion, it is not unusual for time to take precedence over other educational concerns simply because it is "a convenient yardstick for measuring depth and breadth of a high-school graduate's program." We see this tendency continuing even today. Therefore, we must be extremely careful not to take *learning* out of the "time and learning" formula, especially when we are dealing with the high school day.

Elementary School Day

The elementary school day often resembles the modular day of the junior and senior high. Although bells are seldom used to control the ebb and flow of time as they do in the high school, the clock continues to place limitations on how classroom time can be and is used. The limits that are imposed arise from three distinct sources: (1) state mandates and recommendations, (2) guidelines imposed by the school district; and (3) times assigned for special classes and activities such as gym, music, library, and computers. Although teachers are required to schedule a given amount of time for each subject area (e.g., reading, math, language arts, social studies, and science), they are normally given at least some latitude as to when to schedule the subjects during the day. If, for instance, two teachers decide to team teach reading, they can schedule reading for a time that fits into the schedule of both classrooms as long as they take into consideration the schedule of the special classes.

The most frequently suggested way of restructuring the elementary school day is to integrate the subjects across the day, week, and even month. Rather than separating the day into distinct segments based on subject areas (reading, math, science), topics are selected and units are designed around the topics. Each unit incorporates reading, math, science, social studies, art, music, and physical education. The rationale behind the integrated day is that it allows students to become more deeply involved in the topic they are studying. Also, the instructional units allow for more interactive, hands-on learning activities and thus allow students to apply their newly learned knowledge and skills in problem-solving activities.

The danger with the integrated day is that content-specific skills may be short-changed. When subjects are taught separately, it is much easier for the teacher to isolate specific skills and determine whether a student has mastered them. With the integrated day, this becomes much more difficult because the skills are not being taught or applied in isolation. Therefore the teacher must spend more time with record keeping. There is also a real danger of not being aware of when the class is moving more slowly than it should. An assistant superintendent of public instruction once shared his frustrations along this line. According to him, "The teachers know the requirements of the core-curriculum, they know that students must master one level before moving to the next, and they embrace the concept of the integrated day. The problem is that they have no idea how much time the children are spending in reading or math. I know it's an old way of thinking, but I don't see how, if they can't give me an approximation of how much time their students are spending learning math and reading skills, these teachers can evaluate whether their methods are effective. It suggests to me a doctor who would give a patient a pill and say, 'Take this for 9 or 15 or 36 weeks and if it doesn't work we'll try something else.' I want the doctor to know before those weeks are up if the medicine isn't working as well as it should—just as I want my teachers to know if the students aren't progressing as rapidly and effectively as they should."

Other Alternatives to Restructuring School Time

Although the restructuring of the school year and/or day are the most frequently employed strategies for altering school time, some additional ways have been suggested for restructuring or redistributing the time that children spend in school. Among the alternatives are double sessions, alternate day kindergarten, four-day school week, and a shortened school career.

Double Sessions
Schools in the 1950s were faced with a severe overcrowding problem as a result of the post-war baby boom. Many schools went to double sessions as a way of postponing the costs involved in the construction of new buildings. By opening the school earlier in the day and closing it later in the evening, two school sessions could be held, thus doubling the number of children that

could be served by a single building. As soon as construction caught up with the boom, the number of double sessions was reduced greatly. Occasionally, you will hear of a school that has a double session, but usually this is a result of a building problem. For instance, several years ago, the junior and senior school students in a particular Michigan school district were forced to go to a double session because the junior high building had been condemned. Until the problem was finally resolved, the junior high school students met in the senior high building with the senior high students arriving in the morning and the junior high students arriving in the afternoon.

Although there are few schools that choose to go to a double session, there has been some discussion of using a double session at the high school as a way to provide time for community service. Courses would be offered in both mornings and afternoons, but students would attend only three quarters of the day. The other quarter would be spent in some form of community service. The problem with this is that it really increases the length of the students day by 25 percent, and this greatly affects the choices they are able to make regarding part-time work and/or participation in sports and other after-school activities.

Alternate-Day Kindergarten

As we saw in the previous chapter, there has been an ongoing debate concerning which is better, half-day or full-day kindergarten. As a compromise between the two programs, some schools have implemented an alternate-day program in which kindergarten children attend school a full day but only on alternate days. Such a program was implemented in the Pasco School District in Wisconsin in the mid-1980s. According to Beverly McConnell, a consultant with the Research and Evaluation Office of Pullman, Washington, and Stephanie Tesch, an assistant superintendent with the Pasco School District, teachers welcomed the change in scheduling because it provided the students with the equivalent of an extra half day each week of learning time. This time made it possible to teach a concept on one day and provide reinforcement activities on the same day. It was also easier to schedule field trips. In addition, parents liked the idea that older children could accompany their younger siblings going to and from school (McConnell & Tesch, 1986).

Four-Day School Week

During the late 1970s and early 1980s, schools were faced with many problems associated with operating on a fixed budget at a time of high inflation. For many schools, the problems were further complicated because school enrollments were steadily dropping. The drop in enrollments could be traced to a number of factors, including an earlier decrease in the birth rate and an increase in the number of families migrating from rural and city areas to the suburbs. As a result, many schools found it necessary to cut both academic and extracurricular activities. Some schools, however, found such cuts to be unacceptable and looked for other alternatives. Consolidation of schools, sharing of resources, and collection of fees for extracurricular activities were all used as a way of dealing with the budget crisis. And, as you might expect, some schools chose to change the school schedule in order to save money. In Colorado, twelve rural districts moved to a four-day week. The total amount of time that students spent in school was held constant, but the length of the day increased while the length of the week decreased. By going to the four-day week, the schools were able to reduce the amount of money they spent on transportation and utilities. This was especially important because of the energy crisis. An early evaluation of the program, conducted by Colorado State University, indicated that there were some very positive reactions to the shortened week. Almost everyone was pleased with the results. Student achievement was unaffected or increased slightly, teachers felt that they were able to devote more time to planning and professional development activities, and parents noted that they were able to spend more time with their children. The one group that was most negative were the high school coaches. They felt that the long school day drained the energy of the young athletes. In addition, they complained that having the student practice for four days in a row and then having three days without any practice had a negative impact on the athletes' skill training (Richburg & Edelen, 1981).

Shortened School Career

Most suggestions for restructuring the school time revolve around *redistributing* time. Occasionally, however, suggestions are made for *shortening* the amount of time students spend in school. One such suggestion was made in 1931 by Engelhardt:

> Certain authorities are convinced that time could be saved by reduction in the number of school years consumed in carrying on the curriculum prescribed for the public schools. There appears to be ample evidence that an acceptable elementary education can be mastered in a shorter period, and that children exposed to a briefer schooling can pursue without difficulty the work of the secondary school. Many school officials are yet unwilling, in the face of the facts, to adopt any plan which might reduce for all pupils the number of years of elementary and secondary schooling (Engelhardt, 1931, p. 426.)

It would appear that this argument holds little credence today, when many students enter high school lacking the basic skills that make up the elementary school curriculum. There are a number of reasons that can be given for this lack of skill, not the least of which is the exploding curriculum that has drastically increased the number of "basic skills" that elementary students are expected to master. When combined with the extra responsibilities that have been assigned to the school (especially responsibilities dealing with child welfare), it would be unreasonable to assume that the elementary curriculum can be condensed into a fewer number of years.

However, another argument occasionally found hidden in the literature on time and learning does bear examination. According to this argument, if the school year was increased to 220 days and the length of the school day increased by one hour, the length of a student's academic career could be shortened by one to two years. Advocates for the plan often combine the arguments for both year-round and extended-year programs and note that the plan makes sense economically, socially, and educationally.

The proponents of this plan use simple mathematical formulas to prove that the plan is economically sound. They acknowledge that although initially this organization plan would be more expensive, when averaged over the length of the entire school career, the cost of an individual student's education would be reduced. For instance, if you increase the length of the school year by 25 percent at a cost of 15 percent (some costs such as building maintenance and insurance are fixed costs), every four years you reduce the cost of the child's education by 40 percent. Not only does the program save the taxpayer money, but also it contributes to making young adults productive members of society at an earlier age than is true of the normal K-12 program.

According to those who favor it, the plan makes sense academically because it addresses the issue of summer loss and provides for greater continuity in the educational process. In addition, it demonstrates to children that learning is not a part-time activity, but rather a full-time job. Finally, the program assures that students who will eventually drop out of school will achieve a higher level of education because the plan compresses learning into a shorter time span.

Socially, the program aids the school in providing for the needs of the young child, especially the child at risk. Young children who spend all or part of their day or year at home alone or with a teenage baby-sitter would, under this program, spend the majority of their waking hours in the safe environment of the school. In addition, advocates for such programs declare that the violence associated with young teens roaming the streets would also be reduced because they would be under direct supervision during most of the day.

In most instances, the arguments used to support a shortened school career can be pared down to basic economics—children can receive the same amount of schooling (number of hours) for less money. Those who offer supporting arguments often provide an alternative interpretation of the facts that are brought to light by the advocates of both year-round schools and the extended school calendar. For this reason, if for no other, the arguments are worthy of a least a cursory examination.

TIME AND THE SCHOOL SCHEDULE

Since the beginning of the public school, the school calendar has remained an element of debate. Because the time represented by the calendar embodies economic, social, political, and philosophical elements, the debate revolving around the calendar remains strong even today. There are advantages and disadvantages to every calendar, whether that calendar is the customary 180-day calendar, a year-round calendar, or represents an extended-year program. The debate does not stop with the structure of the school year but also incorporates components of the school day. Because there is *no one best-way* of scheduling time, it can be expected that the debate will not subside anytime in the near future.

Anyone involved in school reform needs to be well informed on the scheduling plans currently being discussed. This will require an understanding of the history of the calendar, the different approaches that can be taken to alter the calendar, and the advantages and disadvantages that are associated with the approaches. Most importantly, however, is the understanding that time, in and of itself, will do little to improve, enhance, and or even maintain the current quality of public education. Just as more money is not the answer to every economic problem, more time is not the answer to every educational concern. Nonetheless, just as the prudent appropriation of finances can help to ease the impact of money-related problems, the wise allocation of school time can go a long way toward addressing many of the educational concerns our society now faces.

REFERENCES

Arthur Andersen Company. (1993, May). *Cypress-Fairbanks Independent School District financial analysis of year-round education.* Houston, TX: Author.

Besvinick, S. L. (1961). The expendable Carnegie unit. *Phi Delta Kappan*, 42(8), 365–366.

Engelhardt, F. (1931). *Public school organization and administration.* Boston, MA: Ginn and Company.

Heathman, J. E., & Nafzinger, A. J. (1971, October). *Scheduling for flexibility: A manual for administrators of small schools.* (Educational Resources Information Center, ERIC Document ED056 820).

McConnell, B. B., & Tesch, S. (1986, November). Effectiveness of kindergarten scheduling. *Educational Leadership*, 48–51.

McGregor, P. (1996, August 12). Summer of discontent? Year-round schools seem like a great idea, but some systems have learned the hard lessons. *Ann Arbor News*, pp. B1–B2.

National Association for Year-Round Education. (1996). *Twenty-third reference directory of year-round education programs for the 1996–97 school year.* San Diego, CA: Author.

Richburg, R. W., & Edelen, R. W. (1981). *An evaluation of the four-day school week in Colorado: The final report.* Colorado State University, Fort Collins, CO.

Schoenfeld, C. A., & Schmitz, N. (1964). *Year-round education: Its problems and prospects from kindergarten to college.* Madison, WI: Dembar Educational Research Services, Inc.

Swaab, A. M. (1974). *School administrator's guide to flexible modular scheduling.* West Nyack, NY: Parker Publishing Company, Inc.

Wiley, W. D., & Bishop, L. K. (1968). *The flexibly scheduled high school.* West Nyack, New York: Parker Publishing Company, Inc.

Williamson, R. (1993). *Scheduling the middle level school: To meet early adolescent needs.* Arlington, VA: National Association of Secondary School Principals.

▶ 5

Allocation of School Time

Just as there has been a strong, on going debate revolving around the school calendar, there also has been a constant, spirited debate on how to allocate school time that began with the inception of public education and is rich in historical foundation. The debate arises because, regardless of how much time students are required to be in school or how that time is structured or arranged, decisions must be made concerning how to disperse the hours and minutes among the various school subjects and activities. The debate revolves around such concerns as, "How much time should be allocated to a given subject?" and "Should children spend an equal amount of time in science and music?" But the elements of the arguments can also be found in such questions as, "Should schools only be responsible for the academic needs of children or do they have a responsibility to assure that children's welfare needs are met as well?" and "Should schools be more concerned with preparing students for the workforce or with providing them with a well-rounded, liberal education?"

The first two questions deal directly with the task of allocating school time, but the second two questions are truly at the center of the debate. As we shall see later in this chapter, the debate revolves around the contradictory and often controversial views of the purpose of public education. Even though educational jargon may have changed over time, the elements of the debate have remained relatively stable and have traditionally formed around the following argumentative positions:

1. All school time should (should not) be allocated to academic activities.
2. A portion of the school day should (should not) be allocated to enriching but nonessential elements.

3. The majority of a high school student's time should be spent on vocational (liberal) education.
4. All school subjects should (should not) be allocated an equal amount of time.
5. More time should be devoted to the humanities (sciences).
6. More time should be devoted to meeting the needs of the individual student (general student population).
7. The organization of the school should be subject oriented (student oriented).

Considering that we are talking about the allocation of school time, the last question may bother you. However, remember that the allocation of school time includes not only the allocation of minutes in a day and days in a year but also the total years spent in school. The answer to the last question will determine at what time, if ever, in the school career an individual student will be introduced to new topics and subject areas.

The debate emerges out of the tension caused by the need to assign limited resources (time and money) to school activities. If schools did not have to worry about time or money, they could "be all things to all people." But that simply isn't the reality with which we live, and as Tomlinson and Walberg remind us, "The quantity of school time—the amount of time spent at school—is fixed by arbitrary rules and dates; there are so many hours in a class day and so many days in a school year. Accordingly the allocation of school time is a zero-sum game in which numerous elements compete for a share, and for every winner there must be a loser" (Tomlinson & Walberg, 1986, p. 169)

HISTORICAL PERSPECTIVE ON TIME ALLOCATION

Documentation of the ongoing debate on the allocation of school time is provided throughout the educational literature, starting as early as the 1800s. In Chapter 2, we saw how the emergence of state departments of education, basic changes in lifestyle, and an increasing need for standardization of public schools contributed to the creation of the school calendar. As educational policy makers advocated for more school time, they did so by delineating how the additional time should be allocated among the various responsibilities of the school. For instance, Horace Mann not only recommended that the school calendar be lengthened but also urged that the curriculum be enriched through music, drawing, and hygiene instruction. By the end of the nineteenth century, the debate was carried to more formal bodies for deliberation so that throughout the last century a number of commissions, committees, and groups of scholars convened to focus on the predicament of how time should be allocated in public education. That process continues even today.

Committee of Ten

In 1893, the National Educational Association appointed a Committee of Ten to determine the function of the secondary school and to set standards that could be used to measure the degree to which the functions were met. It has been noted that "the majority of the report advanced the doctrine that it made no difference to a student's future what subjects he (she) studied, as long as the subjects provided "strong and effective mental training" (Harding, 1953, p. 170). However, in its final report, the committee stated that in order to fulfill its purpose it had to consider, among other things, "the proper limits of [each] subject" and "the most desirable allotment of time for the subject." Included in the report was a listing of recommended subjects that should be taught, how many semesters a student should spend on each subject, and the semester(s) when the subject should be taken.

Committee on Economy of Time

In 1911, the National Education Association appointed a committee to study the "general problem of economy of time" in the elementary school. In one of its four reports, the committee noted that:

> We approach now the question of saving time in the elementary period or of accomplishing more within the time. The committee agrees that there is much waste in elementary education. . . . Nearly all our correspondents are emphatic regarding waste and the importance of shortening the entire period of general education. Saving time can be made in the following ways:
> The principle of selection is: first choose the most important subjects and the most important topics; make a distinction between first-rate facts and principles and tenth-rate; prune thoroly (sic), stick to the elements of a subject; do not try to teach everything that is good; confine the period of elementary education to mastering the tools of education. This does not prevent inspirational work, which is a demand on the skill of the teacher rather than time. A great secret of education is to accomplish a maximum of training with a minimum of material. This is especially true of formal subjects; it is true also of inspirational subjects, in that after a general survey of the field emphasis should be placed on a few selected points. Under the conditions enumerated the formal elementary period can end in six years (NEA, 1915, pp. 403–404).

In its 1915 report, the committee continued its attack on what it considered wasted school time, but it was unwilling to commit to reducing the number of years a child spent in elementary school. The authors of the report quoted a Mr. Thompson who observed:

> Not many have indicated very much interest in the shortening of the period of education, but almost everyone, explicitly or by implication, would have much more accomplished with this period. . . . Educators are trying to save time, not to the end of having more time for something else than education, but to the end of having more in it of education; in general, "economy of time" is but a synonym for "efficiency." (NEA, 1915, p. 405).

P. W. Horn, superintendent of schools in Houston, Texas, reacted to the previous quote by asking if educators were certain that eliminating the nonessential elements from the curriculum was most needed for economy of time. Superintendent Horn declared, "It is not always those who do the least work that do the least in the best way . . . No alteration of printed courses of study can ever make it certain that we are employing our time in the best manner possible" (NEA, 1915, p. 415). However, his voice seemed to represent the minority because most of the reactions to the report were favorable. There did, in fact, appear to be consensus that the curriculum should address only those elements needed to function in an industrial society and time spent on anything else should be considered a waste of time.

Commission on the Reorganization of Secondary Education

In 1918, the Commission on the Reorganization of Secondary Education issued seven cardinal principles that it believed "should guide the reorganization and development of secondary education in the United States" (Department of Interior, 1918, p. 5). The principles were actually widely defined objectives that focused on: (1) health education, (2) command of fundamental processes, (3) worthy home-membership, (4) vocational education, (5) citizenship, (6) worthy use of leisure, and (7) character or ethical development.

The ideal high school curriculum, according to the commission, would be composed of three groups or categories of studies—constants, variables, and free electives. Studies that were undertaken by the majority, if not all of the students, were referred to as *constants*. The constants were to focus on health education, command of fundamental processes (basic studies), worthy home-membership, citizenship, and ethical development. The curriculum *variables* were ones that students chose based on their vocational or education goals. The third set, *free electives*, was designed to help the student prepare for increased leisure time. The courses were to be selected based on the individual aptitudes and interests of the student.

It was recommended that seventh grade students spend a majority of their time in the constant courses so that they could gain proficiency in the fundamental processes. It was also recommended that students in grades eight and nine devote one-quarter to one-half of their time to the curriculum variables. The report does provide for some variation in this by stating, "Pupils who will probably enter industry at the end of the ninth grade may well give as much as two-thirds of their time to vocational preparation, but they must not be permitted to neglect preparation for citizenship and worthy use of leisure" (Department of Interior, 1918, p. 24). The commissioners concluded their report by proclaiming:

> The doctrine that each individual has a right to the opportunity to develop the best that is in him is reinforced by the belief in the potential, and perchance unique, worth of the individual. The task of education, as of life, is therefore to call forth that potential worth.
>
> While seeking to evoke the distinctive excellencies of individuals and groups of individuals, the secondary school must be equally zealous to develop those common ideas, common ideals, and common modes of thought, feeling, and action, whereby America, through a rich, unified, common life may render her truest service to a world seeking for democracy among men and nations (Department of Interior, 1918, p. 32).

American Youth Commission

The American Youth Commission was formed in 1935 as a subgroup of the American Council on Education. This was a private commission that had no ties to any professional or governmental agency. The charge presented to the commission was to evaluate the facilities and resources that served the needs of young people and then to recommend procedures and programs that would be effective in solving the problems of youth that the commission identified. In its report, the commission concluded that, "An effective program of education must provide a balance between training for individual ends and training for social objectives." Among the recommendations made by this commission were the following:

1. The curriculum of the secondary school should give less time to the college-preparatory objects and subjects and "much more time to subjects and aspects of subjects more closely allied to the problems of individuals as citizens."

2. Alternative courses in science, mathematics, English, and social studies should be developed "so that differences in interests and abilities among youth will not render the educational program ineffective for a large proportion of them."

3. The concept of schooling should be broadened to include functions that weren't typically thought of as schooling. "Emphasis must be placed on supplementary medical and dental services, the development of character and personality, guidance services and the recreational and extra-curricula possibilities for education."

4. More time should be given to social studies. Economics, geography, sociology, and political science "should be taught in every year of the secondary school and required by all students." (Douglass, 1937, pp. 129–131)

Educational Policies Commission

In 1936, a year after the AYC undertook its work, the National Education Association, through its Educational Policies Commission, began a systematic analysis of the relationship between public schools, welfare and recreation agencies, and public libraries. During the Great Depression (1929–1940), a number of new public agencies were created to help relieve the economic emergency that existed in the country. Many of these were federally funded programs designed to aid children in need. Often the programs were offered outside of the realm of the school and the commission felt that such programs had the potential of usurping the power that had been given to local and state educational authorities. Therefore, the commission declared that, "Public educational authorities must be charged with full powers and full responsibilities for public educational activities. Any other course of action inevitably leads to confusion, authoritarian policies and lack of a unified approach to the educational needs of the individual" (Educational Policies Commission, 1939, p. 21) The commission defined education as the "guidance of the intellectual, moral, physical, and social development of the individual." The home, school, and church held the primary responsibility for the education of the child and of these three the school was the only one that was publicly supported and controlled. Consequently, the commission concluded that, *"It is sound education policy for school authorities to initiate action leading toward the removal of handicaps affecting the education of children"* (p. 24) and recommended that all public services for children should come under the auspices of the local educational authority.

The 1955 White House Conference on Education

This committee undertook the task of answering the question, "What should our schools accomplish?" and they began by stating that "No attempt has been made to answer from the point of view of ultimate philosophical objectives which could be read into the question." A few lines later they state, "As a lay group, the Committee has felt it inappropriate to undertake a discussion of the curriculum content in specific detail." What the committee did do, however, was to provide the following list of "purposes shared by most schools."

1. A general education as good as or better than that offered in the past, with increased emphasis on the physical and social sciences
2. Programs designed to develop patriotism and good citizenship
3. Programs designed to foster moral, ethical, and spiritual values
4. Vocational education tailored to the abilities of each pupil and to the needs of the community and nation
5. Courses designed to teach domestic skills
6. Training in leisure-time activities such as music, dancing, avocation reading, and hobbies
7. A variety of health services for all children, including both physical and dental inspections, and instruction aimed at better health knowledge and habits
8. Special treatment for children with speech and reading difficulties and other handicaps
9. Physical education, ranging from systematic exercises, physical therapy, and intramural sports, to interscholastic athletic competition
10. Instruction to meet the needs of abler students
11. Programs designed to acquaint students with countries other than their own in an effort to help them understand the problems America faces in international relations
12. Programs designed to foster mental health
13. Programs designed to foster wholesome family life
14. Organized recreational and social activities
15. Courses designed to promote safety. These include instruction in driving automobiles, swimming, civil defense, etc. (The Committee for The White House Conference on Education, 1956, pp. 8–9).

The committee endorsed each of these purposes but gave little guidance on how to accomplish any of them. Committee members did agree that "the development of the intellectual powers of young people, each to the limit of his capacity, is the first responsibility of schools" but then insisted that order of priority for the other purposes had to be determined on an individual basis since "all kinds of instruction are not equally important for all children." The commission went on to say, "In adding new, worthwhile activities to the curriculum, nothing of value has to be subtracted if a proper sense of proportion is maintained and enough resources are provided" (p. 13).

National Commission on the Reform of Secondary Education (1972)

The purpose of this commission was to conduct ". . . a comprehensive examination of secondary education and provide the American public with a clear, factual picture of their secondary schools, indicating where and how they can be altered to better serve the nation's young people" (Brown, 1973, p. xiv) According to the commission, the fear inspired by the launch of Sputnik in 1957 caused the nation to focus its educational efforts on math and science in the latter half of the decade. However, by the mid-1960s the country had begun to embrace the concept of the "Great Society." As a result, an increased emphasis was placed on social legislation and the educational focus changed from math and science to the improvement of education for disadvantaged students. "The schools, which only six years before had feverishly geared for a substantial concentration in mathematics and science courses, were required to make an abrupt shift in a massive effort to improve the education of the disadvantaged, especially education in basic skills" (Brown, p. 9–10) This led the commission to conclude that the American high school was a "beleaguered institution" on the "verge of complete collapse." The commission blamed this state of affairs on "society's insistence on sudden and traumatic changes" in the mission of the high school and went on to list a total of 32 recommendations for improving secondary education.

The recommendations made by the commission ranged from the establishment of national goals for education to the creation of additional opportunities for female students to participate in team sports, and even went so far as to indicate the number of cable TV channels that a local school district should have. Eight of the 32 recommendation were directly or indirectly related to how time should be allocated within the high school. They are:

> **Recommendation 3**: The Basis for Curricular Revision. The content of traditional high school curricula should be revised to eliminate busy-work components designed merely to occupy the time of adolescents who are in school only because the law requires it (p. 14).

> **Recommendation 8**: Expanding Career Opportunities. Secondary schools must realign their curricula to provide students with a range of experiences and activities broad enough to permit them to take full advantage of career opportunities in their communities. To meet this objective, basic components of the school program will have to be offered in the late afternoon or in the evening for some students (p. 15).

> **Recommendation 9**: Career Education. Opportunities for exploration in a variety of career clusters should be available to students . . . This

training should involve experiences in the world outside school and should equip the student with job-entry skills (p. 15–16).

Recommendation 12: Alternative Paths to High Completion. A wide variety of paths leading to completion of requirements for graduation from high school should be made available to all students (p. 16).

Recommendation 14: Credit for Experience. Secondary schools should establish extensive programs to award academic credit for accomplishment outside the building, and for learning that occurs on the job, whether the job be undertaken for pay, for love, or for its own sake (p. 17).

Recommendation 19: Flexibility of Alternative Programs. Differing time sequences—hourly, daily, weekly, yearly—must be made available so that educational programs can be adapted to the needs of individual students (p. 18).

Recommendation 28: Compulsory Attendance. The formal school-leaving age should be dropped to age fourteen. Other programs should accommodate those who wish to leave school, and employment laws should be rewritten to assure on-the-job training in full-time service and work (p. 21).

Recommendation 29: Free K-14 Education. The Congress of the United States in conjunction with state legislatures should enact legislation that will entitle each citizen to fourteen years of tuition-free education beyond kindergarten, only eight of which should be compulsory. The remaining six years should be available for use by anyone at any state of his life (p. 21).

Basic to all the recommendations was the underlying belief that education should be tailored to the needs of the individual student and should be directed toward helping the student become gainfully employed, at whatever age that might occur.

National Commission on Excellence

In 1981, the U.S. Department of Education created the National Commission on Excellence to study the quality of education in America. In its final report, *A Nation at Risk*, the commission noted that in many schools the time spent in nonacademic areas such as cooking classes and drivers education counted as much toward a high school diploma as did courses in the academic areas of mathematics, English, chemistry, U.S. history, or biology. This disturbed the commissioners. They were also disturbed that the average student spent only

22 hours a week in academic instruction and that some students spent as little as 17 hours in instruction. They therefore recommended that all high school students take four years of English, three years of mathematics, three years of science, three years of social studies, and one-half year of computer science. It was further recommended that college-bound students take two years of foreign language during their high school years. In order to meet these requirements, the commission noted that schools would need to extend the school day, lengthen the school year, or use the existing day more efficiently (National Commission on Excellence in Education, 1983).

The National Educational Commission on Time and Learning

In 1991, the National Educational Commission on Time and Learning was charged with examining the quality and adequacy of time students spent on learning. In its final report, the commission identified five barriers to quality education. These barriers included a fixed clock and calendar, stolen academic time that was being used for nonacademic activities, a schedule that was unresponsive to changes taking place in life outside of the school, a lack of time for educators to do their job properly, and an insufficient amount of time to meet world class standards. Three of the five—a school calendar that is unresponsive to the changing needs of society, lack of sufficient time for students to reach the mastery required by world-class standards, and the large amount of time spent on nonacademic activities—relate directly to the debate on how best to allocate school time.

The commission asserts that "students bring many more problems to school than children did a generation ago." The commission goes on to note that "It is clear that schools cannot be all things to all people—teachers cannot be parents, police officers, physicians, and addiction or employment counselors. But neither can they ignore massive problems" (p. 17). The implication is that schools have a responsibility to address the needs of the whole child and doing so is a legitimate use of school time—whether that time comes from an extended day or year.

The second barrier—lack of sufficient time required for students to meet world class standards—indicates that more time is needed for academics. In fact, the Commissioners stated unequivocally that "Additional hours and days will be required if new standards in the arts, geography, and foreign languages are to be *even partially attained*" (p. 21).

When discussing the third barrier—the large amount of school time spent on nonacademic activities—the commissioners noted that the number of nonacademic activities has increased over the years. Nonacademic activities include gym, counseling, study hall, pep rallies, driver's training, consumer education, and AIDS education. The commission maintained that while "most Americans believe these activities are worthwhile," the problem is that the only way that schools can find time for these activities is by "robbing Peter (academic activities) to pay Paul (nonacademic activities).

Based on these conclusions, the commission recommended that the school day be reinvented around a core curriculum rather than around scheduled time, that an academic day devoted almost exclusively to core academic instruction be established, and that schools be kept open longer in order to meet the needs of the community.

CONSISTENCY OF CONCERNS

These various commissions that were just reviewed represent only a small fraction of the educational commissions that have convened over the course of the last hundred years. The stated purpose of almost all of these commissions has been to study the state of education and to recommend improvements in the schooling process and their reports consistently reflect the concerns of the period in which they were written. For instance, in the early 1900s the reports stressed the need for schools to impart a sense of nationalism, while in the 1970s the reports emphasized the need for schools to respect the rights of the individual. In the 1930s the emphasis was on the social and welfare needs of indigent children who were living through the depression, and in the 1950s there was concern with meeting the educational needs of a mobile society.

But even as the reports addressed the social concerns of the time, their domain of inquiry remained surprisingly stable. Recurring throughout the reports are the themes of academic versus nonacademic classes, enrichment versus essential elements, vocational versus liberal education, humanities versus sciences, personal growth versus societal concerns, and individual versus mass education. Buried within these themes is the issue of how school time should be allocated. Several of the commissions, such as the Commission on the Economy of Time and the National Commission on Time and Learning, addressed the time issue directly. Other commissions, including the Committee of Ten, attempted to downplay the role of time in the curriculum but ultimately recommended specific courses being taken for a specific number of hours and at a specific time in the student's school career. Still other commissions, like the Educational Policies Commission, chose to ignore the issue of time completely. And finally there were commissions, like the White House Commission of 1955, that provided long lists of goals for the school and then left it up to the local districts to choose among the many goals. The belief was that schools would find the time to accomplish those goals that they felt were most important for the local community. Perhaps these commissions were correct in their assumption because historically, as framed by the following quote, that is precisely what has happened.

Consider the wave (sic) by which a new study is introduced into the curriculum. Someone feels that the school system of his (or quite frequently nowadays her) town is falling behind the times. There are rumors of great progress in education being made elsewhere. Something new and important has been introduced; education is being revolutionized by it; the school superintendent, or members of the board of education become somewhat uneasy; the matter is taken up by individuals and clubs; pressure is brought to bear on the managers of the school system; letters are written to the newspapers; the editor himself is appealed to use his great power to advance the cause of progress; editorials appear; finally the school board ordains that on and after a certain date the particular new branch—be it nature study, industrial drawing, cooking, manual training, or whatever—shall be taught in the public schools. The victory is won, and everybody—unless it be some already overburdened and distracted teacher—congratulates everybody else that such advanced steps are being taken.

The next year, or possibly the next month, there comes an outcry that children do not write or spell or figure as well as they used to; that they cannot do the necessary work in the upper grades, or in the high school, because of lack of ready command of the necessary tools of study. We are told that they also are not prepared for business, because their spelling is so poor, their work in addition and multiplication so slow and inaccurate, their handwriting so fearfully and wonderfully made. Some zealous soul on the school board takes up this matter, the newspapers are again heard from; investigation are set on foot; and edict goes forth there must be more drill in the fundamentals of writing, spelling and numbers (NEA, 1901, p. 334).

Although this statement was made in 1901, it holds at least a nugget of truth even today. The commission reports find their way into the media, the state and local boards of education respond, calling for changes in the school goals, the core curriculum, and/or calendar. Overburdened educators may complain that the changes are unnecessary or that there is no time to accomplish all that is desired even as their professional associations climb on the bandwagon of school reform. Many claim that this situation arises because schools developed with no clearly defined purpose. As the commission reports show, however, the purpose of schools is well defined. The purpose, as outlined by the Educational Policies Committee, is to guide the intellectual, moral, physical, and social development of each student. Therefore, it is not the lack of a clear purpose but rather the articulation of the purpose that creates the need to readdress the issue of how to best allocate school time for each new generation of students, teachers, and policy makers.

CURRENT STATE OF AFFAIRS

The fact that school reform is alive and well today should surprise no one. The news media, professional journals, and local school board meetings serve only to remind us of the intractable nature of the recurring issues in education. "Hot" among today's topics are the core curriculum, school funding, work-to-school transitions, inclusion, and authentic assessment. Embedded in these topics are the issues of the past—essential versus nonessential elements, academic versus nonacademic activities, general versus vocational education, and education of the masses versus education of the individual. These topics go beyond the issue of time, but at a pragmatic level, it is the allocation of time that tips the scale in favor of one side or the other. Year-to-year and day-to-day, schools must address the practical questions that result from the necessity of allocating school time. These questions include: "How much time are we going to allocate for non-academic activities?"; "How much time per day or per week should we allow for each subject or activity?"; "How many vocational education credits should a child be permitted to take?"; "What portion of the school day should we allot for the core curriculum?"; "Should we schedule the same amount of time for each subject or should we allow more time for the more demanding academic subjects?"; "How many semesters of science, math, English and foreign language should be required in order for a student to receive a high school diploma?"; and "Should promotion from grade-to-grade be based on how many years a student has been in school or on the objectives that he or she has mastered?" How these questions are answered will depend, at least to some degree, upon current educational standards and recent social, philosophical, and educational trends.

COMPETING EDUCATIONAL STANDARDS

In the past few years, professional organizations strove to develop new, higher standards of academic achievement for students at all levels. The standards set by each organization help to identify which topics and objectives are considered most important within a specific academic area.

The Mid-continent Regional Educational Laboratory, using the guidelines for academic achievement provided by various professional organizations, identified 157 standards with 1,541 benchmarks for students in grades K through 12.

In the report of their findings, the researchers acknowledged that the number of benchmarks are excessive and that it would be improbable, if not impossible, for all students to obtain each of the benchmarks.

Clearly, a school or district could not expect a student to demonstrate competence in all of these (although they may be a part of instruction). Sheer numbers would make such a system untenable. Given that there are 180 days in the school year and 13 years of schooling (assuming students go to kindergarten), there are only 2,340 school days available to students. If all benchmarks in this report were addressed, this would mean that students would have to learn and demonstrate mastery in a benchmark every 1.5 school days, or more than three bench marks every week. (Kendall & Marzano, 1994, p. 27).

The sheer number of benchmarks puts us at the heart of the time dilemma because, as the NECTL has warned us, "The American people and their educators need to be very clear about the standards movement. *It is not time free* [emphasis added]" (NECTL, 1994, p. 21). It takes time to learn new material and even more time to truly master the objectives. Yet most of the recommended standards ignore the dimension of time. The authors of the standards appear to agree with Bill Spady who believes that education should be outcome based and "geared to what we want the kids to demonstrate successfully at the 'real end'—not just the end of the week, the end of the semester, the end of the year" (Spady, 1992, p. 67). As an educator it is hard to argue with Spady—it is true that our end goal must be geared toward what the students can do once they leave our protective environments. What is of concern, however, is that the standards are often interpreted to mean that it makes no difference how long it takes the students to achieve the goals—just so long as they do. The problem here is that if teachers are unable to prioritize the goals, they are in danger of falling into the trap of feeling that they "must do everything" and do so at the risk of attempting too much and accomplishing too little.

There are those who believe that the only way around this dilemma is to add more time to the school day and year. Others, however, argue that extending school time treats the symptom (not enough time) and not the problem (competing goals). In the spirit of the findings of the Commission on Economy of Time in 1915, members of this group would argue that schools don't need more time, but rather they need to eliminate the nonessentials in the curriculum. In order to do this, of course, it would be necessary to first determine what is essential. Such a determination has always been difficult and this difficulty has eased little over the years as the following quote by Olsen and Zigler demonstrates.

Too often, the debate over what sort of preschool experience should be regularly provided for 5-year old children has been obfuscated rather than clarified by the attention focused on the length-of-day variable. While the issue of whether children should attend school for two-and-a-half, four, six, or eight hours a day clearly needs to be addressed, any resolution of the issue that fails to involve an account of the philosophy and content that shapes and fills those hours is trivial. Children's school performance, their intellectual development, their quality of life will *not* improve simply because they spend longer hours every day in a classroom.

The issue of whether a more "child-centered" or a more "academic" approach to preschool education is preferable is complicated by the fact that it requires us to articulate fairly specifically our expectations of preschool education and how broadly we construe the meaning of "learning" and "education" with respect to the development of young children. The issue relates particularly to the question of length of day because the kind of experience provided becomes more critical the more hours a child spends in school (Olsen & Zigler, 1989, p. 180).

The reality is that the problem of competing priorities is always complex and must be analyzed in view of the current situation, with respect for the lessons that we have learned from the past and with attention to both the present and future needs of our students.

RECENT TRENDS IN TIME ALLOCATION

Most, if not all, schools do attempt to allocate school time in a way that most effectively meets the needs of their students and their community while taking into consideration past practices and present concerns. We have seen how past practices have influenced school time, both at the calendar level and at the allocation level. We now turn our attention to some of the more pressing national trends that are currently affecting the allocation of school time. Among these factors are the "new basics," the growing emphasis on school to work transitions, the move toward outcome-based education, and an increased desire to meet the needs of all children.

New Basics

The National Committee on Excellence in Education (1983) identified what it called the "new basics" for high school students. The basics consist of four years of English, three years of math, three years of science, three years of social studies, and one-half year of computer science. In addition, two hours of foreign language were strongly recommended for college-bound students.

Between 1982 and 1994, the percentage of students meeting the requirements of the new basics increased from 2.7 to 29.2 percent. The percentage of students who met the new basic requirements and took two hours of foreign language increased from 1.9 to 23.2 percent (see Table 5–1). Even more

TABLE 5–1 Percent of high school graduates earning minimum credits in selected combinations of academic courses: 1982 and 1992

Years of graduation and course combinations taken[1]	All students	Sex		Race/ethnicity			
		Male	Female	White	Black	Hispanic	Asian
1982							
4 Eng., 3 S.S., 3 Sci., 3 Math, .5 Comp., & 2 F.L.[2]	1.9	2.0	1.7	2.2	.07	0.5	6.0
4 Eng., 3 S.S., 3 Sci., 3 Math, .5 Comp.[3]	2.7	3.3	2.1	3.1	1.0	0.9	7.1
4 Eng., 3 S.S., 3 Sci., 3 Math, & 2 F.L.	8.8	8.5	9.2	10.1	5.2	3.5	17.0
4 Eng., 3 S.S., 3 Sci., 3 Math,	13.4	14.3	12.6	14.9	10.1	6.3	21.0
4 Eng., 3 S.S., 2 Sci., 2 Math	29.2	29.1	29.3	30.2	28.1	23.5	34.5
1992							
4 Eng., 3 S.S., 3 Sci., 3 Math, .5 Comp., & 2 F.L.[2]	23.2	20.9	25.4	23.6	21.5	19.9	29.3
4 Eng., 3 S.S., 3 Sci., 3 Math, .5 Comp.[3]	29.2	28.0	30.4	29.5	27.0	28.6	32.2
4 Eng., 3 S.S., 3 Sci., 3 Math, & 2 F.L.	36.9	33.9	39.8	38.5	31.9	25.0	46.0
4 Eng., 3 S.S., 3 Sci., 3 Math,	46.8	46.5	47.1	48.5	43.2	35.9	50.8
4 Eng., 3 S.S., 2 Sci., 2 Math,	72.8	72.0	73.6	72.1	77.0	73.0	76.1

[1]Eng. = English; S.S.= Social Studies; Sci. = Science; Comp. = Computer science; F.L. = Foreign language.

[2]The National Commission on Excellence in Education recommended that all college-bound high school students take these courses as a minimum.

[3]The National Commission on Excellence in Education recommended that all high school students take these courses as a minimum.

Source: U.S. Department of Education National Center for Education Statistics. "1990 High School Transcript Study" and "National Education Longitudal Study." Second Follow-up Study. Published in Synder, T. D., & Hoffman, C. M. (1994), *Digest of education statistics 1994*. Washington, DC: U.S. Department of Education, Office of Educational Research and Improvement: National Center for Education Statistics.

impressive is the increase in the number of students who earned credits in the more rigorous math and sciences courses. For instance, the percentage of students who took both Algebra II increased from 26.48 percent in 1982 to 52.42 percent in 1994 and the percentage of students taking both biology and chemistry increased from 27.12 percent in 1982 to 49.62 percent in 1994 (see Table 5–2).

School to Work Transitions

Even as schools move toward implementing the new basics, there is a growing emphasis being placed on the need to prepare students for the "world of work." Fewer than 24 percent of high school graduates earn a bachelors degree. This concerns many who believe that schools have placed too much emphasis on preparing students for college rather than preparing them for the workplace. To support this argument is the fact that as the number of students completing the "new basic" minimuns has increased, the number of vocation courses taken by high school students has dropped from an average of 4.6 in 1982 to an average of 3.8 in 1992 (see Table 5–3).

Schools have begun to treat this concern by incorporating aspects of job-related skills, knowledge, and attitudes into the nonvocational courses. The 1992 report, *Learning a Living: A Blueprint for High Performance*, which was prepared by the United States Department of Labor Secretary's Commission on Achieving Necessary Skills (SCANS) has served as a key resource for schools attempting to integrate job skills into academic courses. Figure 5–1 presents a summary of the basic elements within the report. The commission identified five competencies and three foundational skills that it believed to be critical for quality job performance.

Teachers across the nation are now attempting to integrate these skills and competencies into their courses. Although this is a reasonable approach to developing job-related skills, it does require that time be allocated in different ways—teachers need time to redesign their courses and classroom time must be reassigned if the skills and competencies are to be met by the students.

Outcome-Based Education

There is now a growing interest in the concept of outcome-based education (OBE). As the name implies, outcome-based educational programs stress the end results of learning. Learning is viewed as a culminating process in which new skills and knowledge build upon existing skills and knowledge. The results of learning are applicable to "real-life" situations and are generizable to many different types of situations. The curriculum is designed around the intended outcomes and students progress through the curriculum by mas-

TABLE 5–2 Percentage of high school graduates taking selected mathematics and science courses in high school, by race/ethnicity: 1982 and 1994.

Mathematics and sciences courses credits	Total %		White		Black		Hispanic		Asian/Pacific Islander		American Indian/Alaskan Native	
	1982	1994	1982	1994	1982	1994	1982	1994	1982	1994	1982	1994
Mathematics[1]												
Any mathematics (1.00)	98.94	99.40	98.7	99.6	99.2	99.3	97.2	99.2	100.0	100.0	99.6	98.9
Algebra I (1.00)	46.26	64.72	57.8	67.5	42.4	65.0	42.4	70.7	55.5	61.7	33.2	58.7
Geometry (1.00)	40.70	67.20	51.0	72.7	28.8	58.1	25.6	69.4	64.9	75.8	33.2	60.0
Algebra II (0.05)	26.48	52.42	36.0	61.6	22.0	43.7	18.0	51.0	45.6	66.6	10.8	39.2
Trigonometry (0.50)	11.18	14.80	13.7	18.6	2.2	9.8	2.8	13.9	14.5	33.9	1.8	8.7
Analysis/pre-calculus (0.50)	5.62	16.90	6.8	18.2	2.2	9.8	2.8	13.9	14.5	33.9	1.8	8.7
Statistics/probability (0.05)	.875	1.46	1.2	2.3	0.5	1.7	0.1	1.0	1.7	1.1	0.0[2]	1.2
Calculus (1.00)	5.04	9.32	5.4	9.6	1.3	3.8	1.7	6.0	12.8	23.4	4.0	3.8
AP calculus (1.00)	1.62	7.42	1.8	7.3	0.3	2.0	0.4	4.6	5.5	21.0	0.1	2.2

Continued

TABLE 5–2 *Continued*

Science												
Any science (1.00)	95.28	99.5	96.9	99.7	97.4	99.5	93.8	99.3	96.2	99.3	92.1	99.7
Biology (1.00)	73.98	92.36	78.3	94.4	73.0	91.3	68.2	94.0	83.7	90.0	66.7	91.2
AP/honors biology (1.00)	5.52	4.12	7.4	4.6	4.6	2.7	3.1	3.3	11.9	8.3	0.6	1.7
Chemistry (1.00)	30.04	51.88	34.1	58.5	21.9	43.8	15.5	46.5	52.8	69.3	25.9	41.3
AP/honors chemistry (1.00)	2.58	3.44	3.3	4.3	1.6	2.1	1.3	2.5	5.8	7.7	0.9	0.6
Physics (1.00)	14.44	21.88	16.3	26.1	7.3	14.7	5.7	16.0	34.8	42.3	8.1	10.3
AP/honors physics (1.00)	1.48	2.40	1.2	2.5	0.9	1.4	0.4	1.8	3.4	6.0	0.0[2]	0.3
Engineering (1.00)	0.13	4.25	0.2	0.2	0.1	0.4	0.1	0.1	0.0[2]	1.0	0.0[2]	0.0[2]
Astronomy (0.05)	0.80	1.06	1.3	2.0	0.4	0.6	0.7	0.4	0.0[2]	0.08	0.0[2]	2.2
Geology/earth science (0.05)	12.72	20.46	14.0	23.8	10.0	23.3	11.2	15.3	9.6	16.7	18.8	23.2
Biology and chemistry (2.00)	27.12	49.62	31.3	56.4	19.7	42.2	14.2	45.1	48.5	64.8	21.9	39.6
Biology, chemistry, and physics (3.00)	11.42	18.86	12.2	22.7	4.8	13.0	3.9	13.4	28.4	37.2	7.8	8.0

[1]These data only report the percentages of students who earned credit in each mathematics cours while in high school and does not count those students who took these coures prior to entering high school.

[2]Percent is less than 0.05 and is rounded to 0.0.

Source: U.S. Department of Education National Center for Education Statistics. The 1994 High School Transcript Study Tabulations: Comparative Data on Credits Earned and Demographics for 1994, 1990, 1987, and 1982 High School Graduates, 1996.

TABLE 5-3 Average vocational course units completed

Characteristics	Total Vocational				Consumer and home-maker education				General labor market preparation				Specific labor market preparation			
	1969	1982	1987	1992	1969	1982	1987	1992	1969	1982	1987	1992	1969	1982	1987	1992
Total	**3.7**	**4.6**	**4.4**	**3.8**	**0.5**	**0.7**	**0.6**	**0.5**	**1.1**	**1.0**	**0.9**	**0.7**	**2.1**	**2.9**	**2.9**	**2.5**
Sex																
Male	3.4	4.6	4.5	4.0	0.1	0.3	0.3	0.4	0.9	1.0	0.9	0.7	2.4	3.4	3.3	2.9
Female	3.9	4.6	4.4	3.6	0.9	1.0	0.9	0.7	1.2	1.1	1.0	0.7	1.8	2.6	2.6	2.2
Race/ethnicity																
White	3.4	4.5	4.5	3.7	0.4	0.6	0.6	0.5	1.0	1.0	0.9	0.7	2.0	2.9	3.0	2.5
Black	4.8	4.8	4.5	4.0	0.7	0.9	0.7	0.7	1.6	1.0	1.0	0.7	2.5	2.9	2.8	2.5
Hispanic	5.1	5.3	4.3	3.8	0.4	0.9	0.6	0.5	1.9	1.2	1.0	0.8	2.8	3.2	2.7	2.6
Asian	3.8	3.1	2.9	3.2	0.2	0.3	0.3	0.4	1.6	0.9	0.7	0.5	2.0	1.9	1.9	2.3
American Indian	—	5.1	4.7	4.8	—	0.5	0.6	0.6	—	1.1	0.9	0.7	—	3.5	3.2	3.5
Parents' highest educational level																
Didn't finish high school	—	5.3	—	4.5	—	0.8	—	0.7	—	1.1	—	0.8	—	3.4	—	3.0
High school graduate	—	5.1	—	4.6	—	0.8	—	0.7	—	1.1	—	0.8	—	3.2	—	3.0
Some college	—	4.1	—	3.9	—	0.5	—	0.5	—	1.0	—	0.7	—	2.5	—	2.6
College graduate	—	3.1	—	2.5	—	0.4	—	0.4	—	0.8	—	0.5	—	1.9	—	1.7
Urbanicity of school																
Urban	—	4.2	—	3.5	—	0.6	—	0.4	—	0.9	—	0.7	—	2.7	—	2.4
Suburban	—	4.4	—	3.4	—	0.6	—	0.5	—	1.0	—	0.6	—	2.8	—	2.3
Rural	—	5.2	—	4.5	—	0.9	—	0.7	—	1.2	—	0.8	—	3.2	—	3.0

Source: Smith, T. M., Rogers, G. T., Alsalam, N., Perie, M., Mahoney, R., & Martin, V. (1994). *The Condition of Education of 1994: National Center for Education Statistics.* Washington, DC: U.S. Department of Education, Office of Educational Research and Improvement.

Note: Course units refer to Carnegie units, which are a standard of measurement that represents one credit for the completion of a 1-hour per day 1-year course.

—Not available

Data Source: U.S. Department of Education, National Center for Education Statistics, The 1969 Study of Academic Growth and Prediction, 1992 High School and Beyond Transcript Study, 1987 NAEP High School Transcript Studies, and the National Education Longitudinal Study of 1988 (Transcript Study, 1992).

tering the preceding skills and knowledge. Students progress at individual rates so that different students master the skills and knowledge at different points in their educational careers.

William Spady, a strong advocate for OBE, contends that there are two major obstacles to implementing OBE in the traditional school system. One is "wanting the outcome to happen for all students" and the other obstacle is related to the time-bound nature of our schools. According to Spady:

> What makes implementing OBE even more problematic is the second complicating factor: the totally TIME-BASED nature of our existing educational system in all of its organizational and procedural aspects. When you step back and really come to grips with the issue, you find it almost impossible to identify organizational or procedural features of our system that not both DEFINED BY and REGULATED BY the CALENDAR and the CLOCK. School buildings, school years, semesters, grading periods, courses, grade levels, Carnegie Units of credit, promotion, retention, school entry, graduation, testing programs, and staff contracts are defined and driven by the calendar (Spady, 1992, p. 7).

OBE is consistent with both the new basics and with work-to-school transition programs. OBE is also consistent with recent trends geared toward meeting the needs of all children when, and only when, the intended outcomes are defined in terms of the students' needs and not in terms of the clock and calendar.

Meeting the Needs of All Children

Schools have always existed for the purpose of meeting the educational needs of children. But only recently have public schools extended their mission to meeting these needs for all children—including special education students, children-at risk, and gifted and talented students.

Special Education Students
In 1975, the United States Congress passed Public Law 94-142, the Education for all Handicapped Act (EHA), to ensure a "free and appropriate public education" for *all* students. The law defined handicapped children as "those children evaluated as being mentally retarded, hard of hearing, deaf, speech impaired, visually handicapped, seriously emotionally disturbed, orthopedically impaired, other health impaired, deaf-blind, multi-handicapped, or as having specific learning disabilities, who because of those impairments need special education and related services" (p. 121 a.5). After the enactment of the

WORKPLACE KNOW-HOW

The know-how identified by SCANS is made up of five competencies and a three-part foundation of skills and personal qualities that are needed for solid job performance.

WORKPLACE COMPETENCIES	
Resources	Know how to allocate time, money, materials, space, and staff.
Interpersonal skills	Can work on teams, teach others, serve customers, lead, negotiate and communicate, and work well with people from culturally diverse backgrounds.
Information	Can acquire and evaluate data, organize and maintain files, interpret and communicate, and use computers to process information.
Systems	Understand social, organizational, and technological systems, they can monitor and correct performance, and they can design or improve systems.
Technology	Can select equipment and tools, apply technology to specific tasks, and maintain and troubleshoot equipment.

FOUNDATION SKILLS	
Basic Skills	Reading, writing, arithmetic and mathematics, speaking, and listening.
Thinking skills	Ability to learn, to reason, to think creatively, to make decisions, and to solve problems.
Personal qualities	Individual responsibility, self-esteem and self-management, sociability, and integrity.

FIGURE 5–1   Workplace skills from the Labor Secretary's Commission on Achieving Necessary Skills (SCANS) (SCANS, 1992)

law, the number of students served under federally supported special education students increased steadily from 3.7 in 1976-77 to 5.4 million in 1993-94 (see Table 5–4).

In 1990, PL94-142 was reauthorized and became known as IDEA, the Individuals with Disabilities Education Act of 1990. Prior to the enactment of EHA and IDEA, the majority of special education students were assigned to special classrooms, sent to special schools, or in some cases denied a public education. The law now requires that students be educated in the "least restrictive environment," and as a result the number of special education students who are taught in the regular classroom has increased steadily since the enactment of PL-142.

The law also requires school personnel to develop an individualized education program (IEP) for each special education student. The development, implementation, and evaluation of a student's IEP requires a team approach which in turn requires a number of team meetings between the classroom teacher, the special education teacher, the parents, and perhaps the school counselor and administrator. It may also require the preparation of special instructional materials and the implementation of alternative assessment techniques. Teaching methods may need to be altered so the special child is truly included within the class activities. There is often a need for more individualized instruction than is typical in a more homogeneous classroom.

In order to meet the needs of both special and regular education students, teachers often find it necessary to modify the amount and pacing of instruction that is given, change the sequence in which information is presented, and/or omit some content. Smith and his colleagues note that "Time is frequently a critical element that must be addressed in terms of classroom modifications. For many students with disabilities, modifications in time constraints can be of great assistance in promoting success" (Smith et al., 1995).

Children At Risk

Even as laws, educational policies, and teachers' concerns direct attention toward meeting the needs of the special education student in the regular classroom, there too has been an increased emphasis placed on meeting the needs of children at risk. Educators have identified a number of factors that put children at risk academically. Among those easiest to quantify are the educational level of the parents, literacy level of the parents, living in poverty, and/or a limited proficiency in English.

Educators find it alarming that over 20 percent (21.2% in 1994) of the children in the United States live in poverty, close to 2 million students lack proficiency in English, and over 200,000 mothers between the ages of 18 and 19 have less than 12 years of education (Smith, et al., 1996). Many of these disadvantaged children enter school missing the basic entry skills and lacking an understanding of what is expected of them in the school environment. How do kindergarten and first grade teachers cope with this situation? Do they spend the bulk of the school day helping the children adjust to school? Do they spend most of the day on teaching the skills necessary for reading, writing, and arithmetic and only a small amount on school adjustment? Or do they try to balance the time between the needs of the individual students and in doing so help to widen the gap between the students? These are never easy questions, but as schools and teachers allocate time during the school day, they are answering the questions, even if don't they realize it.

TABLE 5–4 Number of children who were served by federally supported programs for students with disabilities

Type of disability	1977	1978	1979	1980	1981	1982	1983	1984	1985
Number served (in thousands)[1]									
All disabilities	**3,692**	**3,692**	**3,692**	**4,005**	**4,142**	**4,198**	**4,255**	**4,298**	**4,315**
Specific learning disabilities	796	964	1,130	1,276	1,462	1,622	1,741	1,806	1,832
Speech or language impairments	1,302	1,233	1,214	1,186	1,168	1,135	1,131	1,128	1,126
Mental retardation	959	933	901	869	829	786	757	727	694
Serious emotional disturbances	283	288	300	329	346	339	352	361	372
Hearing impairments	87	85	85	80	79	75	73	72	69
Orthopedic impairments	87	87	70	66	58	58	67	56	56
Other health impairments	141	135	105	106	98	79	50	53	68
Visual impairments	38	35	32	31	31	29	28	29	28
Multiple disabilities	—	—	50	60	68	71	63	65	69
Deaf-blindness	—	—	2	2	3	2	2	2	2
Preschool disabled	([3])	([3])	([3])	([3])	([3])	([3])	([3])	([3])	([3])

Type of disability	1986	1987	1988	1989	1990	1991	1992	1993	1994
All disabilities	**4,317**	**4,374**	**4,447**	**4,544**	**4,641**	**4,762**	**4,949**	**5,125**	**5,373**
Specific learning disabilities	1,862	1,914	1,928	1,987	2,050	2,130	2,234	2,354	2,444
Speech or language impairments	1,125	1,136	953	967	973	985	997	996	1,009
Mental retardation	660	643	582	564	548	534	538	519	554
Serious emotional disturbances	375	383	373	376	381	390	399	401	414
Hearing impairments	66	65	56	56	57	58	60	60	64
Orthopedic impairments	57	57	47	47	48	49	51	52	57
Other health impairments	57	52	45	43	52	55	58	65	83
Visual impairments	27	26	22	23	22	23	24	23	25
Multiple disabilities	86	97	77	85	86	96	97	102	110
Deaf-blindness	2	2	1	2	2	1	1	1	1
Preschool disabled	([3])	([3])	363	394	422	441	484	531	587

Note: Counts are based on reports from the 50 states and the District of Columbia only (i.e., figures from the U.S. territories are not included). Increases since 1987–88 are due in part to new legislation enacted in fall 1986, which mandates public school education services appropriate for all disabled children aged 3 to 5. Details may not add to total due to rounding.

(1) Includes students who were served under Chapter 1 of the Elementary Consolidation and Improvement Act (ECIA) and Par B of Individuals with Disabilities Education Act (IDEA).

(2) Includes preschool children aged 3-5 years and 0-5 years who were served under Chapter 1 and Part B of the IDEA, respectively.

(3) Prior to the 197-88 school year, preschool disabled students were included in the counts by disabling conditions. Beginning in the 1987-88 school year, states were no longer required to report preschool students (aged 0-5) with disabilities by disabling condition.

(4) Revised from previously published figures.

—Not available

Source: U.S. Department of Education, Office of Special Education and Rehabilitative Services. Annual Report to Congress on the Implementation of Individuals with Disabilities Act, various years, and National Center for Education Statistics, *Digest of Educational Statistics*, 1995.

The Gifted and Talented

A great deal of attention has been directed toward meeting the needs of the academically slower child but, unfortunately, the gifted student is not always provided the same consideration. Recent research studies conducted by the National Research Center for Gifted and Talented (NRC) found that only a small number of third and fourth grade teachers modify classroom activities to accommodate the needs of the above average student. At the high school level, advanced placement classes are often provided in an attempt to meet the needs of the advanced high student, but these courses may not be available to the junior high student who is highly capable of mastering the concepts presented within the advanced courses. In addition, high schools students who are ready for college-level courses may find it difficult to receive either high school or college credit for such courses. When this occurs, the most gifted and academically capable students in our schools are forced to take courses in which they have mastered 85 to 95 percent of the content or to take courses that hold little interest for them (Ries, 1992).

State laws mandate that students stay in school until a certain age (typically 16 years of age). Most states continue to provide a free education for an additional two to three years (to age 18 or 19) beyond the minimum age of leaving for those students who have failed to meet graduation requirements. However, when students are allowed to take accelerated courses throughout their school career it is possible for them to complete the requirements for high school graduation at the age of 14 or 15 or even younger. This raises a number of questions. Should these student be forced to stay in school taking courses that are of little value to them? Should they be allowed to leave school even though state law mandates that they should be in school until age 16? Should they be allowed to take college courses at the expense of the school district? If advanced students are allowed to take college courses at the expense of the taxpayer, shouldn't all students be allowed to do so, at least until they reach the upper age limit for a free education as allowed by the state? Although these questions seem to have little to do with how time is allocated in schools, the questions force decision makers to focus on the consequences of allocating school time for the gifted and talented student and to develop policies regarding acceleration that are often more reflective of the budget needs of the school than of the academic needs of the more accomplished students.

TIME WASTERS VERSUS TIME ROBBERS VERSUS COMPETING GOALS

The debate over how time in school should be allocated often boils down to the simple question, "Should school time be allocated to academics alone or should some time be devoted to nonacademic activities that help meet the needs of the whole child?" The question could be reworded to read, "Are nonacademic activities time wasters or are they essential to meeting the goals of our educational system?" Time management experts talk about time wasters—activities that waste time and pull you away from your primary goal. If the primary goal of schools is to impart academic knowledge and skills—which seems to be a logical conclusion because schools are evaluated on the scholastic achievements of their students—nonacademic activities would be considered time wasters.

Most educators would be hesitant to define all nonacademic activities as time wasters, but there are many who do believe that such activities distract from the primary purpose of school. Time management experts would say that for these educators the nonacademic activities are time robbers rather than time wasters. Time robbers are activities that are seen as having value but that distract from the primary goal simply because they take away, or steal, time from activities that contribute more directly to the primary goal. If you will recall, this was one of the barriers identified by the NECTL. In its report, *Prisoners of Time*, the commission noted that, "Most Americans believe these activities are worthwhile. But where do schools find the time? Within a constrained school day, it can only come from robbing Peter to pay Paul."

There are several ways to deal with time robbers. One way is to *reduce the amount of time* that the "robbers" are allowed to "steal" from the primary goal. One example of a strategy that schools use to reduce the amount of stolen time is the closed lunch hour. Prior to the implementation of this strategy in the early 1970s, many students went home for lunch and this required schools to schedule 45 minutes to an hour for lunch. When schools went to the closed lunch hour, students stayed on campus and the lunch hour was reduced by 15 to 30 minutes. The minutes that were recovered were then allocated to academic activities.

Another way to deal with time robbers is to *reduce the impact* they have on the primary goal. High schools will often do this by scheduling the pep rally for the last class period on Friday when students tend to be less attentive than they would be, say at 10:00 Monday morning. Another way to reduce the impact of the time robbers is to dedicate a portion of time to the primary goal and declare that time as untouchable by any other goal. This is what the NECTL is recommending when it suggests that schools establish an academic day of 5.5 hours "devoted exclusively to the common core of subjects."

Perhaps the most drastic strategy that can be employed to deal with time robbers is to *redefine the primary goal*. This is a dangerous strategy because of the enormous impact it can have on outcomes. Key resources would have to be diverted from the original goal to the modified goal. With the changing of the primary goal, schools would no longer be judged by the academic achievements of their students, but rather by criteria that more accurately measure the attainment of the new goal. For example, if the schools change their primary goal from academic pursuits to socialization and counseling, there would be a need for fewer teachers and more counselors and psychologists. Some time would be allocated to academic pursuits, but the majority of time would be devoted to helping students get along with one another and to helping them "better understand themselves." The evaluation of schools would no longer be based on the scholastic achievement of the students, but rather on the students' ability to get along with one another. If carried to the extreme, we would have high school graduates who were as compatible as a gaggle of geese and just about as intelligent! (Of course, we must admit that if the academic goal were carried to the same extreme we would have high school graduates who are as intelligent as an isolated scholar—and just about as social!)

The question that automatically comes to mind at this point is "But isn't it possible to have dual, noncompeting goals?" And the obvious answer is, "Yes, of course. We do it all the time." In reality, the answer is "probably not," because even when we have complementary goals they can, and often do, become competing goals. For schools, the problem is that they often find themselves in "forced-choice" positions. There is only so much time and so much money allocated to schools. If the time and/or money is used to meet one goal it (they) can't be used for the other. If we are spending time counseling students on birth control, we can't use that time to teach Ohm's Law. If we are spending money for counselors, then that money can't be used for teachers or vice versa. There have been some creative attempts to resolve the forced-choice nature of dual goals that limit resources for one or the other. For example, one school district decided to train its teachers in the basics of counseling with the idea that this would reduce the need for trained counselors and that the time spent on counseling could be integrated within the school day. The results, however, were less than satisfying. It was found that teachers were spending less time in teaching (their area of strength) and more time in counseling (their area of weakness) under the new plan and, as a result, the quality of both the teaching and the counseling suffered.

There is another possibility, however, and that is that nonacademic activities may be necessary to meet the ultimate goal of education—to help all students reach their full potential. The general public expects schools to produce students who are well-rounded, who are productive citizens, who know how to take care of themselves, and who will become life-long learners. In order to meet these expectations, schools frequently find it necessary to spend time on the nonacademic areas. This then creates a dilemma in helping students reach their full potential: Should nonacademic activities be considered time wasters and consequently removed from the school day? Should they be considered time robbers whose impact should be reduced? Or should they be considered necessary elements in meeting the ultimate goal of education? If nonacademic activities that are stealing time from academics are deemed important, necessary, and pressing, then they are neither time wasters or robbers but rather fundamental contributors to the primary goal. The important thing to realize is that the determination of the primary goal should not and must not be haphazard, impulsive, or reactive. It must be deliberate, proactive, and carefully implemented because, in the words of Alex MacKenzie, a noted time management expert, "Without goals, priorities, and planning, you are leaving the future to chance. And you may be forced to pay the price sooner than you think. If you have not identified your ultimate target, you cannot know which interim objectives to set. Therefore, on any given day your priorities are either nonexistent or hopelessly confused. Without priorities you will tend to react to whatever comes by. You respond to the request of others without passing them through the filter of your objectives." MacKenzie goes on to say: "Now comes the time trap of attempting too much. With no priorities to help you discriminate between the truly important and the not-so-important, you believe that *everything* has to be done" (p. 88).

REFERENCES

Brown, F. B. (1973). *The reform of secondary education: A report to the public and the profession*. New York: McGraw-Hill.

The Committee for The White House Conference on Education. (1956). *Full Report to the President*. Washington, DC: U.S. Government Printing Office.

Committee of Ten on Secondary School Studies. (1894). *Report*. New York: American Book Company.

Department of the Interior. (1918). *Cardinal principles of secondary education, Bulletin No. 35*. Washington, DC: United States Government Printing Office.

Douglass, H. R. (1937). *Secondary Education for youth in modern America: A Report to the American Youth Commission of the American Council on Education*. Washington, DC: American Council on Education.

Educational Policies Commission. (1939). *Social services and the schools*. Washington, DC: National Education Association.

Harding, L. W. (1953). Influences of commissions, committees, and organizations upon the development of elementary education. In Harold G. Shane (Ed.), *The American Elementary School* (pp. 157–193). New York: Harper & Brothers Publishers.

Kendall, J. S., & Marzano, R. J. (1994). *The systematic identification and articularion of content standards and benchmarks: Update*. Aurora, CO: Mid-continent Regional Educational Laboratory.

Mackenzie, A. (1990). *The time trap*. New York: AMACOM.

National Commission on Excellence in Education. (1983). *The nation at risk*. Washington, DC: Office of Educational Research and Improvement.

National Education Commission on Time and Learning. (1994). *Prisoners of time*. Washington, DC: Office of Educational Research and Improvement.

National Educational Association. (1901, July 8–12). *Journal of proceedings and addresses of the fortieth annual meeting*, p. 334, Detroit: NEA.

National Education Association. (1915). *Journal of proceedings and addresses of the fifty-third annual meeting and international congress on education.* Ann Arbor, MI: Author.

Olsen, D., & Zigler, E. (1989). An assessment of the all-day kindergarten movement. *Early Childhood Research Quarterly, 4,* 167–186.

Ries, S. M. (1992, March). *The curriculum compacting study.* The National Research Center on the Gifted and Talented Newsletter.

Secretary's Commission on Achieving Necessary Skills (SCANS). (April, 1992). *Learning a living: A blueprint for high performance—A SCANS report for America 2000.* Washington, DC: U.S. Department of Labor.

Smith, T. E. C., Polloway, E. A., Patton, J. R., & Dowdy, C. A. (1995). *Teaching students with special needs in inclusive settings.* Boston: Allyn and Bacon.

Smith, T. M., Rogers, G. T., Alsalam, N., Perie, M., Mahoney, R., & Martin, V. (1994). *The Condition of Education 1994: National Center for Education Statistics.* Washington, DC: US. Department of Education, Office of Educational Research and Improvement.

Smith, T. M., Young, B. A., Choy, S. P., Perie, M., Alsalam, N., Rollefson, M. R., & Bae, Y. (1996). *The Condition of Education 1996*: National Center for Education Statistics. Washington, DC: U.S. Department of Education, Office of Educational Research and Improvement.

Spady, W. G. (1992, Summer). It's time to take a close look at outcome-based education. *The Quarterly Journal of the Network of Outcome-Based Schools,* 6–13.

Synder, T. D., & Hoffman, C. M. (1994). *Digest of education statistics 1994.* Washington, DC: U.S. Department of Education, Office of Educational Research and Improvement: National Center for Education Statistics.

Tomlinson, T. M., & Walberg, H. J. (1986). *Academic work and educational excellence: Raising student productivity.* Berkeley, CA: McCutrhan Publishing Company.

▶ 6

Time and Learning Models

Model of School Learning and Learning for Mastery

In the previous chapters, we have looked at the first two levels of time in school: scheduled time and allocated time. Scheduled time and allocated time treat the relationship between time and learning from a quantitative perspective. When dealing with quantity issues, the questions to be asked revolve around such concerns as: "How much time should be allocated to a given subject?" "How long should the school year be?" and "How much time should students spend in school during the day?" The answers to these questions take the form of policy decisions and are implemented through the school calendar and the school schedule.

Now we will turn our attention to the relationship between time and learning from a qualitative perspective and will examine the last two levels of school time: engaged rate and academic learning time. Engaged rate is the amount of time students spends working on a task. The phrase time-on-task is often used as a synonym for engaged rate. Academic learning time refers to the amount of time a student spends on an academically relevant task at which he or she is highly successful.

While allocated time and scheduled time are easy to measure (i.e., quantify), quality time is much more elusive, not only because it is hard to measure but also because it is non-static and influenced by many different variables. The amount of time a student needs may vary from day to day. The classroom climate, the ability of the teacher, the nature of the instructional task, and the characteristic of the students will all have an impact on the quality of the instruction given and received and the amount of time needed to deliver the instruction.

Decisions that affect the quality of learning time are most frequently made in the classroom under the direction of the teacher. Teachers deal with this quality issue every time they prepare a lesson plan. It is almost impossible to prepare a working instructional plan without asking questions such as, "How much time will the students need to master this set of skills?" "How long should I allow for hands-on activities?" and "How much time should I allow for this test?"

The overriding question regarding quality of instruction, from a time perspective, is: "How can the ratio between time and learning be improved?" In order to answer this question, we must also answer the questions: "How is classroom time currently being spent?" "How can we improve time usage in the classroom?" and "What distracts from quality time during the existing school day?"

An understanding of the time and learning research, along with an understanding of the nature of instructional tasks, an awareness of the different types of teaching behaviors, and an appreciation of the variations in student characteristics and classroom environments will go a long way in helping to address these questions.

Over the last several decades, researchers have increasingly directed their attention toward the use of time in education. This research has generated several important theories about the relationship between time and learning and has provided a framework that has helped to structure, organize, and reorganize the professional knowledge base associated with the interrelationship of time and academic achievement. The theories have resulted in a number of theoretical models, including Carroll's Model of School Learning (1963), Bloom's Learning for Mastery (1974b), and the Beginning Teacher's Evaluation Model of Academic Learning Model (Fisher, 1978). Both the theories and the models have been tested through quantitative and qualitative studies *and* have been subjected to the "real-life" test of the classroom.

Although the relationship between time spent and amount learned appears to be a relatively simple one—the more time students have for learning, the more they will learn—the testing of the theories has helped to reveal the complexity of the interactions of these two variables. This is especially true when the variables are considered in light of other intervening variables such as quality of instruction and student characteristics. The theories have been instrumental in increasing the professional educator's awareness of the many factors that affect both the amount of time a student will need to master a learning task and the amount of time a student will be willing to devote to learning. The findings from the research have resulted in the development of general guidelines for planning and evaluating instruction and instructional materials, and have served to demonstrate that, although many of the factors are outside the control of the teacher and the school, many of the factors *are* within their control. The research also demonstrates that even factors that are considered outside the control of the school and the teacher can be influenced by school policies and teacher behaviors. Although the research on time and learning is far from conclusive, the findings from the research have provided insights into how to improve the time and learning ratios within the classroom.

This chapter will examine two of the three major models of time and learning—John Carroll's Model of School Learning (MSL) and Benjamin Bloom's Learning for Mastery Model. Chapter 7 will address the Academic Learning Time (ALT) Model of Classroom Instruction.

INTRODUCTION TO THE MODEL OF SCHOOL LEARNING

In 1963, John Carroll introduced his "Model of School Learning" (MSL). The model is founded on the basic principle that a "learner will succeed in learning a given task to the extent that he [she] spends the amount of time that he (or she) *needs* to learn the task" (Carroll, 1963, p. 725).

Carroll defined the task of learning as "going from ignorance of some specified fact or concept to knowledge or understanding of it, or of proceeding from incapability of performing some specific act to capability of performing it" (Carroll, 1963, p. 723). To go from "ignorance" to "understanding" requires that students spend at least the minimum amount of time they need to learn the fact, concept, or skill. The amount of *time needed* will depend on a number of factors including the student's aptitude for the task, the quality of instruction that is received, and the student's ability to understand the task. *Time spent* depends on how much time a student is given for learning a task and how much of that time the student is willing or able to spend in learning. It is important to note that time spent refers to the actual time the student spends on learning, *not* the amount of time that has elapsed since the student began the task or the amount of time that has been allocated to the task.

Carroll reduced his model to the following formula:

$$\text{Degree of learning} = f(\text{time spent} \div \text{time needed})$$

where
Time spent = *the lesser of*

a) amount of time allowed for learning (opportunity)
b) amount of time student is willing to spend learning (perseverance)
c) amount of time needed to learn (aptitude) adjusted for quality of instruction and ability

and

Time needed = amount of time needed to learn (aptitude) adjusted for quality of instruction and ability to understand instruction.

Time Needed to Learn

Several factors affect the amount of time a student needs in order to learn a specific body of knowledge or a particular skill. These factors include a student's aptitude, his or her ability to understand instruction, and the quality of instruction that the student receives.

Aptitude

Carroll defined aptitude as the amount of time a student needs in order to learn, given optimal instructional and motivational conditions. According to the MSL, there is a direct, negative relationship between the amount of time a student needs in order to learn and the student's aptitude. A student with a high aptitude in a particular area requires less time to master learning tasks within that area than does a student who has a lower aptitude in the area. In other words, a student who has a high aptitude in math will require less time to master mathematical learning tasks than will a student with a low aptitude in math. There are a few students who may never master a task in a particular area because they have a very low aptitude in that area. In terms of the model, we would say these students need an infinite amount of time to learn a given task.

Aptitude is defined in terms of *each* task and is dependent upon prior knowledge and learner characteristics. The more experience and knowledge that a student has regarding a particular area, the less time it will take for a student to master new tasks in that area. For instance, let's say two students are taking Spanish I. The first student has spent the better part of one summer with friends in Mexico and occasionally used a Spanish word or phrase to emphasize a point. The second student has no exposure to Spanish or any other language other than English. With all else being equal, it is very likely that the first student will have a higher aptitude for learning Spanish because of his or her prior knowledge. And because of this higher aptitude, the student will be able to complete assignments more quickly than will the second student.

Carroll has suggested that it is possible to increase a student's aptitude through practice and enrichment activities. By providing students with enrichment activities in which they encounter the learning task in many different forms and by providing additional practice activities for the students, the teacher is helping to build the students' background knowledge which in turn should enhance the students' aptitude for learning tasks in that area. The first student in our example had encountered the task in the "real world," and we can assume that the student had been given many chances to practice the skill during the summer which could account, at least in part, for the higher aptitude of the student. The second student had not been afforded these same opportunities and therefore does not have the rich background knowledge upon which to build. The teacher can help the second student by using an assortment of instructional approaches and having the student participate in a variety of learning activities that require the student to use his or her language skills in a number of different ways. By doing so, the teacher may help to reduce the amount of time it takes the student to learn the language.

Ability

Ability to understand instruction, the second factor affecting the amount of time a student needs to learn a task, is defined by Carroll as "that characteristic, general intelligence or verbal intelligence, which determines the extent to which the individual will be able to understand directions and explanations or to infer such directions and explanations from the total content of the instruction, even when they are lacking" (Carroll, 1962, p. 122). General intelligence affects a student's ability to construct knowledge based on reason and understanding. Verbal ability refers to the degree to which a learner can make sense of the spoken or written word. A student who has a high level of both general intelligence and verbal ability related to the learning task will need less time to learn the task than will a student who has a low level of either.

As an example, consider a third student in the Spanish class. This student had also spent extended time in Mexico and used Spanish phrases occasionally, especially when conversing with the first student. However, this third student has a tendency to "take everything literally." In addition, other teachers have noted that "you have to give her step-by-step directions or she'll never get done and she would never assume you meant something unless you actually said it." We can anticipate that this student will have some trouble in the Spanish class and will take longer to complete assignments, not because of low aptitude but because of a generally low verbal ability.

Quality of Instruction

Quality of instruction "is a measure of how clearly the task is presented and explained, and how appropriately it is placed in the sequence of graded tasks to be learned" (Carroll, 1962, p. 121) The organization and sequencing of tasks relates directly to a student's aptitude—i.e., a student with prior knowledge and experience will require less time to learn. If the learning tasks are sequenced so that they build upon one another, the instructional process is ensuring that the students have the necessary prior knowledge to learn. The clarity of the instructional presentation and explanation interacts with the student's ability. A student of high ability who is able to infer directions, even when they are not explicitly stated, will be impacted less by an unclear instructions than will a student of lower ability who is unable to make such inferences. Regardless of the student's ability, however, the clearer the instructional presentation, the less time it will take the student to master the task.

The presentation and organization of instruction affects the rate and efficiency of learning and the elements of quality instruction go beyond the instruction presented by the teacher to all aspects of instruction, including textbooks, workbooks, films, and laboratory exercises. One of the characteristics of a high quality of instruction is the degree to which learners are informed of exactly what is expected of them—they must know what task they are attempting to learn. The learners must be able to see and hear the instruction. For instance, the print must be large enough to see, the teacher's voice must be loud enough that the student can hear it, and the room must be dark enough to make out the detail in a videotape. All parts of the learning task must be presented in a logical sequence so that each step in the learning process prepares the learner for the next step and learners are not presented with new information before they have mastered the prerequisite information. There must be enough detail presented in the lesson so that the students are able to comprehend the subtle parts of the learning task and they should not be expected to master large chunks of information as part of a single learning task. In its ultimate form, quality instruction may demand that a lesson, in all its various forms of presentation, be adapted to meet the individual and special needs of each learner.

Final Note on Time to Learn
Carroll noted in his original presentation of the model that both aptitude and quality of instruction could be eliminated from the model if the assumption was that "a change in the quality of instruction causes an essential change in the learning task itself" (Carroll, 1962, p. 727). If Carroll had chosen to eliminate aptitude and quality of instruction from his model, however, the model would have been less representative of learning in schools because aptitude and quality of instruction are important variables that are within a teacher's ability to influence.

Time Spent in Learning

Even when students have an aptitude for a task, have the ability to understand the instruction, and are provided with a high quality of instruction, they still may not succeed in achieving mastery. Carroll accounts for this failure in terms of the amount of time the students spend in learning the task. If a student needs x number of minutes to master a task but devotes only $x-y$ amount of time to learning the task, the student will fail to master the task. Although this appears to be self-evident, it is remarkable how many times students fail to meet this very basic requirement of success—spending enough time to master the task. In the school setting, this failure can often be attributed to one of two factors. The first is the amount of time available for learning (opportunity to learn). The second is the amount of time the student is willing to devote to learning the task.

Opportunity to Learn

Under normal circumstances, a student is allowed only a limited amount of time to work on a learning task within the school day. If the time available for learning (opportunity time) is less than the time needed (time required based on aptitude and ability) the student will fail to master the task. In schools, the time allowed for learning any specific task is limited and often turns out to be less than what the student needs. And as any teacher can tell you, there are three major reasons for this lack of time.

The first reason for students not being provided with enough time is due to the large amount of material they are expected to master each year. Kendall and Marzano (1994) have noted that if teachers were to follow the national standards that are being recommended by the various professional organizations, students would be required to learn and demonstrate mastery of a benchmark every 1.5 school days. Although most teachers see this as an unrealistic expectation, many feel obligated to cover the content represented by the benchmark. This then limits the amount of time the students have to accomplish any one benchmark.

The second reason that some students are not provided with the time they need for learning is due to the great disparity among students in the amount of time they need in order to learn. Although most teachers do make some attempt to adapt instruction to the special needs of individual students, the classroom structure is geared toward meeting the needs of groups of students. As a result, teachers are forced to use classroom time in a way that they believe will best serve the majority of the students even when this may mean that some students will never have enough time to master a task.

The third reason for lack of student learning time is that the structure of the school day places a constraint upon how much time a student is allowed to work on a learning task in a particular subject. Class bells, school specials, yearly calendars, and even grade placement all place a boundary around school time and serve to limit the amount of time that a student is allowed for learning. Students often react to the frustration of not having enough time by avoiding the task altogether or by taking on an air of seeming indifference toward the task.

The Amount of Time Student Is Willing to Spend

The amount of time students spend on learning is affected not only by the amount of time they are *allowed* to spend on a learning task but also by the amount of time they are *willing* to spend. Carroll referred to the amount of time students are willing to spend learning as "perseverance." He defined perseverance in terms of three attributes that had earlier been described by Paul Brandwein in 1955. According to Brandwein, perseverance, or persistence, was composed of the following.

1. A marked willingness to spend time beyond the ordinary schedule in a given task.
2. A willingness to withstand discomfort . . . it includes withstanding fatigue and strain and working even through minor illness, such as a cold or headache.
3. A willingness to face failure. With this comes a realization that patient work may lead to successful termination of the task at hand (Brandwein 1955, pp. 9–10).

There are a number of reasons why a student may or may not be willing to spend time beyond the ordinary schedule, withstand discomfort, and face failure in order to accomplish a specific learning task. Some of these reasons are conscious and logical and others are emotional and somewhat illogical. The student may believe that the task is too difficult or may become distracted or bored. Part way through the task, the student may lose confidence in his or her ability or may overestimate how much he or she has achieved and simply leave the task before truly mastering it. The student's aptitude, ability, and motivation, the quality of instruction he or she receives, and the amount of time that is allowed for learning will all affect the student's perseverance with a learning task.

CLASSROOM IMPLICATIONS

The following scenarios provide examples of how the model might be applied to the classroom. Assume that Student A needs an hour to learn a concept (learning task). The student is given two class periods of 50 minutes each to master the concept. During any one class period she is able to work about 15 minutes before her mind begins to wander. This means that she can work for 15 minutes and then must take a "mental break" for approximately two minutes. The first six minutes of each period are taken up with announcements and the last ten minutes are devoted to giving homework assignments. If we add the time taken for announcements, the time used to assign homework, and the time for the student's "mental breaks," multiply the time by two (for the two class periods) and subtract this time from the total time that was in the two class periods, we find that the student has the 60 minutes she will need to master the task (see Table 6–1).

TABLE 6–1   Student "A"

Time	Activity
9:00	Class begins
9:00 (6 min.)	Announcements
9:07 (15 min.)	Works on task
9:22 (2 min.)	Mental break
9:24 (15 min.)	Works on task
9:39 (2 min.)	Mental break
9:41 (10 min.)	Homework assignment

Opportunity (a)	Perseverance (b)	Time Needed (c)	Learning Ratio (Time Spent/ Time Needed)
68 minutes (34 min. * 2 class periods)	60 minutes (15 + 15) * 2 class periods	60 minutes	1/1 Perfect match between time needed and time spent

As you review the chart you will see that the teacher has allowed 34 minutes of each 50 minute class period for the student to learn the concept. This gives the student a total of 68 minutes of opportunity time (see letter (a) in Table 6–2). However, because the student takes a two-minute mental break, the total time she spent learning was 60 minutes (letter (b) in Table 6–2). The premise provided at the beginning of this example was that, based on the student's ability to understand the instruction, her aptitude for the task, and the quality of the instruction being employed, she would need 60 minutes to master the concept. Therefore the degree of learning for Student A is 1/1, or a perfect ratio.

Now let's suppose that a second student in the same class, Student B, is a low aptitude student who needs 95 minutes to master the concept. The student's attention span is about ten minutes. Every ten minutes the student becomes bored or distracted and spends an average of three minutes off task. It also takes this student an average of three minutes longer to begin the learning task because he must wait for further direction from the teacher. Using Carroll's formula, we find that the student has a learning ratio of 48/95, which means that the time he spends learning is slightly more than half of the time he needs (Table 6–2).

A third student, Student C, needs only 30 minutes to master the concept. His attention span is 20 minutes, but after a mental break of little more than

TABLE 6–2   Student "B"

Time	Activity
9:00	Class begins
9:00 (6 min.)	Announcements
9:07 (20 min.)	Waits for future instructions
9:11 (10 min.)	Works on task
9:21 (3 min.)	Mental break
9:24 (10 min.)	Works on task
9:34 (1 min.)	Mental break
9:37 (13 min.)	Works on task
9:41 (10 min.)	Homework assignment

Opportunity (a)	Perserverance (b)	Time Needed (c)	Learning Ratio Time Spent/ Time Needed)
68 min.	48 min.	95 min.	48/95 Ratio indicates student is spending only about half the time needed.

a minute he is able to return to his work (see Table 6–3). This means that his learning ratio is 2 to 1, which in turns means that the student is capable of mastering the concept in just one class period. If he is unable to move on to the next task and instead continues to work on the task, he will have spent double the amount of time he needed on learning the task and would have lost the opportunity to move on to a more suitable learning task. The amount of time assigned to learning the task was just as inappropriate for this student as it was for the slower student and could be almost as damaging because excessive learning time can lead to boredom, poor work habits, and even discipline problems. (It should be noted that "excessive learning time" *is not* the same as time allocated to overlearning. Overlearning refers to additional practice after a concept is mastered. Because overlearning has a positive effect on learning, time allocated to overlearning is good, while time allocated to excessive learning is bad.)

These examples demonstrate what can happen when students are forced to adhere to certain time limits, or blocks of instruction (which is the case in most classrooms). If the time limits are less than the time required based on the students' aptitudes, they will be unable to master the learning task (or

TABLE 6–3   Student "C"

Time	Activity
9:00	Class begins
9:00 (6 min.)	Announcements
9:07 (20 min.)	Works on task
9:27 (1 min.)	Mental break
9:28 (13 min.)	Works on task
9:41 (10 min.)	Homework assignment

Opportunity (a)	Perserverance (b)	Time Needed (c)	Learning Ratio (Time Spent/ Time Needed)
68 min.	66 min.	30	60/30 Student is spending twice as much time as needed

benchmark outlined by the new standards). The school day is built around blocks of time and these blocks are adequate for some students and more than adequate for other students. There are, however, some students that simply are not given enough time to master the instructional tasks set before them. The net result of the policies and practices that make time a constant and learning a variable is that some students are condemned to fail in school.

The picture is not as bleak as it appears. The examples just presented treated the allocation of classroom time as a given and the time needed for learning as more or less stagnant. We know, however, that both variables can be altered, at least to some degree, by the actions of the classroom teacher. In our example, the teacher could have spent less time making announcements, given written directions for the homework assignments, and increased or decreased the number of class periods devoted to learning the task. But even more importantly, the teacher, through his or her instructional techniques, may have been able to lessen the amount of learning time required by the students.

THE INTERACTION BETWEEN TIME AND ACHIEVEMENT

The MSL presupposes an interaction between time and academic achievement. Consequently Carroll divided the five basic variables into two classes— those that dealt with time and those that dealt with achievement. The three time variables are opportunity time—the amount of time available; aptitude—the amount of time needed; and perseverance—the amount of time the student is willing to spend. Ability and quality of instruction are treated as achievement variables. With the MSL, aptitude, opportunity, and perseverance are measured in terms of time. Quality of instruction and ability are included in the model because of the impact that they can and do have on the time and learning relationship.

Time Variables

Opportunity Time

Opportunity time is defined as the amount of time a student has available to learn a given task and this time is affected by the school calendar, the daily schedule, the class agenda, and classroom management. Two of the four—class agenda and classroom management—are under the direct control of the teacher and can be altered from day to day. The other two—school calendar and daily schedule—are more rigid and, although designed with input from teachers, are more removed from direct teacher control.

School Calendar

The school calendar, including length of the school year and day and the way the days within the school year are allocated, tends to be the most rigid of the opportunity time variables. The school calendar may include a summer vacation of several months or it may have a number of smaller vacations spread throughout the year. The calendar may contain teacher planning days incorporated throughout the year. During these days, students do not attend school but they are considered work days for the teachers. The calendar may allow for extra days that are to be used if the school closes due to snow but otherwise go unused. Once the calendar is established—including professional days, snow days, student vacation, and the time for school opening and closing—it becomes very difficult to change. This is important to realize because it is the school calendar that provides the upper limit on opportunity time.

The Daily Schedule

How the instructional day is divided is determined in part by state requirements, in part by accreditation requirements, and in part by decision makers within the school. State agencies and accreditation associations require that a certain amount of time be devoted to core competencies. This requirement may be stated in terms of time (i.e., the number of hours or units that a student must have in a certain area in order to graduate) or it may be stated in term of benchmarks and testing. Regardless of which method is used, the way in which the school time is allocated reflects the weight given to the different subject areas.

Within the school, teachers and administrators often meet to determine how they are going to structure the school day. At the secondary level, their decision may result in block scheduling, modular/flexible scheduling, or a seventh period. At the elementary level, teachers and administrators work together to schedule recesses, special classes (e.g., gym, music, art, computers, library time, etc.), and any special events that may occur during the year or semester. Elementary teachers are expected to teach reading, arithmetic, science, social studies, language arts, spelling, and any other subject dictated by the curriculum. How much time they devote to these subjects (how much opportunity time is available for these subjects) is reflected in the daily schedule. In some schools this is a very straightforward process—90 minutes for reading, 60 minutes for math, and so forth. In other schools, especially those that have gone to an integrated school day, the assignment of minutes may not be as obvious, but it's still there.

Classroom Agenda
The classroom agenda is composed of the instructional lesson plan plus other planned events. A well-devised plan will identify the instructional tasks the teacher and students will be involved with, indicate how much time is allocated for the task, list the resources that will be needed, and state the desired outcome from the lesson.

Other planned events are also part of the classroom agenda. For instance, a trip to the local art museum may be planned. The trip will require that the students travel by bus to the museum. The trip must be planned for and it will take part of the classroom time, but it is not part of the instruction and so is not part of the lesson plan *per se*.

The classroom agenda, including both lesson time and the time for other events, reflects how the teacher plans on distributing the minutes within the class period or school day. The planning process takes time and the agenda uses time; both have a great impact on the student's opportunity for school learning.

Classroom Management
Opportunity time is affected not only by the amount of time available, but also by how much of that time is actually used for instruction. Karweit and Slavin (1981) have observed that:

> To increase achievement from a score of 3.4 grade equivalent to 3.8 would require a daily increase of 13 minutes of active learning time. This increase, from 37 minutes to 50 minutes would require either a sizable increase in scheduled time or tremendous improvement in classroom efficiency. Because engaged minutes typically run about 50 to 75 percent of the available time, unless classroom efficiency

were improved, the instructional period would have to be length-ened appreciably. And, of course, engagement rate would likely go down as the length of the period went up. Consequently, realizing significant gains in learning time would have to come from recover-ing lost minutes due to interruptions, waiting, and classroom transi-tions (Karweit & Slavin, 1981, p. 171).

The amount of time lost to interruptions, waiting, and classroom transi-tions can be reduced through sound classroom management techniques, in-cluding arrangement of the physical environment, scheduling of instructional activities, establishing routines, and easing discipline problems. Chapter 9 provides tips and techniques that can be used to increase opportunity time through classroom management.

Aptitude

Aptitude is included as a time variable because it is defined in terms of the amount of time a student will need to master a task. A student with a high aptitude for a task will require less time to master the task than a student with a lower aptitude. Aptitude will vary from task group to task group and is de-pendent upon the student's prior knowledge and experience with the task. For instance, all things being equal, it will take students longer to learn their first word processing program than it will take them to learn a third program. By the third program they will have an understanding of what word proces-sors do and what kind of commands they will need to use (even though the commands may be different from program to program). A teacher can reduce the amount of time a student will require for each new learning task by link-ing new tasks to previously learned ones.

Student Perseverance

Student perseverance is a time variable because it relates to the amount of a time a student is willing to spend learning a task. The amount of time that a stu-dent is willing to spend on a task can be affected by task difficulty, the student's level of confidence, the student's ability to evaluate his or her own learning, and by student motivation. Once the teacher becomes aware of the factors that are influencing a student's level of perseverance, it is possible for the teacher to make adjustments in the instructional format in an effort to increase the stu-dent's level of perseverance. For instance, if the student feels that the task is too difficult, the teacher may want to break the task up into a number of small steps. If the student lacks confidence in his or her ability to perform the task, the teacher should take steps to help the student understand his or her suc-cesses. Sometimes students overestimate their ability to perform a task and in such instances the teacher must work to help the students so that they become capable of evaluating their own learning. Student motivation can be affected by a number of factors including those just mentioned (perceived task difficulty, confidence, and evaluation of learning need). Motivation also is affected by perceived pay-offs, competing priorities, and the student's sense of self-efficacy, among other things.

Achievement Variables

Carroll classified ability and quality of instruction as achievement variables. According to Carroll, "under-achievement" and "over-achievement" both represent situations in which there is a discrepancy between expected achievement and actual achievement. If prediction of achievement were perfectly accurate, there would be no over- or under- achievers. In the words of Carroll, this would be, "an unlikely eventuality to be sure!" (p. 1962, 730). The discrepancy between predicted and actual achievement, according to the MSL, can be explained in terms of the ability of the student and the quality of instruction that he or she receives. As has been noted earlier, the relationship between time and learning appears to be a rather simple, direct relationship—if a student, based on his or her aptitude, is given the time needed to learn and is willing to spend this time learning, then the student will learn. However, the strength of this relationship can be altered by both the ability of the student and the quality of instruction that is received.

Ability
Carroll classified ability as an achievement variable. Ability is composed of both general intelligence and verbal ability. In the MSL, general intelligence refers to the students' abilities to "figure out for themselves what the learning task is and how to go about learning it."

Today we refer to this ability as metacognition. Metacognition requires that a student "understand *what* skills, strategies, and resources are needed to accomplish a task" and knows "*how* and *when* to use these skills and strategies to ensure the task is completed successfully" (Schunk, 1991, pp. 182–83). This may involve deciding how to go about accomplishing a task (planning), deciding how much time to spend on each aspect of the task, evaluating how effective one is with the task, and deciding when to switch to alternative ways of solving the task. General abilities incorporate many of the skills that used to be taught under the heading of "study skills" and teachers are often able to help students develop this general learning ability by pointing out successful strategies that the student has used and/or helping them to analyze why other strategies the student used did not work as planned.

Verbal ability refers to the learner's ability to construct meaning from written or oral directions. This ability can be limited by the students' vocabularies and their reading or auditory skills. Consider the following example. A group of students were to perform a given instructional task. Directions for completing the task were as follows: "There is a set of pictures on page 1. You are to look at the pictures and do as I say. Make certain that you are looking at the pictures and not at me." The purpose of the directions was to help focus the students' attentions on the task before them rather than watching what the teacher was doing. Unfortunately, one member of the group was a hearing impaired student who relied heavily on lip-reading. When she followed the teacher's directions of "look at the picture, not at me," the student missed the next set of directions. As a result, the student was unable to successfully complete the task, so the teacher concluded that the work was too difficult for her and gave her a remedial assignment that was far below the student's actual instructional level.

This may seem like a somewhat simplistic example, but it comes from an actual classroom. Similar examples can be found where students' academic achievements have been underrated because of the students' poor verbal abilities. The problem here is that when teachers fail to recognize the root cause of the problem (verbal ability) they treat the symptom (inability to perform instructional task) and end up wasting valuable instructional time and often frustrating the student in the process.

In the study of school time, the importance of ability (either general or verbal) lies in the fact that if a student is lacking in ability, the amount of learning time a student will need will, of necessity, increase. The additional time the student must spend with the task is then lost to the learning of other important skills, concepts, and more advanced knowledge-building activities.

Instructional Quality

In school, the amount of time allocated to learning is often less than the student will need under optimal conditions. This fact has long been recognized by educational leaders, policy makers, researchers, and practitioners. It is one of the reasons that there is such an interest in increasing the amount of time that students spend in school. One of the tenets of the MSL is that the amount of time students need for learning is greatly impacted by the quality of instruction they receive. Providing students with more time (by increasing the length of the school year or day) possibly could diminish the discrepancy between the time needed and the time provided, but even when this doesn't happen, adjusting the quality of instruction could have the same effect. The quality of instruction can increase (or decrease) a student's level of perseverance, increase (or decrease) the student's aptitude in given areas, and even have a positive (or negative) impact on the student's ability to learn. Although Carroll admitted that "the model is not very specific about the characteristics of high quality instruction" (Carroll, 1989, p. 26), the model did outline four qualities that are essential to quality instruction. First, the model states that a student must be given clear directions in terms he or she understands. These directions should explain what is to be learned and how the learner is to go about learning it. Second, the student must be placed in what Carroll calls the proper sensory contact with material. In other words, the instruction must be presented in such a manner so that the student can hear or see the material. For instance, if the teacher is showing a film, the room must be dark enough for the picture to be seen, or if a lecture is being given the students must be able to hear the speaker. Third, the instruction should be organized and sequenced with enough detail so that each step provides the necessary background to adequately prepare the student for the next step in the instructional sequence. Fourth, the instruction must be adapted to meet the learning needs of the student. This includes providing instruction in different formats (auditory, visually, and kinesthetically) and at a level appropriate for the student.

The quality of the instruction that a student receives can reduce the amount of learning time a student needs. However, the reverse of this also is true. If the quality of instruction is poor, the student will need more time to learn than he or she would need under optimal conditions. If teachers are truly interested in helping students reach their full potential, it is important that they understand how the quality of instruction they provide impacts students' opportunities to learn, their perseverance with learning, their aptitude, and their abilities.

SIGNIFICANCE OF CARROLL'S MODEL

The MSL was developed more than 30 years ago but continues to remain one of the defining models for research on time and learning. The basic concepts in the model were "defined so that they can be measured in terms of *time*" (Carroll, 1963, p. 724) and three of the five variables presented in the model— opportunity, perseverance, and aptitude—are directly related to time. The other two variables—quality of teaching and student ability—are assumed to interact with one another and to influence the amount of time needed to learn.

Almost every major study that has been conducted on time and learning from 1963 on has referenced and/or built upon Carroll's model. Between 1963 and 1986, the *Social Sciences Citation Index* referenced over 300 citations of the article that first presented the model (Carroll, 1989). However, as important as the Model of School Learning is in defining the interrelationship of time and learning variables in a school setting, it must be remembered that Carroll limited his examination to academic learning. Social and emotional variables were ignored by the model. Also ignored by the model were aspects of "overlearning" and "sudden insight." In spite of this, the MSL has provided us with a valuable set of precepts for studying the relationship between school learning and student time and became part of the foundation for the time and learning models that were to follow it—including the Learning for Mastery and the Academic Learning Time model.

MASTERY LEARNING

The concept of mastery learning is based on the belief that most, if not all, students can master the skills and knowledge embedded in the core curriculum if they are given all the time they need and are provided with the appropriate level of instruction that they require. Traces of the mastery learning philosophy can be found in the Jesuit schools of the sixteenth century and in the work of Comenius in the seventeenth century. The philosophy was espoused by Pestalozzi in the eighteenth century and by Herbart in the nineteenth century. Tenets of mastery learning were used frequently at the University of Chicago laboratory school in the 1920s and were embedded in programs of instruction based on the Winnetak Plan of the 1930s. (Bloom, 1974a). However, it wasn't until the early 1970s that mastery learning took the form of a conceptual model.

Mastery learning is an instructional strategy that draws at least part of its theoretical strength from Carroll's Model of School Learning. Mastery learning models take different forms, especially as they are implemented in the classroom; however, most build upon Benjamin Bloom's Learning for Mastery or Fred Keller's Personalized System of Instruction (PSI). In the most current form, mastery learning is embodied within the philosophy of Outcome Based Education (OBE). Unlike Bloom's and Keller's models, which are instructional models that focus on classroom strategies, OBE focuses on the policies related to school learning and there is less focus on instructional strategies and more on educational goals.

LEARNING FOR MASTERY MODEL

Benjamin Bloom's Learning for Mastery model grew out of his interest in Carroll's Model of School Learning. Based on Carroll's model and on research he himself had conducted earlier, Bloom hypothesized that if, in any given classroom, student aptitude (the amount of time individual students needed to learn) followed a normal distribution and students were given the same quality of instruction and the same amount of time to learn, academic achievement within the class would, consequently, follow a normal distribution.

Bloom further hypothesized that if the type of instruction and amount of time were varied to meet the needs of the students, all students could achieve mastery. In terms of grades, this meant that the majority of students would receive A's and *no* student would receive a D or an F.

Bloom's theory regarding the distribution of achievement was supported by data from a comprehensive national study that he and his associates at the University of Chicago had conducted on GED test results from 1943 to 1955.

The study revealed that there was great variation in the level of student achievement from one state in the union to another. After 12 years of formal schooling, the variation was so great that students in the highest achieving states had accomplished in eight years of formal education what it had taken the students in the lowest achieving states 12 years to accomplish (Bloom, 1956).

His theory was further supported by a later study (Bloom, 1973) in which he analyzed standardized test scores from elementary students and found that tasks that had been mastered by only the top 20 percent of the students in the first year, were mastered by 50 percent of the students in the second year and by 80 percent by the end of the third year. Additional research conducted by both Glaser (1968) and Atkinson (1968) upheld Bloom's theory. These researchers found that it took the slowest 5 percent of students five times longer to meet a set learning criterion than it did for the fastest 5 percent of students. These findings led to the conclusion that the ratio between the amount of time a student spent learning and the amount of time a student needed to learn was highly predictive of student achievement and could account for as much as 20 percent of the variation in achievement.

Bloom's Model

Bloom postulated that, given enough time and a high quality of instruction, 80 percent of all students could master the learning tasks that were expected of only the top 20 percent of the students. In order for this to occur, the amount of time the slower students spent with a learning task would need to be increased by 10 to 20 percent and the amount of increase would depend upon the quality of instruction that a student received. Based on these assumptions, Bloom developed the Learning for Mastery Model (LFM).

The Learning for Mastery model is designed to be used with group-based instruction and assumes a fixed amount of classroom time. The teacher begins by determining what is meant by mastery. In other words, the teacher determines the learning objectives and the standard against which these objectives are to be measured. Next, the teacher designs and develops a set of evaluation instruments. The instruments are used to inform the teacher of the student's progress and achievement relative to the objective. Lessons are broken into small units that last about two weeks and at the end of the unit the teacher administers the evaluative test. Students who have failed to master the objectives are then given individual assignments, called correctives. Correctives are designed to provide the student with further instruction and additional practice with the learning objective or task. Correctives are designed so that each student spends additional time working only on those tasks he or she has failed to master. The plan calls for the majority of classroom time to be spent on some form of group instruction and assumes that the *majority* of corrective work will take place on the student's own time, for example, at recess, during study hall, or as part of his or her homework.

Time and Learning for Mastery

The Learning for Mastery model views time from several different perspectives. First there is *classroom time*—the way in which the teacher allocates the minutes within the classroom. There is little difference in the utilization of classroom time from a more conventional approach to instruction. The major difference is that with this model less time is spent on individual practice and more time is spent on direct, large-group instruction. In fact, very little classroom time is devoted to individual practice and any additional work that is needed is performed on the students' own time (for example during recess or after school).

The second perspective is *elapsed time*—the total amount of time that expires before a student masters a learning task or objective. Remember that Bloom had found that the material that had been mastered by the top 20 percent of students during the first year had been mastered by an additional 60 percent of the students by the third year. In other words, at the end of the first year, only the top 20 percent had mastered the objectives, but by the end of three years 80 percent of the students had mastered the objectives. For the top students, elapsed time amounted to one year while for the other 60 percent of the students who did reach mastery elapsed time varied from two to three years.

The third perspective is *time-on-task*. Time-on-task is the time a student spends actively working on a task and is similar to Carroll's "time spent in learning." Bloom found that the amount of time a student spent on task was highly predictive of student achievement and that variations in the amount of time spent "account for about three fifths of the *achievement* variation of students" (Bloom, 1974b, p. 686). Bloom and his researchers also found that the amount of time a student spent on task was determined by "the student's achievement over the preceding units of the course, by his [her] interest in the subject, and by the *quality of instruction provided.*"

Bloom was interested in reducing the gap between the amount of time it took slower students and faster students to reach the same level of academic achievement because he felt that such discrepancies were costly in terms of both time and resources. According to Bloom:

> The costs in years of learning are very great. Not only are these costs enormous in terms of resources spent, but they mean that many students must forego a great deal of other learning because so much time (years) is spent in bringing them up to a satisfactory level of

competence in the tool subjects of language, reading and arithmetic (Bloom, 1974b, p. 683).

Bloom believed that the "cost of learning" could be reduced by making better use of classroom time and by improving the quality of classroom instruction. In other words, he believed that classroom time, elapsed time, and time-on-task were all important elements to consider when attempting to improve student achievement and that each of the elements could be affected by classroom practices.

Assumptions of Mastery Learning

The Learning for Mastery Model is an instructional design model that is designed to be used primarily in a whole-group instructional format. One of the assumptions upon which the model is built is that if students are left to do individual assignments during the greater part of the instructional day, they will spend less time on task than if they are in an environment that is teacher-directed and in which each of their peers are working on the same task. This increase in time on task will reduce the amount of time it takes a student to achieve mastery.

Another major assumption within the model is that the amount of time a student is willing to spend on task is determined by the student's prior achievement, his or her interest in the subject, and the quality of instruction that the student receives.

Prior Achievement

The model assumes that tasks build upon one another, and that if a student has failed to master the prerequisite skills he or she will have a difficult, if not impossible, time mastering the subsequent skills. Therefore, instruction is presented in small steps (usually units that last no more than two weeks) and the student's progress is monitored at each step to make certain that the skills are mastered before moving to the next level.

Interest in Subject

According to this model, a student's interest in a subject is based on how well the student has done in the past. According to Bloom, "as students reach adequate levels of achievement over the preceding tasks, their confidence and interest in the task increase, while if they do not reach such levels of achievement they become frustrated and despair of their ability to learn the tasks, and they tend to develop some dislike for or disinterest in the subject" (Bloom, 1974b, p. 687). Student interest in the subject is important because it will affect how much time the student is willing to spend on task. According to the model, students will be more successful if they have mastered the prerequisite skills and if the teacher provides quality feedback that is both corrective and supportive.

Quality of Instruction
According to the model, quality of instruction is dependent upon four basic factors that are incorporated into the design of mastery lessons. These factors include (1) the instructional cues provided to the student by the teacher, (2) the degree of active participation demanded of the student, (3) the quality of feedback provided, and (4) the appropriateness of the corrective tasks assigned. The Learning for Mastery model also stresses the importance of timing in instruction. For instance, initial instruction should begin only after the student has mastered the prerequisite tasks and student evaluation must occur at intermediate points so that corrective feedback can be given before a student incurs some misconceptions or develops poor habits in the learning of a new skill or the acquiring of new knowledge. The trick in mastery learning is to develop a system of whole-group instruction and independent corrective activities so that when the class begins a new unit all students will have the necessary prerequisite skills and knowledge.

Trade-Offs in Mastery Learning

When using the mastery learning approach to instruction, there are five major trade-offs in the development of the program: (1) mastery versus coverage, (2) achievement-based versus time-based promotion, (3) criterion-referenced versus norm-referenced assessment, (4) facilitation of learning versus allowing learning to occur, and (5) task-oriented versus activity-oriented instruction.

Mastery versus Coverage
Many teachers consider covering the material presented in the textbook to be one of their primary duties. They see their central tasks being to direct the learning of their students, to keep the students' attention, and to cover a syllabus. In other words, a teacher's work is defined as the management of students' attention over time and curriculum (Anderson, 1984). The Learning for Mastery Model places the focus on the mastery of the objectives in the syllabus rather than simply covering the material in the syllabus. Mastery, therefore, is based on time required to reach the objective, not simply on covering the material.

Achievement-Based versus Time-Based Promotion
Education has hotly debated the issue of student promotion and retention with such recurring questions as: "Does retention at a grade level improve a student's chances for success?" and "Should we have social promotions?"

The mastery learning model attempts to alleviate this problem by making the movement from one task to the next contingent upon the achievement of the proper skills. As a result of this portion of the mastery learning model, many ungraded, nongraded elementary schools emerged. By eliminating first, second and third grades, it was believed that students would be able to reach achievement of a basic unit before advancing to the next unit and the effects of fixed time would vanish.

Criterion-Reference versus Normative Testing
Under mastery learning, each student is evaluated on some predetermined (criterion-referenced) standard rather than on some norm-referenced standard which states that the students at a given age or grade level should be able to perform specific tasks simply because of their age.

Facilitating Learning versus Allowing Learning to Occur
This relates directly to Bloom's concept that not only time but also timing is important in education—by properly timing instructional events we will be facilitating the learning process. When we simply cover the content and then test on how well the students perform on achievement tests based on the content, we are allowing learning to occur rather than facilitating it.

Task-Oriented versus Activity-Oriented Instruction
The question here is: "When does an activity become a task (and vice versa)?" The most accepted definition of task, from a mastery learning perspective, is that it is a learning activity which is goal oriented (Anderson, 1984; Doyle, 1979). When students are given worksheets to complete, or pictures to draw, or stories to write to "keep them busy" until the teacher "can get to them," they are involved in activity-oriented tasks rather than in goal-oriented activities. Although most teachers are aware of the difference, it is often difficult to keep all activity in the classroom at the task level rather than at the "busy work" level.

FINDINGS FROM MASTERY LEARNING RESEARCH

One of the important findings from the mastery learning research was that when students were placed in a mastery learning environment, student time-on-task *in* the classroom tended to increase even though allocated time remained unchanged. In one set of studies, for instance, students were divided into mastery learning groups and non-mastery learning groups. Both the mastery learning and the non-mastery learning groups were given the same classroom instruction. Under these conditions it was found that:

On the first learning task both groups were equal in average time on task in the classroom—about 65% of the time. The mastery students were then given extra time and help until they reached the criterion of this first unit, while the students in the conventional group were given no help after they took the formative test. On the second task, the mastery students increased their percent of time on task in the classroom while the nonmastery students decreased their percent of time on task. This trend continued over several learning tasks until on the final task the mastery students were spending about 85% of the classroom time on the task while the nonmastery students were spending about 65% of the time on task (Bloom, 1974b, p. 686).

Carroll would not have been surprised by these findings because, as you will recall, he believed that a student's level of perseverance (the amount of time he or she was willing to spend on learning or "on task") is influenced by the student's aptitude, ability, and the quality of instruction he or she received. Under normal conditions, a student's ability and aptitude increase as the student gains knowledge and experience with a learning area. As a result, new tasks in the same area require less time to master and the student tends to devote more concentrated time (time on task) to learning.

COMPARISON OF BLOOM'S AND CARROLL'S MODELS

In an article written in 1989, Carroll compared his Model of School Learning to Bloom's Learning for Mastery Model in this way:

> . . . we should seek mainly to achieve equality of *opportunity* for all students, not necessarily equality of *attainment*. In this respect, the model of school learning differs from Bloom's mastery learning concept, which seems to be focused on achieving equality of attainment. In view of the model's emphasis on the role of individual differences in aptitudes and in students' ability to understand instruction, I doubt that true equality of attainment can ever be realized, even if this were desirable (a point that is at least debatable). Emphasizing equality of opportunity means not only providing appropriate opportunities to learn (*appropriate*, not necessarily *equal*, for all students), but also pushing all students' potentialities as far as possible toward their upper limits (Carroll, 1989, p. 30).

The distinction between equality of opportunity and equality of attainment is an interesting one since it is reflective of many of the arguments revolving around the purpose of schooling (e.g., Is the purpose to help each student reach his or her potential or is it to ensure a well-educated citizenry?). And as we have seen earlier, the arguments for and against arranging school time in one way or another often relate to this fundamental difference of view.

PERSONALIZED SYSTEM OF INSTRUCTION

Bloom's Learning for Mastery Model was most frequently implemented in K-12 schools. This does not mean, however, that universities were exempt from the mastery learning movement. The most popular of the mastery learning models in higher education was Fred Keller's Personalized System of Instruction (PSI). The model eventually found its way into secondary education and into some of the open-concept elementary schools of the late 1970s.

Classroom Time

Keller's model focused on self-paced, individualized learning—as opposed to Bloom's model that was directed at whole-group instruction. In the Personalized System of Instruction, instruction was most frequently provided through the use of a self-instructional package called a "module." In the modular approach, students work at their own pace throughout the course of study and very little classroom time is actually spent on direct whole-group instruction. The teacher serves as a learning facilitator by diagnosing the skills that a student needs to work on, assigning the appropriate module for that student, and providing corrective feedback and encouragement. During the class period, students work independently on their modules as the teacher moves from student to student, offering help as needed. Once the student has completed a unit of study, he or she is given a test that will determine if the student is ready to move on to the next unit. If it is determined that the student has failed to master selected skills, additional work will be assigned but the work will focus only on those skills that were not mastered. A variety of instructional methods are incorporated into the units, including printed materials, audio/visual equipment, and computers. Students are able to assert some control over which parts of the module they complete and which methods of instruction they use. The only criterion that remains in place is that the students must master all of the skills in one unit before moving to the next.

Elapsed Time

Under the PSI model, it is expected that elapsed time will vary from student to student. The model recognizes that students differ not only in their abilities (the degree to which they can understand instruction) and aptitudes (amount of time they need to reach mastery) but also in their potential for learning (the level of achievement that they can be expected to reach). Each of these will affect how much time elapses from the time a student first begins a module to the time her or she reaches mastery.

Time on Task

Time on task under the PSI is affected by the same elements that affect time on task under most time-based models. Students' perseverance, distractions within the learning environment, and mis-diagnosis of needs can all influence how much time students spend working on the learning task. However, because students complete only those modules that address their learning needs, the PSI model theoretically leads to a greater amount of time on task than does the Learning for Mastery Model, which requires that all students share at least some instructional time (i.e., during the whole-group instruction period). Learning for Mastery advocates, however, would disagree with this theoretical view because they believe that students become easily distracted without the teacher there to guide the learning process.

COMPARISON OF BLOOM'S AND KELLER'S MODELS

Both the Learning for Mastery and the Personalized System of Instruction models are instructional strategy models that start from the assumption that all students can and will learn. The Learning for Mastery model assumes that the reason for variation in student achievement results from a variation in the amount of time they need to reach mastery and that quality of instruction can be used as a mediator to reduce the amount of variation. The PSI model also assumes that students vary in the amount of time they need to reach mastery and that the amount of variation can be eased through instruction. The PSI model does not assume, however, that time is a variable to be manipulated in order to reach what Carroll called *equity of achievement* but rather to reach *equity of opportunity* so that each student is spending his or her instructional time only on those objectives he or she has yet to master.

Under both models, PSI and LFM, it is the teacher's responsibility to design the instruction so that the learning occurs in the most time-efficient manner possible. This is accomplished by first defining what is meant by mastery (specifying the objectives) and then deciding how mastery will be measured. The objectives are then grouped into small units of instruction that are sequenced so that the skills from one unit build upon the skills mastered in the previous unit. By monitoring the students' progress and providing corrective feedback where necessary, the teacher is able to guarantee student success.

Evaluation of the students is based solely on what the student has done, not on what other students have accomplished.

The use of classroom time is one of the major differences between the two models. As has already been noted, the Learning for Mastery Model uses the majority of classroom time for whole-group instruction while the Personalized System of Instruction uses the majority of the time for independent, individualized learning.

It is interesting to note that the Learning for Mastery model was utilized most at the elementary level and the PSI model was used most frequently at the high school and post-secondary levels. What makes this interesting is that the Learning for Mastery model is very similar to what happens in most college classrooms. The professor lectures during the allocated class period and then students are expected to devote as much out-of-classroom time as necessary in order to master the objectives. At the same time, elementary classrooms had long focused on the individual needs of the children and teachers often rearranged the classroom schedule so that more or less time could be spent on the different subject areas (reading, math, social studies, etc.). Students were often taught in small groups that were formed according to the students' abilities and seatwork and learning centers were assigned based on the student's instructional needs. In other words, classroom time was used in much the same way that Keller recommended in the PSI model.

CRITICISM OF THE LEARNING FOR MASTERY MODEL

Throughout the latter part of the 1960s and into the early part of the 1980s, mastery learning models were embraced by researchers and practitioners alike and, as a result, nongraded and ungraded schools sprang up across the country. In nongraded schools, children were grouped according to ability rather than by their age or by the number of years they had spent in school. In ungraded schools, the grades of "A", "B", "C", "D," and "F" were replaced with "√+" (highly satisfactory), "√" (satisfactory), and "√−" (unsatisfactory). The purpose of the new marking system was to move from a norm-based evaluation system to a criterion-based system that recognized individual differences. The nongraded/ungraded schools were based on the belief that lock-step programs were obsolete and that students should be allowed to progress at their own learning rates rather than on the basis of how much time they had spent in the school building.

In other schools, mastery learning manifested itself in the form of direct instruction and explicit teaching. Lessons were goal-oriented and teacher-directed. Students were reinforced for correct responses and provided with corrective feedback when necessary. Extra assignments were given to those students who needed additional time to master the content. These assignments were expected to be completed on the student's own time—e.g., after school or during recess.

By the middle of the 1980s, the programs had begun to grow out of favor for a number of reasons. The conflict between practical application of mastery learning and the philosophical and theoretical view of learning was difficult to reconcile. Cox and Dunn have noted that:

> At any point in time individuals will vary both in terms of innate ability and possession of teachable prerequisites. Faced with these innate and environmentally determined differences that exist among individual learners, the instructor or instructional designer must realize that certain instructional objectives have a higher probability of achievement for some learners than for others. Obviously, time and resources for recycling and rebuilding of the missing prerequisites are not unlimited. So it naturally follows that some objectives or sequences of objectives differ in the appropriateness for various learners (Cox and Dunn, 1979, p. 28).

In addition to a limited number of resources and the vast extent of individual differences within the classroom, there were practical problems involved with designing instruction in the way that was required by the Learning for Mastery Model. Inherent in the model was the belief that teachers had the time to redesign each lesson to meet the individual needs of their students. Groff reacted to this belief rather strongly when he wrote, "It is something of a slur on the work habits of present-day teachers to aver that hidden away in the normal school day is an unused deposit of teacher time, the extra time necessary if teachers using mastery learning strategies are to give students *all the time* the students need to learn to mastery" (Groff, p. 90).

Even if the teachers had the time necessary to design individual units for individual students, there were the problems of making the units meaningful and of designing the units to the right depth and in the right sequence. When teachers first wrote learning objectives, they tended to be too broad and almost unmeasurable. In an effort to correct this situation, the teachers often overadjusted and the objectives became almost trivial. A number of companies developed instructional materials that were designed to overcome these problems, but these were expensive and hard to maintain in the typical classroom. Finally, teachers were often left with the impression that they were spending more time testing than actually teaching.

Besides the practical problems associated with mastery learning, some researchers called into question the findings from the research on time and learning. In 1987, Robert Slavin did a "best evidence synthesis" of the research on mastery learning and he found "essentially no evidence to support the effectiveness of group-based mastery learning on standardized achievement measures" (Slavin, p. 175). However, a thorough study of Slavin's research reveals that his concern was more with the research methods used than with mastery learning itself. In fact Slavin stated rather strongly that:

> The findings of the present review should not necessarily be interpreted as justifying an abandonment of mastery learning, either as an instructional practice or as a focus of research. Several widely publicized school improvement programs based on mastery learning principles have apparently been successful . . . and many effective nonmastery learning instructional strategies incorporate certain elements of mastery learning—in particular, frequent assessment of student learning of well-specified objectives and basing teaching decisions on the results of these assessments. Further, the idea that students' specific learning deficits should be remediated immediately instead of being allowed to accumulate into large and general deficiencies makes a great deal of sense (Slavin, 1987, p. 207).

REFERENCES

Anderson, L. W. (Ed.). (1984). *Time and school learning: Theory, research and practice.* New York: St. Martin's Press.

Atkinson, R. C. (1968). Computer-based instruction and the learning process. *American Psychologist, 23,* 225–239.

Bloom, B. S. (1956). The 1955 normative study of the tests of general educational development. *School Review, 64,* 110–124.

Bloom, B. S. (1973). Recent developments in mastery learning. *Educational Psychologist, 10,* 204–221.

Bloom, B. S. (1974a). An introduction to mastery learning theory. In J. H. Block, (Ed.), *Schools, Society, and Mastery Learning* (pp. 4–14). New York: Holt, Rinehart and Winston, Inc.

Bloom, B. S. (1974b). Time and Learning. *American Psychologist, 29*(9), 682–688.

Brandwein, P. F. (1955). *The gifted student as future scientist.* New York: Harcourt Brace.

Carroll, J. B. (1962). The prediction of success in intensive language training. In R. Glaser (Ed.), *Training Research and Education* (pp. 87–136). Pittsburgh: University of Pittsburgh Press.

Carroll, J. B. (1963). A model of school learning. *Teachers College Record, 64*(8), 723–733).

Carroll, J. B. (1989, January/February). The Carroll Model: A 25-year retrospective and prospective view. *Educational Researcher,* 26–31.

Cox, W. F., & Dunn, T. G. (1979). Mastery learning: A psychological trap? *Educational Psychologist, 14,* 24–29.

Doyle, W. (1979). Classroom tasks and students' abilities. In P. L. Peterson & H. J. Walberg (Eds.) , *Research on teaching: Concepts, findings and implications.* Berkeley, CA: McCutchan.

Fisher, C., et al. (1978, June). *Teaching behaviors, academic learning time and student achievement: Final report of phase III-B, beginning teacher evaluation study* (Technical Report V-1.) San Francisco, CA: Far West Laboratory for Educational Research and Development.

Glaser, R. (1968). *Adapting the elementary school curriculum to individual performance. Proceedings of the 1967 conference on testing problems.* Princeton: Educational Testing Services.

Groff, P. (1974). Some criticisms of mastery learning. *Today's Education, 63*(4), 88, 90–91.

Karweit, N., & Slavin, R. E. (1981). Measurement and modeling choices in studies of time and learning. *American Educational Research Journal, 18*(5), 151–171.

Keller, F. S. (1968). "Good-bye, teacher . . .". *Applied Behavior Analysis, 1,* 78–89.

Kendall, J. S., & Marzano, R. J. (1994). *The systematic identification and articulation of content standards and benchmarks: Update.* Aurora, CO: Mid-continent Regional Educational Laboratory.

Schunk, D. H. (1991). *Learning theories: An educational perspective.* New York: Macmillan Publishing Company.

Slavin, R. E. (1987). Mastery learning reconsidered. *Review of Educational Research, 57*(2), 175–213.

▶ 7
The Academic
Learning Time Model

One of the most influential of the time learning models was the Academic Learning Time model that resulted from an extensive study conducted by the California Commission for Teacher Preparation and Licensing with funding from the National Institute of Education. The project, which began in 1972 and ran through 1978, was initially designed to study the relationship between behaviors of beginning teachers and the academic achievement of their students and was aptly named the Beginning Teachers Evaluation Study (BTES). As the study evolved, the emphasis changed from the behaviors of beginning teachers to the behaviors of teachers in general even though the name of the study remained unchanged.

The purpose of the study, as stated by the researchers, was to:

1. Develop hypotheses about the relations of teaching performance and pupils' learning
2. Develop a measurement system that might be useful in subsequent phrases of the BTES project
3. Estimate the influence of teacher characteristics and the teaching environment on teachers' performance and, correspondingly, the influence of the pupils' characteristics and background on pupils' learning (McDonald and Elias, 1975, and reported in Fisher et al., 1978)

The study was conducted in three phases—Phase I: Methodology Design and General Project Planning; Phase II: Field Research; and, Phrase III: Data Analysis and Model Development and Testing. Phase III was divided into two subphases. In Phase III-A, researchers from the Far West Laboratory for

Educational Research and Development summarized and categorized the data gathered during Phase II and analyzed it in light of other research that had been conducted on teacher effectiveness and classroom learning (including the work done by both Carroll in 1963 and Bloom in 1974). Based on their analysis of the data they had collected and the research that had preceded them, the researchers developed a general model of instruction (see Figure 7–1). In Phase III-B, the model was tested through an extensive field study that focused on the math and reading instruction of 261 second and fifth grade students in 47 different classrooms throughout California.

GENERAL MODEL OF INSTRUCTION

The BTES general model of instruction, presented in Figure 7–1, is basically a systems model made up of inputs, outputs, and processes. In this model, aptitude serves as an input and student achievement is considered the output. The process portion of the model is made up of student classroom learning (student behavior), instructional procedures, and classroom environment.

Student Aptitudes

In this model, aptitude is defined as the "Characteristics of the student which are 'brought to' the learning situation." This is different from the way that Carroll defined aptitude in the Model of School Learning. In Carroll's

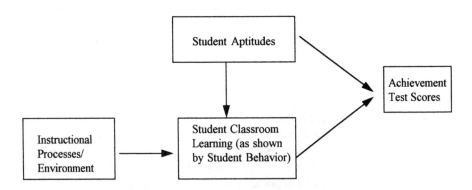

FIGURE 7–1   The BTES general model of instruction

Source: Fisher, C., et al. (1978, June). Teaching behaviors, academic learning time and student achievement: Final report of phase III-B, beginning teacher evaluation study (Technical Report V-1.) San Francisco, CA: Far West Laboratory for Educational Research and Development.

Used with permission.

model, aptitude was defined in terms of the amount of time a student would need to learn. Another major difference between the way aptitude is treated in the two different models is the role that it plays in the analysis of time to learn. In the BTES model, aptitude served as an input to the instructional process. Because the focus of their research was teaching behaviors rather than student differences, they examined aptitude only when it had the potential of explaining differences in instructional processes and classroom procedures. Carroll's research, on the other hand, focused on the student and therefore aptitude played a more central role and was more concretely defined.

Student Achievement

In the BTES general model of instruction, student achievement was considered an output of instruction and was measured in terms of student performance on standardized tests. This differs from the way in which achievement was measured by Bloom in his Learning for Mastery Model. In that model, achievement was measured through the use of criterion-referenced tests and was closely aligned with the objectives that were the target of instruction. The difference in treatments of achievement between these two models can also be accounted for by the difference in focus. The BTES model of general instruction is basically descriptive in nature, whereas the Learning for Mastery Model is prescriptive. The general model of instruction attempts to describe what occurs in the classroom and the effect it has on time and learning. The Learning for Mastery Model, on the other hand, attempts to provide guidelines, format, and structure for manipulating instruction elements so that the amount of time a student needs to learn can be reduced. Once again, the difference between the treatment and measurement of student achievement is created by the difference in focus of the two models.

Student Classroom Learning

The major focus of the BTES research was on the process portion (student classroom learning and instructional procedures) of the general model of instruction. As a result of the research conducted during Phase II of the project, the researchers developed a metric, or formula, for measuring the process of student classroom learning. They called the metric academic learning time (ALT) and defined it as "the amount of time a student spends engaged on a task that produces few student errors and which is directly related to a defined content area" (Fisher et al., 1978, pp. 1–2). The four variables that make up ALT are: (1) allocated time, (2) student engagement, (3) error rate, and (4) task relevance. According to the theory, classroom learning is a function of these four variables and can be represented by the following formula.

ALT = *f*(allocated time, engaged rate, error rate, task relevance)

Allocated Time

Allocated time, as the name implies, refers to the amount of time assigned to the completion of a task and is a function of both school time and classroom management. It is similar to Carroll's opportunity time and Bloom's classroom time. Allocated time is dependent on how much time is allocated for a given subject, such as reading, and how much of that time is lost to classroom management functions such as discipline problems, taking attendance, or resource management.

Student Engagement

Student engagement is the proportion of the allocated time the student actually spends on task, or goal, oriented activities. It should be noted that allocated time is a function of teacher behavior or school policy whereas engaged rate (student engagement) is a function of student behavior. Student engagement is affected by a student's level of perseverance as noted by Carroll in his research

Error Rate

Error rate refers to the number of errors a student makes when working on an activity. When the researchers first identified this variable, they referred to it as "task difficulty." They were concerned, however, that the phrase "task difficulty" would be somewhat misleading because it placed the emphasis on the task while what they were trying to capture with the variable was the complex interaction of the student with a task. Therefore they chose to refer to the variable as error rate because it placed more emphasis on the student than on the task.

Student error rate is considered low if the student understands the material and makes primarily "careless" errors. If the student makes correct responses primarily as the "chance" level (i.e., has a 50/50 chance of getting the answer right) the error rate is high. When a student understands most of the material but makes mistakes because of partial understanding, the error rate is considered medium.

Task Relevance

"Time spent learning" and "time-on-task" are measured in terms of the amount of time a student spends actively engaged in learning tasks and it is assumed that the tasks are related to the objectives to be learned. The BTES researchers found, however, that students were often actively engaged with a task that the teacher had assigned, but the task itself was irrelevant or not related to the actual learning needs of the students. For instance, as part of their spelling assignment, students might be required to write a story. The students could be actively engaged in writing the story, but the story might include only a limited number of the assigned spelling words. If one were to measure the relationship between the amount of time a student spent studying spelling and the student's success on the spelling test, the results would be negatively skewed because the majority of the time the students were engaged with learning was not spent in learning to spell. If, on the other hand, the objective was to practice using correct spelling in a written document, the relationship between achievement and time spent would be more accurate.

THE TEACHING PROCESS

The ALT model is part of the general model of instruction (Figure 7–1) and represents "learning as it is happening" (as opposed to achievement testing that measures learning that has already happened). According to the model, ALT is greatly influenced by the actions and behaviors of the teacher and are presented in the general model as "instructional process." The researchers identified five teaching process that affected both student classroom learning and academic achievement. These processes, (diagnosis, prescription, presentation, monitoring, and feedback) occur in a more or less cyclical order and are interrelated. The interrelationship of these functions is presented in Figure 7–2.

Interactive Teaching Behaviors

Presentation, monitoring and feedback are considered interactive behaviors because the teachers interact directly with the students. These variables are further divided into substantive and procedural behaviors. Substantive behaviors are those that related directly to the academic content of the lesson. Procedural behaviors are those behaviors that have more to do with preparing the students for instruction ("get out your book and turn to page 20") or with informing the student about the acceptability of his or her behavior (as opposed to informing the student about how he or she is doing on an instructional task). Table 7–1 explains the makeup of these variables and provides definitions for each.

Presentation
The first teaching function, presentation, is subdivided into three types. The first type is teacher explanation of academic content that has been planned. The most common format for teacher explanation would be the lecture. But any time a teacher presents content in a planned fashion, it would fall under the category of explanation-planned. The second type of presentation is explanation-needed. Whenever a teacher responds to a student need by providing more content information, it falls under the category of explanation-

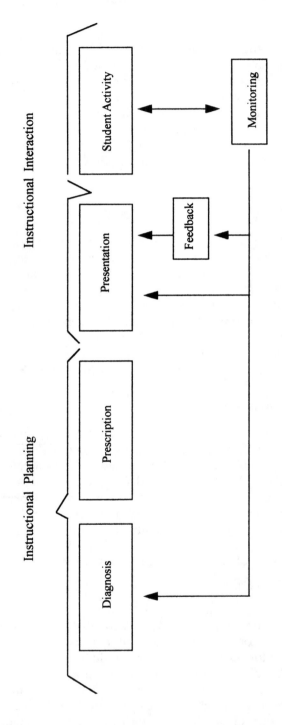

FIGURE 7–2 Schematic configuration of instructional functions in the academic learning time model

Source: Fisher, C., et al. (1978, June). Teaching behaviors, academic learning time and student achievement: Final report of phase III-B, beginning teacher evaluation study (Technical Report V-1). San Francisco, CA: Far West Laboratory for Educational Research and Development.

Used with permission.

TABLE 7–1   Interactive teaching behaviors

General Function	Specific Behavior	Description	Example
		SUBSTANTIVE BEHAVIORS	
Presentation	Explanation— Needed	The instructor explains academic content in response to a clear and immediate student need for help.	During a seatwork assignment on short vowels, the teacher notices that Sonia is having trouble, so she goes over the sounds with her.
	Explanation— Planned	The instructor explains academic content but not in response to a specific or immediate student need. This often takes the form of a lecture.	The class comes to a section in the reading workbook on compound words. The teacher introduces this concept and puts some examples on the board.
Monitoring	Academic Observation	The instructor looks at or listens to student academic responses in order to see how the student is doing.	While Eric is doing seatwork, the teacher looks at his paper to make sure he understands what to do.
	Academic Question	The instructors asks the student for a written or oral answer in order to observe and assess academic performance.	During group discussion the teacher asks Mary to give the meaning of a word from that day's reading lesson.
Feedback	Academic Feedback	The instructor tells the student whether his wrong. Could involve giving the right answer. Does not involve explanation.	The teachers asks Johnny to read out loud to the arithmetic problems. In oral reading circle, Susan hears Jim reading out loud while she reads along silently.
		PROCEDURAL BEHAVIORS	
Presentation	Structure/ Direct	The instructor states the goals of instruction or gives directions about the procedures and activities the student should carry out.	At the beginning of the math lesson, the teacher says "Today we are going to work on 10's and 1's like we did yesterday. Turn to page 20."
Feedback	Task Engagement Feedback	The instructor acts to control inappropriate behavior or to praise appropriate behavior. The focus is on the student's actions rather than the correctness of his answers.	Billy is out of his seat and standing by the pencil sharpener. The teacher tells him to "hurry up and get back to work."

Source: Fisher, C., et al. (1978, June). *Teaching behaviors, academic learning time and student achievement: Final report of phase III-B, beginning teacher evaluation study.* (Technical Report V–1.) San Francisco, CA: Far West Laboratory for Educational Research and Development. p. 5–3. Used with permission.

needed. For instance, a teacher presents a lesson on presidential elections (explanation-planned) and in the process, a student asks, "Why do we have an electoral college? Why don't we just use the popular vote?" In response, the teacher reviews the content that had been previously presented and then adds some detail to that information hoping to clarify the students' understanding. Because this exchange was unplanned, it would be included in the model as explanation-needed. Both explanation-planned and explanation-needed are considered to be substantive behaviors because they sustain the instruction flow and are key to understanding the lesson begin presented.

Other presentation processes include giving students directions and explaining the purpose of a lesson. These are considered to be procedural behaviors rather than substantive behaviors because they do not relate to the substance of the subject matter but rather serve to inform the students of what is expected of them during the lesson.

Monitoring

The second of the interactive teaching functions is monitoring which is defined as behavior that "provides information for the teacher about how well a student can perform a particular task" (Fisher, et al., 1978, pp. 3–20). In other words, the teacher attempts to assess a student's understanding of content through observing the student's work and/or questioning the student regarding his or her understanding of the content.

Feedback

The third interactive teaching function is feedback. In the ALT Model of Classroom instruction, *feedback* takes one of two forms. When the teacher informs the student of a right or wrong answer (without giving additional explanation), it is considered *substantive* teaching behavior, again because it relates directly to the skills and or concepts that are being taught. The second type of feedback is *procedural* and it includes any feedback that relates to the appropriateness of the student's behavior and/or that praises the student for his or her actions.

Instructional Planning

The two remaining teaching process variables, diagnosis and prescription, are classified as planning variables. In the model, diagnosis is broken into the subcategories of prediction, knowledge of subject matter, and differentiated perceptions. Prescription variables are subdivided into the three subcategories of goal orientation, program change based on need, and flexibility in use of curriculum.

Prediction

Prediction relates to the degree to which a teacher is able to estimate the level of proficiency that a student will reach by the conclusion of the lesson. Teachers routinely predict how well their students will do with a particular lesson. The length of the lesson, the amount of content to cover in an instructional setting, the number and types of examples to use, and the amount of practice to incorporate in the lesson are normally based on the teacher's prediction of student performance.

Knowledge of Subject Matter

The second diagnostic subcategory is *knowledge of subject matter*. This category relates to how well a teacher understands the subject matter he or she is teaching. When teachers are limited in their understanding of the content area, it can, and often does, have a negative effect on their ability to deliver instruction, the quality of instruction feedback they are able to provide their students, and/or their ability to assess the students' instructional needs. Although knowledge of subject matter is a positive attribute of the classroom teacher, if it is not balanced with an understanding of the teaching process it can create problems for the student. Teachers who are well grounded in a subject matter, but not as well grounded in the teaching process, have a tendency to lose some of their objectivity about the content. When this happens, teachers have trouble assessing the instructional needs of their students and often tend to present more information than is necessary for the students to master the required objectives.

Differentiated Perceptions

The final diagnostic category, *differentiated perceptions* deals with the teacher's ability to identify individual differences among his or her students. Students will differ in a number of areas including: (1) attitudes toward the learning task, (2) aptitudes for the task, (3) interest in the topic being presented, (4) ability to understand the instruction, (5) ability to think logically, (6) ability to work independently, (7) level of perseverance, and (8) learning styles. The effective teacher will recognize these individual differences and be able to diagnose the learning needs of the students based on these differences.

Goal Orientation

The first *prescriptive* category under instructional planning is *goal orientation*. Goal orientation is measured by the degree to which a teacher's lesson plans correlate to specific instructional goals or objectives and how he or she measures and evaluates the students' attainment of the goals. In a highly goal-oriented classroom, students work primarily on those tasks that relate to the objectives to be learned and are seldom, if ever, assigned "busy work." Tests and other evaluations are related directly to the objectives being taught. In other words, instructional goals guide both the selection of learning activities and the manner in which student achievement is measured.

Program Change Based on Student Need

The second prescriptive category is *program change based on student need*. This variable describes the frequency with which a teacher changes teaching plans based on his or her observations concerning student learning. For instance, a teacher might alter the plans if students need extra help in processing the information being presented, if they process the information more quickly than anticipated, if they lack the prior knowledge necessary to comprehend the instruction, or if they appear to lack interest in the learning task. It is important to note that the category "program change based on student need" is a planned change whereas "explanation-needed" is a presentation behavior that is unplanned.

Flexibility in the Use of Curriculum Material

The final prescriptive category is *flexibility in the use of curriculum material*. This category is concerned with the degree to which a teacher alters teaching materials in order to meet the specific needs of his or her students. Teachers who create their own teaching materials or adapt existing materials to meet the specific needs of their students would rank high in this category. Those who routinely follow the procedures and sequence of the textbook or other curriculum materials would rate low in this area.

Interaction of the Teaching Process

The teaching processes occur in a more or less cyclical fashion. The teacher begins planning for instruction by first diagnosing the needs of the students. The quality of the diagnosis is based on the teacher's understanding of the subject matter, his or her skill in isolating individual differences within the classroom, and in predicting the amount of time the students will need for learning. Generally, the diagnosis made by the teacher should result in establishing instruction goals designed to meet the learning needs of the students and in creating or adapting instructional materials so that they help the students obtain these goals. Occasionally the diagnosis may also require changing an instructional program if it is required to meet the needs of individual students. The effectiveness of the lessons that are planned will depend a great deal upon how effective the teacher is in diagnosing the students needs.

Once the lesson is planned, the teacher presents the material to the students, monitors their behavior, and provides them feedback on how well they are doing. Throughout this process, the teacher continues to diagnose the students' needs and will often make notes for future planning. If the lesson is not well planned, or if the presentation of the lesson is flawed, the amount of time that the student spends engaged in learning, the relevance of the learning task, the level of success the student has with the task, and the amount of the time allocated that is actually spent learning will be negatively effected.

Classroom Environment

The BTES researchers found that the relationship between ALT and the teaching process was often mediated by the classroom environments. The researchers noted that, "classes may differ widely on such dimensions as enthusiasm, warmth, competitiveness, cooperation, and task orientation" (Fisher et al., 1978, pp. 2–11), and they found that the differences in classroom environments had a direct influence on a student's ALT. However, the interaction between teaching processes and classroom environments is almost a "which cam first, the chicken or the egg" type of relationship, but in this case the question becomes, "Which is the cause (teaching processes or classroom environment) and which is the symptom?"

As intriguing as this question may be, it is not nearly as important to lay blame or give credit for origin as it is to understand the closeness of the relationship between the teaching processes, classroom environment, and academic learning time. By improving the quality of the teaching processes, we can have a direct positive impact on the quality of both the classroom environment and the student's academic ALT, which in turns affects the student's level of academic achievement.

STUDENT ACHIEVEMENT AND ALT

The BTES investigators defined student learning in two ways. *ALT* (allocated time, engaged rate, error rate, and task relevance) was used to measure "in-progress" learning, and *academic achievement* was measured through the use of paper and pencil tests (an "end-of-process" measure). Based on the extensive field research that they conducted during Phase III-B of the project, the BTES researchers were able to draw a number of conclusions regarding the relationship between ALT and student learning as measured on achievement tests. Following is a brief discussion of these findings.

Time allocated to instruction in a content area is positively associated with learning in that content area.

Allocated time is affected by the school calendar, the school schedule, events and conditions within the classroom, and decisions made by the teacher. The BTES finding that the amount of time allocated to a particular subject increases student achievement in that area is often used as one of the arguments for extending the length of the school day or year and for increasing the amount of time allocated to the core subjects of math, science, and the language arts. However, one must be cautious in interpreting this finding, because as the researcher have warned us:

> Even if it is true that allocated time causes learning, it only does so under certain conditions and up to some limit. If the student engagement rate is zero, then no amount of allocated time will cause any learning. Furthermore, even under the best of conditions, there is a limit to the amount of work that a student can accomplish within a day (Fisher et al., 1978, p.4–40).

Student engagement rate during allocated instructional time in reading or mathematics is positively associated with learning.

The BTES researchers found that variation in student engagement rate helped to explain at least some of the differences in student achievement levels in reading and math. (Remember that the researchers were only looking at these two areas.) In one case they found that differences in engagement rate accounted for as much as 20 percent of the variance in student achievement. Although their findings were not always this strong, they did find that engagement rate and student learning were positively related in all areas examined (second and fifth grade reading and second and fifth grade math).

The proportion of allocated time spent by students on tasks where they have low error rates is positively associated with learning. The proportion of allocated time spent by students on tasks where they have high error rates is negatively associated with learning.

Low error rate means the students are making mistakes at the "careless" level. High error rate means that the students are working at the "chance" level and they have about a 50/50 chance of making mistakes or getting the right answer. There are a number of components that may account for the negative impact of a high error rate, including frustration, failure to attempt the task, or lack of confidence on the part of the student.

In this study, the researchers found that, "The average student in this study spent no more than half of his/her time at a low error rate level. *Relative to this average*, more time at the low error rate was associated with greater increases in achievement." They went on to conclude that, "A moderate proportion of instruction at the medium error rate level, where the student is exposed to some problems he/she is unable to solve, may be advantageous" (Fisher et al., 1978, pp. 4–40).

Greater quantities of ALT are not associated with declining student attitudes toward the subject matter they were studying or toward school itself.

During the course of the study, the researchers became concerned that, "the learning behaviors represented in the ALT model may consist, essentially, of hard work in the "sweatshop" tradition. This might result in short-term achievement gains, but a long-term deterioration of academic attitudes and enthusiasm for learning" (Fisher et al., 1978, p. 9–1). Therefore, the researchers incorporated an attitude measure within their study. As a result they found that there was "an encouraging *lack* of association of time allocation and engagement rate with student attitude change. This indicates that relatively high levels of time allocation and engagement are no generally associated with aversive, "nose-to-the-grindstone" classroom environments" (Fisher et al., 1978, p. 9–20).

The association of the combined ALT variables with student learning is of considerable practical importance in terms of student learning in schools

In the BTES study, ALT was found to account for at least 10 percent of the variance in student achievement. The researchers felt that the actual percentage rate was even higher but had been "considerably reduced by error of measurement, so that the "true" association of ALT and learning is much stronger" (p. 11–10). The researchers went on to speculate that, because the relationship between each of the individual variables and student learning was so strong, the combined relationship would be even stronger and that a deliberate change in one variable would have a change in the effect of the other variables and on the total effect of ALT. They did not, however, test this assumption in the field research and so it remained a speculative finding.

The association of low error rate with student learning is due to that part of low error rate that is an instructional treatment, rather than the part of low error rate that reflects student skills and abilities. The effects of low error rate are greater for hose students who are lower in pre-achievement.

The researchers found that there was a positive effect between low error rate and student achievement and that, conversely, there was a negative effect between high error rate and student achievement. They also found that this relationship was affected by the students' skills and abilities *and* by the instructional techniques used by the teacher. What is both surprising and encouraging is that the relationship was more positively affected by instructional treatment than by prior knowledge and skills. It was acknowledged that there is a limit to the degree to which instruction can compensate for lack of prior knowledge and skills. However, it was found that the relationship between low error rate and student achievement was most positive for those students who were low in pre-achievement. One explanation give for this is that students' gained confidence in their learning ability through "a series of successive successes" and the more confident they felt, the more likely they were to stay with a task until it was successfully completed.

It is interesting to note that in the summary of their findings of the relationship between the ALT variables and student achievement, the researchers failed to explain the relationship between task relevance and student learning. At several points in their report, however, they do suggest that task relevance is incorporated into "appropriate instruction" and that "Ongoing student learning behaviors have been successfully measured in the form of attentive involvement in a relevant instructional activity for which the student is able to respond correctly most of the time" (pp. 4–51).

INSTRUCTIONAL PROCESS AND ALT

Just as the researchers found that there was a positive correlation between ALT and student learning, they also found a relationship between teaching processes (planning and instruction) and both ALT and academic achievement. This led to the conclusion that student learning can be increased by increasing academic learning time and academic learning time can be increased through the use of instructional practices. The researchers based this conclusion on a number of findings regarding the relationship between teaching processes and ALT. Following is a brief discussion of each of these findings.

Teacher awareness of the academic strengths and weaknesses of individual students (diagnosis) is positively associated with student learning.

Diagnosis requires that a teacher understand the students' level of motivation and interest in the task, prior mastery of skills, basic ability in the content area, and "staying power." It also requires that the teacher understand the subject matter well enough so that when a student makes a mistake the teacher is able to identify the most probably cause of the mistake. Without these skills, the teacher is in danger of prescribing the wrong instructional treatment and the relationship between ALT and student achievement will be negatively affected.

Prescription of instruction that is appropriate to the needs and level of performance of individual students is positively associated with student learning. Appropriateness of prescription is related to the student error rate component of ALT.

Prescription draws its strength from the diagnosis that the teacher has made. But even if the teachers are able to accurately diagnose a student's learning needs, they may be less effective in prescribing the appropriate treatment. Appropriate treatment refers to instruction that is relevant to the learning task and requires student interaction at a low error rate level. Again, it is interesting to note that the researchers imply that task relevance is important (instruction which is appropriate to the needs of the individual needs of the student) but focus on error rate more directly than they do on the relevance of the task.

More substantive interaction between the student and an instructor is associated with higher percentages of student engagement.

The BTES researchers found that the engagement rate was higher when the instruction time was used for substantive interactions in which the teacher and student focused on the content of the lesson. They also found that substantive interactions occurred more frequently in large group or whole group settings than when students worked in small groups or independently. Within the group instruction, engagement rate increased when the time was filled with instructions related to the content (substantive behaviors) than with organizational tasks (procedural behaviors). Engagement rate also increased in direct proportion to the amount of instruction attention the student received from the teacher.

A word off caution is necessary at this point. According to the researchers, "A student was considered to be engaged in an activity whenever he/she was involved in the academic substance of activity" (Fisher et al., 1978, pp. 4–3). When students reacted to the teacher's nonsubstantive directions, they were not considered to be engaged. Hence, because of the way engaged rate was measured, it would have been almost, if not totally, possible for the researchers to reach any other conclusion!

Structuring of the lesson and/or giving directions on task procedures is/are positively associated with low error rate.

Structuring of the lesson and/or giving directions is measured by observing the percent of student instructional time that is devoted to receiving directions or in which the format of the lesson is discussed. When this percentage goes up, the error rate goes down. And, as you will recall, as the error rate goes down, achievement goes up.

Explanation specifically in response to student need is negatively associated with low error rate and positively associated with high error rate.

This finding appears to be almost self-evident. It makes sense that a student needs more explanation when the learning activity is at an inappropriate academic level (e.g., the student hasn't mastered the necessary prerequisite skills) or when the previous explanation was not sufficient for the student to comprehend what is expected of him or her. If either case holds true, one could expect the student's error rate to be higher than that of a student who is assigned a task at a more appropriate level or who was provided with adequate directions at the start. It is also possible, however, that asking questions of the teacher may be delaying technique used by students when they are unmotivated or lack interest in the subject. In any case, when students need more explanation, their error rates tend to go up, and conversely, when they need no additional explanation, their error rates go down.

Academic feedback is positively associated with student learning.

Academic feedback, as defined by the BTES researchers, refers to feedback regarding whether the student's answer is correct. The correct answer may be provided by the teacher, but the feedback would not include explaining why the student's answer was right or wrong. Any further discussion of the answer is considered explanation rather than feedback.

Academic feedback takes many different forms, including direct responses from the teacher, student-to-student responses, student-to-teacher responses, and checking the answers against a code sheet. It is also considered a form of feedback when students read a passage silently while listening to another student read the passage aloud.

More frequent negative feedback to students about their behavior is associated with lower student engagement rates.

Again, this is another finding that is almost self-evident. Students seldom receive negative feedback about their behavior when they are "on-task," so of course negative feedback about their behavior would be associated with lower engagement rates. In fact, the researchers found that, on the average, positive feedback regarding task behavior accounted for less than half of one percent of the students' instructional time. The finding does serve to remind us that lack of engagement often has a negative impact on student behavior.

Teacher emphasis on academic goals is positively associated with academic learning and teacher orientation toward the affect to the exclusion of academic instruction is negatively associated with learning.

The researchers found that, "When the teachers and students turn their attention *primarily* to affective concerns, this leads away from academic instruction. If teachers focus on social characteristics such as the background and personalities of their students, rather than cognitive performance, they may be unaware of or unwilling to tolerate high error rate" (pp. 7–19). The researchers also concluded that, "different instructional variables are involved in promoting attitude from those effective in increasing achievement" (pp. 8–7). Therefore, ALT is higher in classrooms that are goal oriented and lower in classrooms where, tot he detriment of academic achievement, there is greater emphasis placed on the affective.

A learning environment characterized by student responsibility for academic work and by cooperation on academic tasks is associated with greater learning.

"Student responsibility" refers to the degree to which students are responsible for classroom activities, both academic and nonacademic. "Cooperation" relates to how well the students work with one another by sharing materials and space, by performing tasks together, and by generally helping each other. The level of learning is higher in classrooms where students work well together and take responsibility for their work.

ADDITIONAL OBSERVATIONS

The findings and conclusions that have just been discussed were based on statistical analysis of the data collected throughout the research. The researchers also made a number of other observations which they discussed in their final report. Among those were observations regarding the relationship between summer vacation and learning retention, the use of non-academic time in the classroom, and the impact of the instruction setting on ALT.

Summer School

The BTES investigators were curious about the effects of ALT on retention, especially after an extended summer vacation. They specifically sought to answer the question, "What is the pattern of student achievement scores when considered over a period with regular school instruction followed by a period with no instruction?" (Fisher e t al. 1978, pp. 10–11). In order to answer this question, the students who participated in the study were tested at different times throughout the school year—October, December, and May—and then again in September of the next year. Some of the students attended summer school, some attended year-round-school programs, and some had no formal instruction during the summer months, thus making it difficult to control for varying amounts of instruction. To further complicate matters, the last testing in the school year was done in early May, but for many of the schools, summer vacation didn't start until some time in June. This meant that some students received additional instruction during June while others did not.

In spite of these differences, the researchers found that, for *all* the classes included in the study, achievement scores increased from October to December and from December to May. Testing done in September revealed that, for all students, achievement either increased or remained the same over the summer months. The researcher found no indication of the "summer loss" that advocates for year-round-schools often put forth. They did find, however, that the increase in achievement was greater for those students in year-round programs than for those children who either attended summer school or who had no formal instruction during the summer. This would tend to indicate that while there is no "summer loss" per se, shorter periods of instruction followed by a brief vacation has a more positive effect on academic achievement than do longer periods of instruction followed by an extended vacation.

Non-ALT

Perhaps one of the greatest impacts of BTES was to draw attention to how time was being used in the classroom. The researchers, in their final report, noted that:

> A great deal of student time in class consists of "Non-ALT" because the student is not engaged in any academic task or because the academic task in which the student is engaged products an inappropriate error rate. The usefulness of the concept, "Non-ALT", lies in the specification of its cause, either lack of engagement or an unreasonable student error rate. Hence, it is possible to analyze, in terms of student variables, *why* learning does not occur (Fisher et al., 1978, pp. 2–7).

Immediately following the release of the report, a flurry of research studies was conducted to aid in the understanding of how time was used in the classroom. (For a review of this research see Anderson, 1984; Karweit, 1988.)

Even as these studies were being conducted, teachers and administrators rushed to find ways to reduce the amount of Non-ALT in the school day. It wasn't long until the ALT Instructional Process Model was reduced to its simplest denominator, time-on-task. Task was taken to mean any activity that the teacher assigned to the student, regardless of whether it met the criterion of being instructionally relevant. In addition, when tasks were assigned, the concept of error rate was almost totally ignored. For instance, teachers assigned "bell work" as a way of increasing time-on-task. The same work was often assigned to all students within a class irrespective of their varying abilities and academic needs. The assignments would be given to the students to work on while the teacher took attendance, prepared the lunch count, and completed other "beginning of the day" activities. In many cases, the work assigned to the student had little to do with the learning needs of the student and often the teacher would fail to collect or review the student work once it was completed.

Educational writers began to discount the findings of BTES with most of their reactions directed toward time-on-task (or engaged rate) rather than toward the total concept of ALT. The ALT aspects of allocated time, error rate, and task relevance were ignored as was the general instructional model that result from the research. In spite of the criticism by members of the educational community, the quality of classroom time did, at least for a while, improve as a result of the Beginning Teacher Evaluation Study.

THE INSTRUCTIONAL SETTING

In order to study the effects of the classroom setting on student achievement, the researchers selected eight second-grade classrooms to study. They chose three types of classrooms to examine: classes where student achievement was exceptionally high in *both* reading and math, classes that rated average in achievement in both reading and math, and classes where student achievement was exceptionally low in reading *and* math.

When the researchers compared the high achievement classes to the low achievement classes they found a number of interesting comparisons. Among those related to time and learning were:

1. The average amount of time that students had to wait for assignments was much higher in the low-achieving classrooms than in either the average or high-achieving classrooms
2. In the lower-achieving classrooms, students spent less instructional time in math and reading than did students in either the average or high-achieving classrooms
3. Variability in student engagement rate was much smaller in the high-achieving classrooms than in either the classrooms of average or low achievement.

The researcher also looked at the effects of self-paced versus other-paced instruction on ALT. In *self-paced* instruction, students work independently and determine for themselves how much time to spend with different aspects of the task. This determination is made within the total time limited provided by the teacher. For instance, a student might need to read a story and then answer questions about the story. The teacher allocates a total of 20 minutes for this activity. One student might spend ten minutes reading and ten minutes answering questions while another student spends 15 minutes reading and only five minutes answering questions. During this time, the teacher is busy with other activities or is circulating around the room to see how the students are doing.

Other-paced instruction includes all other types of instructional settings, including those where students work in large group; small, teacher-led groups; and small, cooperative groups. The pace of instruction is determined by the teacher and is beyond the control of the individual student.

When comparing different instructional settings, the researchers found the following:

- Students received more explanation in math than in reading in all three settings.
- Academic feedback was greater in math than in reading in all settings.
- Most instructional interaction took place in either small or large groups.
- The average engaged-rate in self-paced settings was 13 percent lower than the average engaged rate in other paced-settings.
- Student were more attentive and there were fewer discipline problems in other-paced settings as opposed to self-paced settings.
- When a great percent of group-based instruction time was devoted to giving directions and/or providing information about the lesson format, engaged rate during self-paced instruction increased.

When considering the findings of the impacts of classroom setting, one must take into consideration the age of the students involved because there is a developmental factor that comes into play. The younger a child is, the less likely it is that the child will be capable of self-direction. Being able to monitor their own learning needs come through experience and the younger the students, the less experience they have in this area. Nonetheless, other researchers have had similar findings in both the middle school and in high school.

THE LEARNING STUDENT/THE LEARNING CLASSROOM

The BTES research is important because it provides us with insight into ways to evaluate student learning while it is occurring and helps us to understand how to establish classrooms that will encourage learning to take place. From the research, we can conclude that the learning student is one who is actively involved "in an activity that is directly relevant to some content area, where this involvement is generally success" (Fisher et al., 1978, pp. 11–21). When you observe a learning student you will find that the student:

- Has an activity or task that is designed to result in increased skill or knowledge
- Is very attentive
- Is actively involved with the activity at hand and is probably enthusiastic about the task—the student isn't sharpening pencils, looking for a book, waiting in line, or socializing with another student
- Enjoys what he or she is doing and pays attention to the task for a long period of time

- Spends a lot of time with practice and review activities, although the amount of time spent with these kinds of activities decreases in the later stages of learning and the time is devoted to application type activities
- Undertakes new tasks only when the previous tasks have been mastered.

In classrooms that encourage learning, you will find that:

- Students are given tasks they haven't mastered but they have the skills and knowledge that are necessary to work through the task.
- The stress is on academics and there is a high expectation for student outcomes.
- Tasks are grouped so that they build upon one another.
- Teachers spend time giving directions and informing the students about the lesson structure of format.
- There is a regular routine for beginning each lesson.
- Students need little additional explanation once the lesson has begun.
- When the students are in a group setting, the teacher uses questions to monitor the degree of their understanding.
- When the students are working independently, the teacher circulates around the room checking on how well each student is doing on his or her assigned task.
- Students receive frequent feedback on how well they are doing academically.
- Students are held accountable for their work.
- Good work is rewarded.
- There is a spirit of cooperation among the students and students work together to accomplish academic goals.

CRITICISM OF THE BTES RESEARCH

The BTES research was successful in focusing attention on the quality of classroom time and its effect on student learning. It would be wrong, however, to assume that everyone embraced the BTES research. Shortly after the release of the study, a number of educators began to criticize the research as being too restrictive and not as relevant to educational practice as the researchers had led the educational community to believe. The criticism set forth by Jere Confrey in 1984 is typical of most of the negative reactions that have been directed toward the study. Confrey felt that by choosing the subject areas of reading and math, the researchers had confined themselves to areas that were primarily skill oriented, which led to the concept of cognitive learning being narrowly defined. The research ignored critical thinking and other process-related skills and by doing so added to the "crisis of understanding" wherein students attain procedural or algorithmic competence without understanding why or how the procedures work" (Confrey, 1984, p. 33).

On one level, Confrey's criticism is accurate and yet on another level it is less than accurate. It is true that the researchers looked only at reading and math, and that at grades two and five the content of the lessons do build heavily on skill development. However, the pencil and paper tests used to measure student achievement did require the students to apply critical thinking and non-algorithm processes in order to answer the questions properly.

Confrey went on to argue that the types of learning associated with affective goals were completely ignored by the researchers. Included in the affected skills that were ignored were topics related to "independent learning, self-responsibility, self-esteem, curiosity, and appreciation of knowledge" (p. 33). Once again, the criticism is valid on one level and less than valid on another. It is true that the researchers did not measure or evaluate the affective learning. They did, however, examine the causal relationship between the affective attitude within the classroom (cooperative learning, independent learning, student responsibility) and the effect on the students' levels of ALT.

According to Confrey, the BTES research was weak because the "interactions between the way something is taught and what is learned is ignored in considering ALT" (p. 340. For instance, skills are often taught in task-oriented, teacher-dominated environments. When dealing with other, nonskill oriented processes such as critical thinking and affective interactions, student-dominated discussions and student-initiated projects are more prominent and inquiry or discovery learning become more important. However, during this process, students may appear to be "off-task," especially at the initial stages of the critical thinking process.

It is unlikely that the BTES researchers would argue with Confrey on this point, for in their final report they stated that:

> Schooling has many different purposes. One purpose is cognitive learning. Others might be development of independent work habits, learning social interaction skills, feeling good about oneself, enjoying work, appreciation of fine arts, keeping kids off the street, etc. Most teachers value and work toward a number of different outcomes. Because the BTES study focused primarily on cognitive outcomes, we cannot fully evaluate classroom instruction. Our data do point out, though, that choices must be made and that teachers should be aware of the choices they make (Fisher et al., 1978, pp. 11–38).

In spite of the criticism of the ALT model set forth by Confrey and others, it is hard to argue that time doesn't play an important role in all types of learning. It is true that it is harder to measure the impact of time on critical thinking and other nonskilled directed learning. However, just because we lack the skills to measure the impact does not mean that the impact does not exist. Common sense tells us that the more time a student spends in learning, the more he or she will learn. Common sense also tells us that time, and time alone, is not the only factor that impacts learning. Research (including the research of Carroll, Bloom, and the BTES researchers) supports this common-sense notion, and as leading educational researchers Borg and Gall remind us, "The consistency of results indicates that amount of instructional time reliably increases student learning: The more instructional time, the more students learn. The effect has been found by many researchers in many school systems" (Borg & Gall, 1983, pp. 5–6).

REFERENCES

Anderson, L. W.(Ed.). (1984). *Time and school learning: Theory, research and Practice.* New York: St. Martin's Press.

Bloom, B. S. (1974). Time and learning. *American Psychologist, 29*(9), 682–688.

Borg, W. R., & Gall, M. D. (1983). *Educational research* (4th ed.). New York: Longman.

Carroll, J. B. (1963). A model of school learning. *Teachers College Record, 64*(8), 723–733.

Confrey, J. (1984). Review of time to learn: Subject-matter specialists. *Journal of Classroom Interactions, 17*(2), 32–36.

Fisher, C., et al. (1978, June). *Teaching behaviors, academic learning time and student achievement: Final report of phase III-B, beginning teacher evaluation study* (Technical Report V-1.) San Francisco, CA: Far West Laboratory for Educational Research and Development.

Karweit, N. (1988, February). Time-on-task: The second time around. *NASSP Bulletin,* 31–39.

McDonald, F. J., & Elias, P. J. (1975, November). *Beginning teacher evaluation study: Phase II Final Report,* Volume, I. Princeton, NJ: Educational Testing Service.

▶ 8

Student Engagement Rate

One of the major findings from the research on time and learning is that a surprisingly large amount of school time is spent on noninstructional activities. Rossmiller (1983) calculated that the amount of time that the average student spends on-task during a school year of 1,080 hours to be approximately 364 hours, or slightly more than a third of the time. Burns (1984) found that, on the average, only 75 percent of the elementary day is actually spent in the classroom and 37 percent of that time is spent on noninstructional activities. Karweit, a leading researcher on time and learning has noted that:

> Adding 40 days to the school term might increase the actual usable learning time by as little as five days if those schools retain their same rates of student absence, disorder, and lack of effective classroom management and instruction—all of which drastically reduce the available instructional time (1988, p. 32).

She goes on to say:

> The variable we must affect is the amount of active learning time— the time in which a student is actively engaged with learning new materials. Although active learning time takes place primarily in the classrooms, classroom events and practices are not the only factors that affect it. Indeed, active learning time lies at the end of a long chain of decisions and actions by many persons and organizations. To plan strategies for changing active learning time, we must disaggregate it into its constituent parts and then identify the sources of variations for each part (Karweit, 1988, p. 33).

The belief that active learning time is an important component of school learning is not new. Carroll's Model of School Learning (1963), Bloom's Learning for Mastery Model (1974), and the BTES Academic Learning Time Instruction Process Model (1978) all include student engagement as one of the key elements in student learning. Student engagement rate, like Karweit's active learning time, is defined as the amount of time a student spends actively involved with an instructional activity. The terms time-on-task and productive learning time also are used frequently in the educational literature to refer to engagement rate.

Within the school day, the amount of time allocated to learning provides the upper limit of student engagement rate, but it would be safe to argue that this upper limit is seldom, if ever, reached. This is not to say that educators are uninterested or unconcerned about the level of student engagement. In fact, many practitioners, concerned about quality instructional time within their classrooms, have taken steps to improve time usage within their settings. Among the more common ways of recovering instructional time are beginning lessons on time, organizing the classroom so that students can retrieve and replace learning materials with little effort, reducing the amount of time it takes to move from one task to another, and establishing classroom routines that reduce confusions about classroom expectations.

Once a teacher becomes aware of the elements that are having an effect on student engagement rate, he or she can take steps to ameliorate the negative effects of those elements. Among the most common factors that influence the degree of involvement that a student will have with an instructional task are classroom environment, classroom management, the way students are grouped, teacher expectations, the nature of the instructional activity, and the characteristics of individual students.

THE CLASSROOM ENVIRONMENT

It is not unusual to hear teachers say, "That's good in theory, but it will never work in the real world of the classroom." The "real world" that the teachers refer to is often limited to one classroom—their own. As Good and Brophy have noted, the problem with viewing the world from such a narrow perspective is that, "Teachers are often unaware of much of what they do, and this lack of perception sometimes results in unwise, self-defeating behavior." They go on to say:

> If teachers can become aware of what happens in the classroom and can monitor accurately both their own behavior and that of their students, they can function as decision makers. To the extent that teachers cannot do this, they are controlled by classroom events. When

teachers fail to coordinate classroom events, students will not make optimal progress (Good and Brophy, 1991, p. 1).

The classroom environment is a complex one, and because each classroom is a "world unto itself" what usually works in one classroom doesn't always work in the same way in a different classroom. In spite of the uniqueness of each classroom, Walter Doyle (1986) has identified a set of six distinct characteristics that all classrooms share. These are multidimensionality, simultaneity, immediacy, unpredictability, publicness, and history. The degree to which teachers understand these dimensions impacts how well they are able to control and coordinate classroom events, and the better able they are to control and coordinate events, the more time students spend on-task and the less time they spend on nonacademic activities.

Multidimensionality

Multidimensionality refers to the large number of events that take place in a classroom. Doyle describes multidimensionality in this way:

> A classroom is a crowded place in which many people with different preferences and abilities must use a restricted supply of resources to accomplish a broad range of social and personal objectives. Many events must be planned and orchestrated to meet special interests of members and changing circumstances throughout the year. Records must be kept, schedules met, supplies organized and stored, and student work collected and evaluated. In addition, a single event can have multiple consequences: Waiting a few extra moments for a student to answer a question can affect that student's motivation to learn as well as the pace of the lesson and the attention of other students in the class (Doyle, 1986, p. 394).

Each of the events outlined by Doyle requires time to accomplish. In many instances, the time required is subtracted from the time allocated to instruction and therefore has a negative impact on student engagement rate. How much time is required for record keeping, meeting schedules, organizing and storing supplies, and collecting and evaluating classroom work will depend to a great degree on the teacher's classroom management abilities, skills, and techniques. Classroom management therefore becomes a key in the puzzle of how to increase quality time in the classroom.

Simultaneity

Not only do a large number of very different types of events occur in the classroom, but many of these events occur simultaneously. For instance, some students may be working independently at their desks while the teacher works with a small group of students, giving them instructions and responding to their questions. A volunteer works with another two students helping them to catch up on work they missed because of illness. The teacher routinely glances about the classroom, catching the eye of any student who is off task, acknowledging the request of a student who wishes to go to the library, and assessing how the students are progressing in relationship to how much time has elapsed and how much time remains within the instructional period.

Most of the events occur simultaneously and relate to monitoring student behaviors—acknowledging requests for assistance, listening to students answers, watching for signs of comprehension or confusion, and scanning the class for possible misbehavior. And, as we have seen from the earlier studies, the more effective the teacher is in monitoring student behavior, the greater the time on-task or the level of engagement rate within the classroom.

Immediacy

Immediacy refers to the rapid speed with which classroom events happen. Doyle has noted that a number of researchers have documented the classroom characteristic of immediacy. Among the studies that Doyle reviewed were those done by Gump (1967) and Jackson (1968) who found that elementary teachers had over 500 exchanges with individual students in a single day. He also reviewed a 1979 study conducted by Sieber on informal student activity. Based on his classroom observations, Sieber estimated that teachers evaluated pupil conduct on the average of 15.89 times per hour, or 87 times a day. In other words, teachers interactions and evaluations of students are very fluid and occur on an ongoing, rapid, and immediate basis.

When routines are set and students know what is expected of them, it is easier to maintain the flow of classroom events and to reduce the negative impact of the classroom characteristic of immediacy. Students tend to live up to expectations and, when they know what is expected of them, there tends to be less negative feedback regarding their behavior. The establishment of classroom routines helps to inform students of expectations and, as a result, the amount of additional explanation and/or negative feedback is greatly reduced. When negative feedback and additional explanation is reduced, the rate of student engagement increases.

Unpredictability

Events in the classroom are often unexpected and hence there is an element of unpredictability in the classroom. A child may become ill, give an unexpected response to a question, or may accidentally bump into another student when moving about the room. There may be an unannounced fire drill, the principal may stop by with a message for the teacher, or a parent may drop by for a visit. Each of the events are unplanned and has the potential of creating a disruption or interruption in classroom proceedings and will more than likely impact what occurs next in the classroom.

Because of the nature of the classroom, it is impossible to completely eliminate distractions and interruptions, but they can be managed if not completely controlled. The teacher can reduce the number and frequency of such events by establishing classroom routines, by understanding the specific needs of his or her students, and through planning and scheduling. Established routines and schedules should take into consideration recurring events that, if left unscheduled, lead to distractions or interruptions. Consider the following example.

> Sally was working on her seatwork assignment in math when her pencil broke and she immediately headed for the pencil sharpener. Johnny had been meaning to ask Sally for a date, but hadn't had a chance. When Sally headed for the pencil sharpener he saw his chance and he too headed for the sharpener. Billy saw what was happening and he punched Jim, who sat next to him. Johnny had to pass by both boys on his way to the sharpener and as he approached their desks, they began to tease him. The teacher, who had been helping Beth with one of her problems, was distracted by the noise. She asked Beth to wait while she went to see what was happening. Of course, by this time other students in the class had caught on and their work was also interrupted by the events.

While it is true that classroom routines cannot stop raging hormones and Johnny may have been distracted by Sally regardless of what was expected of him, it is also true that the teacher could have established a classroom routine that would have reduced the distractions and consequent interruption for the other students. For instance, if the class had had a simple rule that only one student was allowed at the pencil sharpener at a time, Johnny might not have been as anxious to follow after Sally, the other boys would not have been taken off-task, and Beth's instructional flow would not have been interrupted.

Although this is a very simplistic example, it does serve to demonstrate how interruptions and distractions can be reduced with a little forethought. Classroom rules must be made in light of realistic student needs (e.g., a sharpened pencil), the characteristics of the students, and the history of recurring interruptions and distractions. By doing so, the teacher will reduce time-off-task and increase student engagement rate.

Publicness

Classrooms are public places and therefore most classroom events are observed by the majority of those who are present in the classroom. The public nature of the classroom not only affects the general classroom climate, but it also can have a dramatic effect on a student's perception about his or her own ability. For instance, if a student makes a mistake and the teacher corrects it in front of other students who have not made a mistake, the first student may feel that he or she is "not as smart as the other kids." This in turn can affect the student's level of perseverance, which in turn can affect his or her engagement rate, which will ultimately affect the student's academic achievement.

History

Each class shares a common set of experiences that Doyle defines as the class history. The common experiences could also be called the classroom culture. The rules of the classroom, past interactions among the students, how other perceive the students as a group, and the collection of events that happen throughout the school day and year all impact this "history."

Anytime the "history" of the classroom is altered through changes in patterns (whether those are related to changes in routines or changes in group composition), it can, and usually does, have some impact on student engagement rate. The impact may be slight, lasting only for a short time, or it may have a more or less permanent impact on the engaged rate of the students within the classroom. Take, for instance, the case of Mrs. Smith's classroom. Beginning early in the year, Mrs. Smith had established a set routine with her students. As part of the routine, students were expected to hand in their homework at the beginning of the class period and do the practice problems that were listed on the board while she attended to the day's start-up activities. By October, the students had the routine down pat and it had become part of their "history" or the "classroom culture." In late October, Mrs. Smith was in car accident and as a result was unable to return to school until January. When she had left in October, the students had begun work immediately, but when she returned in January it took up to ten minutes before she could begin instruction. Many of the students "forgot" to hand in their homework when they first entered the room. They would begin to work on the problems on the board and then remember that they hadn't handed in their work so they would wander to the front of the room to do so. In the process they would often stop to talk to another student and this would disturb other students who were doing their work. Not only did these students cause a disruption in the classroom, but it seemed to Mrs. Smith that all of the students were taking longer to complete the problems on the board. In order to stem what she saw as a growing problem, Mrs. Smith began the second week of her return by reminding the students of the routines they had established early in the year. She told them that she understood that they had established a new routine while she was gone but the new routine wasn't working very well. To drive home her point, she noted that the problems on the board were important practice problems and that if they weren't completed during the class period they would have to be added to their homework assignments. She added the last comment because she knew how much the students disliked homework. Drawing upon the history of the class, Mrs. Smith was able to reestablish the earlier classroom routine and increase the students' in-class engagement rate by five to seven minutes per class period.

In this case, the classroom history was shaped by the events established early in the year by Mrs. Smith. That history was affected by the absence of Mrs. Smith and the consequent actions and expectations of the substitute teacher(s). In attempting to regain control in the classroom, Mrs. Smith was wise enough to realize that she had to "take into account the broader context of the class history." She did not expect the classroom routine to revert back to the October routine simply because she was now in the room. Instead, she reminded the students about why the routines had been established in the first place, and then added a little incentive for returning to the routine by calling upon the student's dislike of homework. In doing so, she recouped valuable instructional minutes that had been lost.

CLASSROOM MANAGEMENT

The classroom attributes of multidimensionality, simultaneity, immediacy, unpredictability, publicness, and history all have an impact on the amount of time students spend on-task, and usually the impact is negative. However, the negative impacts of these classroom dimensions can be reduced through sound classroom management techniques. Sound classroom management practices lead to fewer discipline problems, less time spent in transitions from one activity to another, fewer interruptions in the school day, and a reduction in the amount of time that a student must spend waiting for help. In other words, sound classroom management leads to a higher level of student engagement.

Discipline

Classroom management is frequently used as a synonym for discipline. In reality, discipline is just one part of classroom management, but it is one of the overriding concerns of educators. When a student misbehaves, it often forces the teacher to take time away from instructional tasks. Seifert and Beck (1984) found that, "Each incident of discipline reduces the number of minutes of engaged learning time from two to four minutes, depending upon the seriousness of the discipline problem. Each time the teacher stops the engaged learning process to discipline a student the entire class is placed in an off-task mode" (p. 30). If you multiply the number of students in the class by the number of minutes they are off-task you begin to see the magnitude of the impact of discipline problems on student engagement rate. Let's say that there are 25 students in the room and a discipline problem erupts that requires the teacher's attention for a total of two minutes. The class has lost a total of 50 minutes of instructional time. If this occurs several times during the day, the impact becomes even greater. Many may want to argue that if the students are working independently and if the teacher is acting as a facilitator rather than a "dispenser of knowledge" the impact will be less. This may be true. But remember that the classroom is a "public place," and even though the interaction is between the misbehaving student and the teacher it will more than likely draw the attention of the other students, taking them off-task.

Transitions

Transitions from one activity to another involve putting materials away, getting out new materials, changing classes, handing in papers, and numerous other activities. Researchers have found transitions from one activity to another usurp as much as 25 percent of the allocated instructional time in the elementary classroom (Rosenshine, 1980). Within the high school, time scheduled for moving from one class to another can account for as much as 50 minutes per day, or 15 percent of the day. The time devoted to beginning and ending of each new class (for example, getting homework out and putting away textbooks) is also considered transitional time, and it is not unusual for these activities to take another five to ten minutes away from the allocated instructional time. Such activities can account for as much as one hour per day.

Transitions also occur when students move from one activity to another within the classroom. For example, consider a high school chemistry class that is scheduled for 55 minutes. The students begin the class in a large group where they pass in their homework assignment, which takes about one minute. The teacher then distributes the homework from the day before, which takes about two minutes. Three minutes are spent discussing the homework, after which the students are assigned to lab partners and stations. The assignment of lab partners takes five minutes and moving to the stations takes another two minutes. One student from each group is sent to retrieve the equipment that is to be used in the experiment. This takes approximately two minutes, during which time the other students are allowed to talk quietly among themselves. Once everyone is back at their stations and the teacher has their attention, directions are given, which takes two minutes, and the students are given 20 minutes to complete their experiments. At the end of the 20 minutes they are expected to clean up their lab areas, wash the equipment that they used, and to return it to the storage place. This takes approximately five minutes. The students return to their seats and prepare for the discussion that is to follow by getting out their notebooks and sharpening their pencils, if necessary. Two minutes pass before everyone in the class is ready for the discussion. The discussion continues for five minutes, after which the teacher distributes worksheets that are to be completed as part of the students' homework. Distributing the worksheets takes an additional two minutes. The last four minutes of the class period are spent discussing the homework assignment.

In this example, transitional activities take 21 minutes, or slightly more than 38 percent of the allocated instructional time. The transitional time is spent in handing in homework (1 minute), distribution of graded homework (2 minutes), assignment of lab partners (5 minutes), moving to lab stations (2 minutes), retrieving equipment (2 minutes), returning equipment (5 minutes), returning to seats (2 minutes), and distribution of homework assignment (2 minutes).

There is no way to completely eliminate transitional time in the classroom. But, through the use of sound classroom management techniques, the amount of time spent in transitions can be reduced. The students in our example could hand in their homework and pick up the previous days homework before the bell rings, which would reduce transitional time by three minutes. Rather than reading the lab assignments to the class, the teacher could have distributed a printed list of lab assignments, which would have saved another five minutes. Because not all students finish at the same time, one of the students from the first group to finish could be assigned to distribute the worksheets, saving another two minutes. By these very simple methods, transition time could be reduced by almost 50 percent. Additional time might be recouped by looking at better ways of retrieving and returning the lab equipment. Time might also be saved if the students went to their lab stations when they first entered the room rather than going to their seats and then moving to the stations. Such a strategy might not work if the students needed to discuss the homework prior to doing the experiment. The point is, however, that minutes lost to transitions often can be recouped through minor changes in the classroom routine and by a little planning on the part of the teacher.

Classroom organization and arrangement also can affect transition time. Traffic patterns that reduce bottlenecks, storage techniques that allow for easy retrieval of materials and that require little movement by the students can also reduce transition time. For instance, if the pencil sharpener, the box where students hand in their assignments, and the bookshelf that holds supplemental materials are all located in the same area, students may be able to take care of these transitional activities in a smooth flow—hand in the assignment, sharpen a pencil, and get the materials for the next task. However, if a student can't get to the bookcase if someone is sharpening a pencil, the transition time is likely to increase. Likewise, if students need a supplemental textbook for an assignment but the textbooks are stored haphazardly, they will have to spend time looking for the books and the transition time will increase.

Teachers are concerned that when too much emphasis is placed on reducing transition time students end up being placed in an "assembly line" environment where they are working or "being worked on" every moment of the day. However, from the examples that were just provided, it should be obvious that reducing the amount of time spent in transitions does not necessarily mean that the time pressure on students increases. Just the opposite is true. Time pressure is reduced because students are given more time to complete instructional tasks and less time is wasted.

Interruptions

Doyle contends that interruptions are one of the most common characteristics of all classroom settings. Interruptions are unexpected or unplanned events, and they come in numerous formats including announcements from the main office, visitors entering the room, children becoming ill, students pausing in their work to sharpen pencils, fire drills, and teachers stopping to fill out forms.

It is difficult to estimate how much time is lost to interruptions, but it is safe to say that some of the lost time has been recouped in schools where teachers and administrators have implemented interruption-reducing policies. The amount of time lost to interruptions can never be completely recovered, but it can be reduced through the use of sound classroom management techniques. Because the classroom is such a complex environment, with many things going on at once, it is easy for both the teacher and the student to forget even simple tasks. Establishing daily routines helps to develop an almost automatic response to routine tasks to such a degree that they are seldom "forgotten." Planning for classroom activities also helps to maintain a smooth instructional flow because there are fewer interruptions from students asking for help, looking for materials they can't find, and/or trying to determine what they should do after they complete their work.

Within the school setting, interruptions to the instructional flow can be reduced by implementing policies that reduce the number of external interruptions. For instance, many schools will only allow announcements at the beginning or ending of the day. The only exception to this rule is in the case of an emergency. Before entering a classroom, a visitor must report to the office and be escorted to the room. The escort provides the visitor with instruction on the best way to enter the classroom to cause the least amount of disruption. If classes are involved in activities that should not be disrupted, the teacher hangs a "Do Not Disturb" sign on the door and everyone within the school is expected to respect this request. In the past, this procedure was only followed when the students were taking an exam. Today many schools are using this procedure during instruction as well as during exams.

Wait-Time

Wait-time is one of those educational terms that has multiple meanings. It is often used to mean the amount of time that a teacher waits for a response from a student or waits until a student has clarified his or her answer. In this sense wait-time is used as a positive instructional strategy. The term wait-time also refers to the amount of time a student must wait for help from the teacher or the amount of time that a student must wait for a resource (such as a book, a computer, or a handout). In this sense, wait-time has a negative impact on student engagement rate.

Wait-time often results in behavioral problems as in this scenario provided by Everston:

> At one point, five students were at the teacher's desk, and most of them were waiting for help . . . Having so many students in such close proximity to each other frequently created problems and led to the misbehavior to which the teacher was forced to respond (Everston, 1982, p. 341).

This scenario can be used to demonstrate the compounding effects of time off-task. Let's say that it took the teacher an average of one minute to help each child. Under "normal" circumstances, the last child in line would have had to wait four minutes before it became his or her turn. However, while the child was waiting, a discipline problem erupted. The teacher was forced to respond to the problem, which took her approximately one minute and it took another two minutes to get everyone back on task. If we total up the minutes, we find that the last child in line waited a total of seven minutes to get the help necessary before he or she could continue with the instructional activity.

Wait-time also occurs when students must wait for instructional resources. It is not uncommon for students to be forced to wait to use a computer, to wait for a piece of software, or to wait to check out a book at the library. It would be financially impossible for a school to purchase all of the resources that would be needed to provide each student with his or her own copy of a resource, be that resource a supplemental text, a computer, or a set of lab materials. Instead, schools calculate what they believe will be an adequate number of instructional materials and they base this number on the sharing of resources by the students. If they are successful, the amount of time that students must wait is greatly reduced. If they miscalculate, the students will frequently be taken off-task and placed in a wait mode, and valuable learning time is lost.

Just as transitions and interruptions can be reduced by sound classroom management techniques, so can the amount of time lost to waiting be reduced through careful planning and scheduling, by establishment of classroom routines, and by the organization of the classroom.

Procedural Behaviors

The BTES researchers referred to the teaching processes associated with classroom management as procedural behaviors (as opposed to substantive behaviors). Included in procedural behaviors are those behaviors that have to do with preparing students for instruction and providing them with feedback concerning their nonacademic behaviors. Robert MacDonald (1991) has divided the procedural behaviors into three categories: (1) initiatory behaviors, (2) corrective maintenance behaviors, and (3) preventive maintenance behaviors. All three types of behaviors take place concurrently with the instructional process. Procedural behaviors also include those that are involved with organization of the classroom and take place prior to the beginning of instruction.

Initiatory Behaviors

Initiatory behaviors are, as the name implies, behaviors that occur at the beginning of a lesson or a lesson segment. MacDonald has identified several of these behaviors including, cueing, tuning, pausing, and restarting.

Cueing
Cueing involves providing students with an indication that the class is about to begin. The teacher may ask the class to "take your learning positions" or "open your books to page 15." Often these cues are nonverbal such as turning on the overhead, moving to the chalkboard, or picking up a book. Cueing serves to inform the students of what is expected of them and can aid in moving students from one activity to another with a minimum amount of confusion, turmoil, and off-task behavior.

Tuning
Tuning is the process used to help students "tune-in" to the instructional activity. A teacher may start by asking questions about the previous day's assignment, by asking students for their opinions about a specific topic, or by sharing a brief anecdote that will help to focus the students' attention. The teacher also may give directions for the upcoming activity as part of the tuning process. Focusing the students' attentions on the topic at hand makes them more receptive to the instructional task or activity that follows and reduces the amount of time that might be needed for restating the directions.

Pausing

Often the teacher will find it necessary to pause before continuing with directions. If the students are not ready to begin, it makes little sense to give directions or start an instructional activity. Letting students know that the teacher is waiting for them and does not plan on continuing until they are ready should be a "first impulse" for all teachers, according to MacDonald. Once students become aware of this policy, it can be very effective, especially if the teacher makes it clear that there are consequences for not proceeding in a timely fashion. The consequences may be stated in a very direct manner such as "Only work finished during the class period will count toward your grade, and you will need all the total class time if you are to finish." The consequences can also be implied and be part of the regular classroom routine; for example, "any work not finished during the class period will be included in the homework assignment."

Restarting

A teacher may choose to start and then restart the instructional activity. This should not be a consistent approach, but can be used effectively when the students become inattentive at the beginning of an instructional activity or when it becomes apparent that the students are confused by the instructions that are being given. If a teacher finds himself or herself restarting the instruction on a fairly routine basis, he or she needs to reflect on the situation and attempt to analyze why it is necessary to restart the instruction so frequently, because this strategy causes a delay for all of the students and can consume valuable instructional time.

Corrective Maintenance Behaviors

The second set of procedural behaviors identified by MacDonald is corrective maintenance behaviors. These are the behaviors that BTES researchers referred to when they discussed the feedback that teachers provided to students regarding their nonacademic behaviors. Most of these techniques are familiar to the classroom teachers who use them frequently. These include making eye contact or gesturing to a student as a subtle reminder to a student to return to the instructional task. Teachers will often move closer to a student who does not see or respond to the eye contact or the gesture. Sometimes the mere physical presence of the teacher will cause, disruptive behavior to cease or a touch on the shoulder will cause an inattentive student to return to his or her work. Occasionally students will have to be moved away from one another in order to maintain order in the classroom. A teacher may use the time-out strategy by having students stop what they are doing and review the rules or directions that have been given to make certain they are not only on-task but also accomplishing what is expected of them. Occasionally the teacher may find it necessary to discuss nonacademic behaviors with individual students and/or refer the students to a counselor or the principal when the students' behavior is out of control and unyielding to the normal classroom procedures and methods.

In each of these cases, the teacher is responding to student behavior that is robbing the student of learning time. The degree to which these responses is unobtrusive depends upon how consistently the teacher uses them and upon how quickly the teacher responds to the poor behavior. How effective the responses are will depend upon the teacher's ability to assess the situation and respond to it in a positive manner. The effectiveness also will depend on the consequences of being off-task from the students' point of view. If the teacher simply draws attention to the off-task behavior, the student may see little need to return to the instructional task. Furthermore it is important to note that students tend to spend more time on-task when the consequences of being on-task are positive than when the consequences of being off-task are negative. Remember that the BTES researchers found a negative correlation between negative feedback regarding on-task behaviors and both student achievement and academic learning time. In other words, the more time a teacher spends in corrective maintenance, the less the students' time-on-task. It is important to understand why the teacher spends so much time on corrective maintenance, because steps can then be taken to reduce the need for the corrective measures.

Preventive Maintenance Behaviors

MacDonald's third set of procedural behaviors are those that teachers use on an ongoing basis in order to keep students on-task. These include scanning, I-messages, synchronizing, prepping, renewing, and positive framing. Effective preventive maintenance strategies result in the decreased need for corrective maintenance. Although this appears to be somewhat self-evident, it is important to note because, unlike corrective maintenance, preventive maintenance increases both students time-on-task and student achievement.

Scanning
Even as the teachers are involved in tasks such as working with an individual student or working with a small group, they routinely scan the classroom to make certain that students are on-task. Teachers may "catch a student's eye" as a subtle reminder to "get back to work" or may gesture to the student as a clue as to what they are to do next. As a matter of course, teacher's scan the classroom to determine whether the students are on-task, to see how much additional time the students may need to complete the task, to find out if they are ready to move on to the next task, and/or to determine

if they need additional directions for the current task. The more adept a teacher becomes at scanning, the more likely it is that his or her students will be on-task.

I-Messages

Teacher expectations often set the mood in the classroom. If the teacher expects students to be on-task and conveys this expectation to them, students' time-on-task increases. There are a number of ways that teachers can inform students of the teachers' expectations, including sending them I-messages such as, "Johnny, I like the way you are working" or "I would like everyone to think really hard about this problem." Although some may argue that sending I-messages places too much emphasis on what the teacher wants and hence suggests an autocratic classroom, the truth is that the teacher is the instructional leader in the classroom and once the teacher understands and acts on this instructional role, the students will respect the role. The key here, however, is to remain consistent in expectations, establish consequences for meeting and not meeting expectations, and to follow up when expectations are not met. I-messages are a necessary element in the process of establishing expectations.

Synchronizing

This is often one of the hardest classroom management techniques to master. Well-managed classrooms develop a rhythm in which teacher and students "work in harmony" and move in synchronization with one another. In other words, the teacher does not move from one activity to another until the students are ready to move and students move quickly from activity to activity with little direction from the teacher. In classrooms that are well-synchronized, less time is spent in transitions, repeated instructions, and corrective feedback. Correspondingly, the students also spend more time engaged in learning.

Prepping

Prepping is the process of preparing the students for an instructional activity. Students should be informed of all necessary procedures and responsibilities, including procedures for obtaining instructional materials, roles they are to play within a group, time restraints that are being placed on them, and procedures for obtaining help when necessary. Preparation goes beyond simple directions on the instructional task, and are especially critical when students spend time working in small groups or independently. Without such preparation, the teacher can expect the transitions to be less than smooth, the time students spend waiting for help to increase, and the amount of time spent in correcting inappropriate behavior to be greater.

Renewing

The process of renewing involves refreshing students' memories about the instructional goal, reviewing where they currently are in the instructional process, and restating directions as needed. When students are involved in complex learning activities that take place over several class periods, they often need to review what they have accomplished and where they are headed. By doing so, the teacher assures that the students will experience a higher level of success with the instructional task and will be more likely to remain engaged with the learning task.

Positive Framing

The teacher is often responsible for setting the affective climate within the classroom. Saying such things as "I know you don't like story problems" or "This period of history was never my favorite either" sends the students a negative message about the subject matter to be taught. Many students will take such a message to mean that it's okay if they don't do well on the assignment—after all the teacher has admitted that it's not really that important. With positive framing, the teacher tries to avoid such statements altogether or adds a qualifier to each statement such as "I know you don't like story problems, but you're getting much better and before long you are going to be a real whiz at them." Or "This period of history was never my favorite either, but did you know that teenagers during that time were allowed to marry by the age of 15?"

More damaging than the negative messages about content are negative messages about a student's ability to deal with a learning activity. Although generally teachers are very sensitive to the messages they send to students, they can, and often do, send messages that are misinterpreted by the student. For instance, a teacher who knows that a student is having a hard time at home may try to help the student by requiring less work from the student or grading the student's paper a little more leniently. Students often interpret such "acts of kindness" to mean that the teacher thinks that they are incapable of accomplishing what is required of the other students or that this is a time that they can "sluff off." In either case, the result is often the same—a reduction in the student's perseverance or the amount of time he or she is willing to spend on learning.

This does not mean that a teacher should be insensitive to the student-in-need, but rather that the teacher must always be aware of how his or her actions are being interpreted by the student. Positive framing means that teachers react to students and subjects in a positive fashion. Students are encouraged to do their best, interactions between the students' and the teacher are more positive than negative, and teachers encourage and nurture the students' sense of self-worth and academic ability. In classrooms where positive framing is the rule rather than the exception, students' levels of perseverance are higher, as is their level of academic engagement.

STUDENT GROUPING

The amount of time that students in a particular classroom spend in waiting or in transition from one activity to another is influenced not only by the way in which the classroom is managed but also by the way students are grouped within the class. Everston (1982), in comparing classrooms composed of high-ability students with those composed of lower-ability students, found that the lower-ability classes required a great deal more individualized help from the teacher than did the higher-ability group. According to Everston, "multiple individual demands for help from the teacher meant that more students had to wait a considerable time before getting help" (p. 342).

Beckerman and Good (1981) did a similar study, comparing favorable classrooms (less than one-third of students were lower-ability students) and unfavorable classrooms (more than 1/3 were lower-ability students). They found that "teachers in a more favorable classroom have more time to provide individual help to low-ability students, because there are fewer demands on the teachers" (p. 324). Everston, Sanford, and Emmer (1981) found that students in extremely heterogeneous classes spent more time-off task than students in other classroom organizational patterns.

Although these findings are not surprising, they do reinforce the idea that the way children are grouped in a classroom affects the amount of time that individual children spend waiting for help, and this in turn can affect their level of academic achievement. The following example will be used to examine how three different grouping patterns affect the amount of time a student must wait for assistance from a teacher when the student is working independently.

There are 60 students in two classes. A typical student can complete a lesson in 40 minutes. Twenty percent of the group, however, are considered "fast" because it takes them, on the average, only 30 minutes to complete the lesson. Likewise, 20 percent of the group is "slow" because, on the average, it takes them 50 minutes to complete a lesson. After a lesson has been completed, it takes the students approximately five minutes to check their work. Once their work has been checked, the students report to the teacher for the next assignment. Each teacher can advise a member of the fast group in one minute, a member of the average group in one-and-a-half minutes, and a member of the slow group in two minutes. This information is summarized in Table 8–1.

For purposes of this example, three different ways of grouping the students will be considered. In grouping pattern I, all of the students are placed in one group and the two teachers team teach. In grouping pattern II, the students are assigned to two different groups. One group is comprised of the ten fast students, and 15 of the average students. The second group contains the ten slow students and the remaining 15 average students. In the final grouping pattern,

TABLE 8–1   Hypothetical comparison of student time requirements

Group	Number of students	Completion time	Checking time	Time for directions from teacher
Fast	10	30	5	1
Average	30	40	5	1.5
Slow	10	50	5	2

the fast and slow students are grouped with five of the average students and the remaining 25 average students are in a group by themselves. Table 8–2 presents a summary of the amount of wait time in the three different grouping patterns. In Group I, the average time it takes students to receive help before they can move to the task is 1.5 minutes, so the teacher can help an average of 40 students in one hour Table 8–2 presents a summary of the findings.

An examination of the data presented in Table 8–2 reveals that team teaching (Group I) reduced the amount of time that students spent waiting

TABLE 8–2   Hypothetical comparison of classrooms with various grouping patterns

Number of students	Time-on-task	Time spent getting help from the teacher	Number of students requiring help (per hour)	Average time spent waiting (entire class)
Group I				
10 Fast	35 working + 5 Checking work	1	15	
30 Average	40 (working) + 5 checking work	1.5	40	2.95
10 Slow	50 (working) + 5 checking work	2	10	
Group II-A				
10 Fast	35 (working) + 5 Checking work	1	15	4.02
15 Average	40 (working) + 5 checking work	1.5	20	
Group II-B				
15 Average	40 (working) + 5 checking work	1.5	20	9.6
10 Slow	50 (working) + 5 checking work	2	10	
Group III-A				
10 Fast	35 (working) + 5 Checking work	1	15	
5 Average	40 (working) + 5 checking work	1.5	6	5.52
10 Slow	50 (working) + 5 checking work	2	10	
Group III-B				
25 Average	40 (working) + 5 checking work	1.5	33.5	7.68

for help from the teacher. In can be expected that such a reduction in wait time would result in a *fewer number* of students being off-task during the instructional period and in a reduction of the *total time* spent off-task. Under the traditional teaching pattern of one-teacher, one-class, a greater number of students waited for help from the teacher, and they had to wait for longer periods of time than they did under the team-teaching format. Such waiting could result in an increased number of discipline problems which in turn would increase the amount of time students are off-task.

Although the data presented in this problem are purely hypothetical, the problem does serve to demonstrate how grouping patterns can affect the amount of wait-time that students spend in class. One of the factors that was not taken into consideration in our example was that in Group III the students are all at approximately the same level, so it is likely that a greater amount of the instruction would take place in a large group setting, reducing the amount of time the students spent waiting for help. In fact, this is often used as the basis for an argument to support both ability grouping and direct teaching. As the argument goes, when students are grouped according to ability, it is possible to provide more instruction in the form of direct teaching because all of the students are at approximately the same level. In addition, students tend to be more engaged with the learning task in the large-group setting because it is easier for the teacher to monitor their behaviors, guide their instructional performances, and provide feedback, both directly and indirectly.

Direct, large-group teaching is less effective in heterogeneous classrooms where student ability follows a normal distribution. It has been estimated that the range of academic achievement within such a class is approximately two-thirds of the mean chronological age of the students. This means that in a fourth-grade classroom where the average age of the students is nine years, the academic achievement of the students (as measured by a standardized test) will range from fourth grade plus and minus three years. In other words, the students' academic achievement will vary from first through seventh grade. In a first-grade classroom where the average age is six, the academic achievement will range from pre-kindergarten to third grade.

When there is such a large variation of academic achievement within a single classroom, it is almost, if not totally, impossible to keep each child actively engaged in a *meaningful* learning activity. One way of dealing with the large variation is to group the students according to their ability, or to group them homogeneously. However, as First and Gray (1991) remind us:

> In reality, homogeneous grouping does not provide teachers with truly homogeneous groups, just dangerous illusions of homogeneity. Any group of twenty-five to thirty-five elementary school students will vary widely in terms of learning speed and style, interest level, or

aptitude. When this reality is denied, the failure of instruction may be attributed to the child, rather than to the school or the teacher (p. 68).

Regardless of whether the students are normally distributed over the total population or within their own limited population, it has been found that students vary in the amount of time they will need to complete a learning activity. Gettinger (1984) has noted that:

> Most schooling is organized to provide group instruction with definite time periods allocated for various learning tasks; however, this time is likely to be too much for some learners and not enough for others (p. 15).

Teachers often make adjustments in their instructional materials, format, and style in order to accommodate the individual differences within their classrooms. The degree to which they are able to make such accommodations is what Carroll refers to as the quality of instruction and, as you will recall, the quality of the instruction can and will impact the amount of time a student needs for learning. However, simply understanding and adjusting for variation in learning time will do little to improve the quality of instruction if the teacher is unaware of the student characteristics that lead to the variations.

STUDENT CHARACTERISTICS

Educators have long noted that children vary widely in terms of learning speed and style, interest level, and aptitude. This is supported by the work done by Carroll and Bloom as well as by other researchers who have studied the influence of student characteristics on student achievement. Carroll defined student aptitude as the amount of time a student would need to accomplish a learning task. Carroll went on to say that the amount of time a student would need was moderated by the student's level of perseverance and ability in the subject area. Bloom found that students initially varied in the amount of time that they needed to master a task, but the gap between the amount of time needed by the fastest and slowest students could be reduced if the slower students truly mastered one task before moving on to the next, higher level task. Entwistle has found that student characteristics such as prior knowledge, intellectual skills, types and levels of motivation, interest in the topic being taught, anxiety about the subject matter, expectations, and the match between learning style and task requirements all affect student achievement and the amount of time they are willing to spend on-task.

Often, teachers attribute student perseverance, and hence achievement, to one of the previous characteristics without examining how and why the characteristic has developed. In other words, they assume the characteristics to be stable and inborn rather than unstable and influenced by the environment. Consider the following two scenarios to see how time can help to shape student characteristics rather than just being a symptom or a result of the characteristics.

Student 1:

During her first introductory course in science, Jenny repeatedly runs out of time in the science lab and fails to complete lab assignment after lab assignment. She did very well on written assignments, but because she seldom turns in a completed lab report, her grade was affected. At first she tried several strategies to overcome her problem. She asked the teacher for help, but the teacher just said she would have to work faster. She went to a couple of her friends and asked what she should do. They recommended that she copy their reports, but she really didn't want to do that. As the semester went on she became more and more frustrated and her grades on the written assignments began to slip even though she understood most of the material when it was presented in class. Her parents were concerned about her grades and demanded to know why she was doing so poorly. Her explanation was simple. "I'm not good in science and it takes me longer than anyone else to do the stupid lab assignments. Besides, it's dumb for us to have to take a science class when we'll never use the stuff again."

Student 2:

Cal was a third-grade student who liked to make up stories to amuse his younger cousin. He would spend hours at writing the stories and then drawing pictures to illustrate them. His parents encouraged this behavior because they enjoyed his stories and they felt that his writing was, in their words, "a real talent." They were somewhat disappointment and confused, therefore, during the fall parent/teacher conference, when Cal's third-grade teacher told them that she was having trouble getting Calvin to participate in any creative writing activity. The teacher had tried letting him choose a topic from several that she provided, letting him choose his own topic, and letting him work with a partner, but nothing seemed to help. Cal refused to write and when the teacher asked him why he would just shrug his shoulders. Working together, the teacher and parents came up with a series of strategies for encouraging Cal to participate in the creative writing activities, but none of them seemed to help. Throughout this period, however, Cal continued to write at home.

The day before winter break, the teacher told the class that they could spend the entire morning doing whatever they wanted, as long as "it was something that we have done before in class." Calvin chose to write a story, and a wonderful story it was. The teacher praised him and told him she wished he would write more stories for her during class. His response was, "I'll write you more stories, but I have to do them at home." When she asked him why, he responded, "Because I never get them done here and I don't like to write stories that don't end."

Both Jenny and Cal became frustrated when they were not given enough time for a learning task. Jenny reacted to this frustration by developing an indifference to the task, while Cal reacted by avoiding the task altogether. Their reactions are not unusual. Many students experience these same frustrations every day within our classrooms, and their reactions, to greater and lesser degrees, are similar to Jenny's and Cal's. If a student experiences the frustration brought on by a lack of time frequently enough, the frustration often is transferred to the entire subject area—be that subject area math, science, reading, art, or physical education.

Time Needed to Learn

In the two examples just provided, it is obvious that the students were not provided with the amount of time they needed in order to complete the instructional tasks. Students vary greatly in the amount of time they require. Most educators are aware that students with special needs require different amounts of learning time. These special needs may include learning disabilities, physical impairments, emotional distress, bilingualness, and giftedness. They also are aware of, but may not be as in tune to, the fact that students with "regular" needs also vary in the amount of time they require for learning. Both Jenny and Cal appear to be "normal" students with "normal needs," and yet it is obvious that they differ from their classmates in the amount of time they need to complete their class work. We are not given enough information in Jenny's case to diagnosis why it was taking her longer in the lab. We do know, however, that the teacher's suggestion that she work faster was of little help. The teacher needed to help Jenny analyze why it was taking her so long. Did she tend to wait for everyone else to get their equipment before she went after hers? Was she being overly careful in setting up the lab experiment? Did it take her longer to read the lab procedures or to write up her findings? Or is it that she learns better from written material than from hands-on work? Until we are able to diagnose the reason behind her "slowness," we will be unable to help her.

In the case of Cal, we are provided with some insights into why he was unwilling to complete his creative writing assignments. Cal needed more time to do his work not because he was slower than the other children but because he could, and wanted to, do more than was required by the teacher. When time restricted his performance, he became frustrated and stopped performing altogether.

Every day teachers are forced to estimate how much time a class will need to complete an instructional activity. Teachers who are proficient at such estimations usually allocate enough time for 90 percent of the students to complete the activity comfortably in the time allocated. However, even at this high level of proficiency, some students will finish in far less time than the majority of the students and some will not be able to complete the task within the allotted time. For instance, if the teacher has 30 students and allows 20 minutes for a task, approximately 27 will complete the task within the 20 minutes, one or two students will take only eight to ten minutes, and two to three students, like Jenny and Cal, will not be able to complete the task. The danger is that when students are not given enough time to learn it affects not only their achievement on the given activity, but ultimately affects their aptitude in that area.

Time Students Are Willing to Spend Learning

Even when students are given an adequate amount of time to learn, they may not be willing to spend all of the time they should. Carroll referred to the degree to which students were willing to spend in learning as perseverance. Bloom later referred to this as the amount of time the student was willing to spend on-task. Subsequent research has identified a number of factors that affect a student's persevering, including their level of self-efficacy and whether they attribute their successes and failures to something that is within their control or to something outside of their control.

Efficacy

Self-efficacy is the perception that one can or cannot successfully execute the behavior required to produce a particular outcome. How a student perceives his or her ability will influence that student's behavior in at least three ways. First, when given a choice of learning activities, the student's sense of efficacy will often affect the student's choice. Cal, the third-grade student who refused to participate in creative writing activities during the regular class period, may have suffered from a case of low self-efficacy. He didn't expect to be able to finish his stories to his satisfaction, so he chose not to write. When given a choice of activities and unlimited time, he did choose to write because he knew he could finish the story (his expectation efficacy was high).

Second, a student's sense of efficacy will affect the quality of the student's performance. Jenny's inability to complete lab assignments caused her to draw the conclusion that she was poor in science and therefore she did not work as hard to complete her reading assignments. This resulted in her performing poorly on her reading assignments as well as on her lab assignments.

Third, the amount of time a student is willing to persevere with a learning task may be either positively or negatively affected by his or her sense of efficacy. It is not unusual to see students "give up" when they believe they are unable to complete a task. Again we look to Cal as an example. When his expectation efficacy was low, he "gave up" and was unwilling to work on the creative writing assignment.

A student's self-efficacy can have a positive impact on perseverance. For instance, it is not usual to see students who are struggling with a learning task to stay with the task for an extended period of time and even go so far as to decline help from an outside source. These students feel they are able to complete the task on their own and find the work to be challenging rather than frustrating. For these students, the sense of self-efficacy is very high.

Attribution of Success or Failure

A student's sense of self-efficacy is often reflected in his or her perception of what has contributed to his or her success and failure. Students frequently identify the most common causes of their successes and failures as ability, effort, task difficulty, and luck (Weiner 1974; Frieze 1976).

Ability

Comments such as, "I'm not good at math, but neither are my parents, so what do you expect?" or "I'm tone-deaf so of course I can't carry a tune" or "I can draw really well because I inherited it from my grandfather" indicate that the student is attributing his or her success or failure to ability. Students often see ability as something they "were born with," which they have no control over, and which they cannot change. In other words, ability is seen as a stable, internal, and uncontrollable characteristic. When students attribute their successes to ability, they are more willing to persevere with a task until it is mastered. Likewise, if they believe that they are having difficulty with a learning task because they lack the ability necessary to complete the task, they are less likely to stay with the learning activity for any extended period and, as a result, may not spend as much time as they need to master the task.

Effort

Comments such as, "I tried really hard" or "I didn't have time to study last night, that's why I didn't do well on the test" indicate that the student is attributing success or failure to effort. Students see effort as something that changes from day to day and that is under their control. In other words, effort is seen as both changeable and controllable by the student. When students attribute the quality of their work to effort, they are more likely to persevere with a task and will spend as much time as is required to master the task.

Task Difficulty

The difficulty of learning tasks is often seen as consistent and outside of the control of the student. Comments such as, "Mr. Smith always gives hard tests," "You never know what Miss Jones really wants," or "History 101 has lots of easy assignments" indicate that the student is attributing success or failure to the difficulty of the task. When students believe a task is too difficult, they are less likely to spend the time needed to learn. Student perseverance also is affected negatively when students believe that a task is too easy. In such cases, the students fail to devote the time that is necessary to master the task and hence do not perform as well as they could and should.

Luck

Luck is seen as external to the student, relatively unstable, and totally uncontrollable. Comments such as, "I was lucky, I studied just the right chapters," "I lucked out and got Mrs. Curtain for chemistry," "It's just my luck that she always assigns homework on the night I have ball practice" indicate that the student is attributing the quality of his or her performance to luck. Because students see luck as outside of their control, such attribution will usually have little impact on their perseverance. However, over time, the attribution of "luck" will often change to that of ability or effort and this in turn will affect the student's level of perseverance. For instance, a student might change from saying, "I was lucky" to "It was easy for me because I'm really good at that stuff," or "I really worked hard to pass that test."

Attribution Change

Margaret Gredler (1992) has identified three major steps in changing a student's perception of causes (attributions) for their success or poor performance. First, the teacher must identify what the student believes caused his or her performance. Next the teacher should "identify and implement alternative behaviors that can serve as attributitional cues." This could be in the form of: (a) praising the students to demonstrate that they do have the ability to perform, (b) helping students analyze what they did that affected the quality of their performance, and (c) helping them come up with alternative strategies for approaching instructional tasks. Finally, the teacher should implement group activities that foster realistic goal-setting so the students understand that the tasks before them are well within their abilities to achieve.

When students believe that the quality of their academic performance is dependent upon the actions they take, rather than upon luck or ability, their level of perseverance is usually higher. Correspondingly, the longer students are willing to persevere with a task that they are capable of mastering, the more likely it is that they will master that task and will reach a higher level of academic achievement. Therefore, it behooves everyone who is interested in the educational welfare of the student to help the student understand that his or her actions have the most direct impact on how academically successful the student will become.

SUMMARY

Engagement rate, the first micro level of time in school, has been defined as the amount of time students spend actively involved with a learning task. There are a number of factors that affect the amount of time that is spent in active learning within the classroom. The complexity of the classroom setting—multidimensionality, simultaneity, immediacy, unpredictability, publicness, and history; the way in which the classroom is managed—discipline policy, organization, time spent in transitions, condoned interruptions in the school day, and control of student wait-time; the grouping of students—homogeneous, heterogeneous, multiage; and the characteristics of individual students, all play key roles in determining the engagement rate within a classroom. Additionally, as we shall see in the next two chapters, the level of student engagement is determined in great part by the nature of the instructional activity and the expectations of the teacher. Each of these factors can add to or distract from the portion of allocated time that is actually used for instruction.

REFERENCES

Beckerman, T. M., & Good, T. L. (1981). The classroom ratio of high—and low aptitude students and its effect on achievement. *American Educational Research Journal, 18*(3), 317–327.

Bloom, B. S. (1974). Time and learning. *American Psychologist, 29*(9), 682–688.

Burns, R. B. (1984). How time is used in elementary schools: The activity structure of the classroom. In Lorin W. Anderson (Ed.), *Time and School Learning: Theory, Research, and Practice.* NY: St. Martin's Press.

Carroll, J. B. (1963). A model of school learning. *Teachers College Record, 64*(8), 723–733.

Doyle, W. (1986). Classroom organization and management. In M. Wittrock (Ed.), *Handbook of Research on Teaching,* 3rd ed. (pp. 392–431). New York: Macmillan.

Everston, C. M. (1982). Differences in instructional activities in higher- and lower achieving junior high English and math classes. *The Elementary School Journal, 83*(4), 329–350.

Everston, C., Sanford, J., & Emmer, E. (1981). Effects of class heterogeneity in junior high school. *American Educational Research Journal, 18*(2), 219–232.

First, J., & Gray, R. (1991). *The common school.* Boston: National Coalition of Advocates for Students.

Fisher, C., et al. (1978, June). *Teaching behaviors, academic learning time and student achievement: Final report of phase III-B, beginning teacher evaluation study* (Technical Report V-1.) San Francisco, CA: Far West Laboratory for Educational Research and Development.

Frieze, H. (1976). Causal attributions and information seeking to explain success and failure. *Journal of Research in Personality, 10,* 293–305.

Gettinger, M. (1984). Individual differences in time needed for learning: A review of the literature. *Educational Psychologist, 19*(1), 15–29.

Good, T. L., & Brophy, J. E. (1991). *Looking into classrooms,* 5th ed. New York: Harper & Row.

Gredler, M. (1992). *Learning and instruction: Theory into practice.* New York: Macmillan Publishing Company.

Gump, P. V. (1967). *The classroom behavior setting: Its nature and relation to student behavior* (final Report). Washington, DC: U.S. Office of Education, Bureau of Research. (ERIC Document Reproduction Service No. ED 015 515).

Jackson, P. (1968). *Life in the classroom.* New York: Holt, Rinehart, & Winston.

Karweit, N. (1988, February). Time-on-task: The second time around. *NASSP Bulletin,* 31–39.

MacDonald, R. (1991). *A handbook of basic skills and strategies for beginning teachers: Facing the challenge of teaching in today's schools.* New York: Longman.

Rosenshine, B. (1980). How time is spent in elementary classrooms. In C. Denham & A. Lieberman (Eds.), *Time to Learn.* Washington, DC: National Institute of Education.

Rossmiller, R. A. (1983, October). Time-on-task: A look at what erodes time for instruction. *NASSP Bulletin,* 45–49.

Seifert, E. H., & Beck, J. J. (1984). Time-on-task observations: How principals can improve instruction. *NASSP Bulletin, 68*(47), 29–34.

Sieber, R. T. (1979). Classmates as workmates: Informal peer activity in the elementary school. *Anthropology and Educational Quarterly, 10,* 207–235.

Weiner, B. (1974). An attributional interpretation of expectancy-value theory. In B. Weiner (Ed.), *Cognitive views of human motivation* (pp. 51–69). New York: Academic Press.

▶ 9

Time and the Instructional Task

Common sense tells us that the more time students spend in learning, the more they learn. This commonsense notion is one of the most consistent findings in educational research today (Walberg, Niemiec, & Frederick, 1994, Borg & Gall, 1983). Research has shown that time spent learning (engaged rate) and opportunity to learn (scheduled and allocated time) are essential to academic achievement. If, however, students spend time working on tasks that are irrelevant or only slightly relevant to what they are attempting to learn, the amount of time they need to learn will be greater and their academic achievement will be less than when they spend time on relevant tasks. Task relevancy, however, is dependent upon a number of interacting factors, such as the level of learning desired, the learning characteristics and developmental level of the student, and the subject matter skills and knowledge to be learned.

DEFINITION OF AN INSTRUCTIONAL TASK

In the early studies on time and learning, "task" was defined very broadly to mean any activity that led to learning. As a result of Bloom's work on mastery learning, task became more narrowly defined. Under this model, tasks were considered to be procedural behaviors that were hierarchical in nature. Each task built upon the preceding task and was considered "mastered" when a very specific behavior was observed. In the academic learning time model (ALT), "task" was once again defined in a broad sense. The ALT model defined "task" as a learning activity that the teacher prescribed. In today's educational literature, the term "task" is used rather inconsistently. For some writers the term still conveys Bloom's narrow definition. For others, the terms "task" and "activity" are interchangeable. Regardless of which definition is used, the term "task" embodies the concept of a learning goal. The difference between the two definitions rests in how the instructional plan is operationalized—through small, well-defined, and sequenced steps that are hierarchical in nature or through a series of activities that are more fluid and allow for a more personalized approach to instruction. In other words, tasks are composed of an instructional activity, or series of activities, used by the teacher to help students interact with the subject matter so that they will meet a specific learning goal. Therefore, for the purpose of this chapter, a learning task is defined as "a learning activity that serves the purpose of bringing the student into contact with the subject matter both in terms of content and procedural techniques." This definition is in line with both Carroll's and the ALT definition and, although not as narrowly defined as the mastery learning definition, is not incompatible with either model.

IMPORTANCE OF THE INSTRUCTIONAL TASK

The strength of the relationship between time spent learning and the amount learned is greatly influenced by the nature of the instructional task. Through the process of accomplishing a task, a student acquires information or knowledge about the subject content embodied in the task. The knowledge base may include facts, concepts, rules, principles, procedures, and/or recurring problem-solving techniques. A task also allows the student to practice operations and techniques that are demanded by the task. The student may be required to memorize facts, classify items according to their attributes, develop information from the data provided, analyze the data in order to draw conclusions, evaluate the information provided, and/or create new solutions to the problem.

The nature of the instructional task is important because, according to Walter Doyle:

- Students' academic work in schools is defined by the academic tasks that are embedded in the content they encounter on a daily basis. Tasks regulate the selection of information and the choice of strategies for processing that information.
- Students will learn what a task leads them to do, that is, they will acquire information and operations that are necessary to accomplish the tasks they encounter (Doyle 1983, p. 162).

If students' work in school can be defined by the tasks that they encounter, the changing of a task can, and will, alter the learning experience. For instance, if a student is required to listen to a selection of classical music as part of a music appreciation class, the affective experience and consequent learning outcome will be different than if the student is required to listen to "rap music". This is true even if the instructional goal—"to develop an appreciation of how emotions can be expressed through music"—is the same for both experiences. This does not mean that one approach is better than the other or that one experience would lead to more success with the instructional goal. It does mean that the learning experiences are different and the learning outcomes are likely to be at least slightly different. Teachers must be astute enough to understand this subtle difference if they are to provide sound and relevant learning tasks for their students.

TASK RELEVANCE

The relationship between both the amount of time a student will need to learn and the amount of time a student is willing to spend in learning is directly proportional to the relevance of the instructional task. A task is relevant if it relates to (1) the subject matter or material to be learned, (2) the type of learning outcome desired, *and* (3) the specific learning needs of the student. All three elements must be present if a task is to be considered relevant.

Material to Be Learned

A task is relevant to the degree to which it relates to the subject matter to be learned. This means that if a student is supposed to be learning basic addition facts, the task assigned to the student should relate to basic addition facts. As simple as this may sound, it is not always easy to evaluate. For instance, if the students within a first-grade class were given a worksheet and provided with the following directions, "Color all the words with the long 'a' sound green and all the words with short 'a' sound red," would they be developing their coloring skills or their ability to distinguish between the long and short 'a' sounds? What if students in a high-school technology education class were given the task of building a bookcase following a set of plans provided by the instructor. What are the students to learn—how to follow a technical plan or how to build a bookcase? The answer to these questions may be that the students are learning both skills. However, the answer may also be that they are learning one of the two, or neither of the skills. The answers to the questions will depend upon the learning level of the students and their prior knowledge with the content. It may also depend upon how much time they spend on each aspect of the task. For instance, if first graders spend more time coloring than sounding out words, then more learning time is devoted to art than to phonics. The same is true for the student building the bookcase. If the student spends more time reading the plans than building the case, then the emphasis for that student may well be on reading rather than on developing the psychomotor skills needed to build the bookcase. What is learned from the task is also dependent upon how adept the student is at developing shortcuts for accomplishing the task. The first grader may figure out rather quickly that the flower is red and the stem green and therefore be able to complete the task without sounding out any words. The high schooler, through trial and error, may be able to build the bookcase without referring to the plans and thereby totally bypass the need for reading the plans.

Many times we find that students are assigned instructional tasks that only indirectly relate to desired learning outcome. Consider the following example.

> Jim Flowers is a first-year history teacher at Rosemont High. The district has a policy that at the end of the first year each new teacher must be evaluated by both the building principal and the director of elementary or secondary education. Mr. Flowers received his evaluation from the principal early in May. The evaluation was very good and Jim received exceptionally high marks in instructional effectiveness. The written evaluation stated that his students were motivated by the instructional activities he developed and there was a high level of student engagement in his classes. In discussing the evaluation with Jim, the principal shared some of the feedback he had received from the parents of Mr. Flowers' students. "Jim, I have to tell you these are some of the most glowing reports I have ever received on a first-year teacher. The parents are thrilled with your homework assignments, they say the kids come home and discuss what happens in your class, which is rare at this age, and even Mr. Marks says his son Clay is more enthused about school than he has been since second grade. But I'll tell you what impresses me most. I see the students leaving your class discussing the content of your lessons. Just the other day, I heard Jack and Bill talking about how they would feel if they, as seniors, were facing the draft and how it might have been different in 1945 than it is today. This is exciting stuff. I am really pleased with your performance. Keep up the good work."

> Two weeks later Jim is scheduled for his meeting with Dr. Bookman, the director of secondary education. Jim was looking forward to this meeting, especially after the glowing evaluation he had received

from Mr. Marks. Imagine his surprise when Dr. Bookman begins by saying, "Jim, I have some grave concerns about your teaching. I have just gone over the achievement scores for your students on the state's basic skills test. Your students did very poorly, the worst that I have seen in many years. They don't know dates, they don't know the names of those who played major roles in historical events, they don't know where things happened. Timelines escape them. What have you been doing in your classes? Why don't your students know even the most basic historical facts?"

Jim was left speechless. He simply didn't know what to say, so he sat there and shook his head. Finally, Dr. Bookman said, "Tell me about the unit you taught on the events leading up to World War II. What did you do on Monday, Tuesday, and so on." And so Jim went through the week, day by day.

Monday: On Monday we began our unit on World War II. I showed a documentary film that discussed the events leading up to the War.

Tuesday: Because there wasn't enough time on Monday, we spent the class period discussing the film. I listed the key events on the board and the students provided examples from the film and then we discussed each of the events and their relationship to one another. At the end of the period, the students were told to read Chapter 7,—"Factors Contributing to World War II," and to be ready to discuss it the next day.

Wednesday: We spent Wednesday discussing the chapter, focusing on economic, political, and social issues that were prevalent just prior to World War II.

Thursday: I had three guest speakers share their experiences about World War II. One of the speakers was a soldier stationed at Pearl Harbor, another was a woman who had worked in one of the ammunition factories, and the third one was a woman who had been married two weeks before her husband was sent overseas, where he was killed by enemy fire.

After the speakers had concluded, I had the students divide into groups to discuss how they might feel if the year were 1945 and they were high-school seniors. Just before they broke into groups I reminded them to think about the political and economic climate at the time.

The group discussions were very lively and everyone lost track of time. Before we knew it, the bell rang dismissing class and so there was no time to share the small group discussions. As the students prepared to leave, I did have time to remind them that they would have a quiz the next day.

Friday: On Friday I gave the students this quiz.

Dr. Bookman took one look at the quiz and began to nod. "Having students share their opinions with one another and to think about how they would have reacted in a historical setting is a good instructional method, especially when you are trying to get them to think critically. The problem, however, is that you never ask them how their opinions and analyses build upon the historical facts. The students spent the entire class period on Thursday focusing on the social, political, and economic issues leading to World War II. This was 25 percent of their instructional time, yet they were never evaluated on the impact of this activity on their understanding of history. This would have been an excellent activity if you had taken it a little further and helped the students to understand that everyone has opinions, but an educated person, especially a historian, builds his or her opinion on data and facts rather than on limited personal experiences. Using this as a springboard, you could then help the students understand how data and facts are derived, why it is important to understand the relationship between key events and the timing of those events, and how individual decisions combine to make history. However, all of the questions on your quiz evaluate how effective your students are at memorizing facts and none have to do with evaluating their ability to critically think about the events."

Jim and Dr. Bookman went back to look at the achievement test results and to analyze how the activities that had so excited and engaged Jim's students could be improved to help the students learn the elements of history that the educational community deemed important.

The question that should come to mind at this point is, "But isn't it true that the students were learning even if they were not being evaluated?" The logical answer is, "of course." However, we must go one step further and ask, "Were the students using the classroom time to help them meet the instructional objective that would eventually be used to measure their academic achievement?" If, for instance, one group of Mr. Flower's students used the class time on Thursday to discuss teenage issues of today and never related those issues to the conditions prevalent in 1945, then, for those students, the task wasn't relevant. Even though the students were engaged in the learning activity, it could be expected that they would need more time to achieve the objective than would other students who were discussing the issues relative to the historical time period.

This example serves to demonstrate that even when students are actively engaged with a learning task that is at the appropriate level, if the task is not specific to the material to be learned, the relationship between time spent and academic achievement will be weakened.

Types of Learning

Just as important as matching the task to the subject matter to be learned is matching the task to the type and level of learning outcome that is sought. Educators have long attempted to classify the different types and levels of learning. It is now widely accepted within the educational community that there are a minimum of three domains of learning—cognitive, psychomotor, and affective. Each of these domains has been further subdivided into levels of learning called taxonomies. Perhaps the best known and widely accepted of all learning taxonomies is Bloom's Taxonomy of Cognitive Learning. In his taxonomy, Bloom identified six distinct levels of cognitive learning—knowledge, comprehension, application, analysis, synthesis, and evaluation.

Taxonomies have also been developed for both the psychomotor and affective domains of learning. For instance, Heinich, Molenda, and Russell (1993) have also developed a taxonomy of psychomotor learning in which they divide the domain into four levels—imitation, manipulation, precision, and articulation, and Krathwohl and his colleagues developed a taxonomy of affective learning that contains five levels—receiving, responding, valuing, organizing, and characterizing.

Cognitive Learning

At the first level of cognitive learning, the knowledge level, students are able to recall specific information or experiences that they have learned. This type of learning is most commonly measured by having students identify key concepts, list components, or restate the information that has been presented.

Instructional tasks at the knowledge level call for a large amount of time to be spent on drill and practice. Students repeat, verbatim, the information that is presented. Preschool children who are heard singing the alphabet song, students who work with flash cards (be they multiplication or the periodic table), and students who listen to language tapes and repeat the information over and over are all working at the knowledge level. It is important that an adequate amount of instructional time be devoted to "learning the facts" over and over so that they become automatic. This is true whether you are working at the early elementary level or at a highly technical level. This is so important because more instant recognition of the basic facts and components are necessary for more complex information processing. Therefore, it is essential that enough instructional time be devoted to drill and practice so that basic skills become automatic.

It is important to remember, however, that knowledge is the lowest level of the cognitive skills as defined by Bloom. In a "real world" setting, it is not uncommon to see individuals demonstrate their knowledge by quoting others or referring to information that was in the newspaper or on TV. A person may be very good at communicating his or her knowledge but not understand the significance of the information he or she is relaying. For instance, young children will often repeat something they have heard on TV or rephrase an adult conversation that they have overheard. They mimic the adult and use the same word patterns, intonations, and colloquialisms. When they do this frequently enough, they come across as exceptionally bright. Many such children, however, do poorly in school, much to everyone's surprise and dismay. This occurs because these children are cognitive foolers, that is, they appear to be very enlightened when they are actually operating at the lowest level of learning—the knowledge level.

The second level of cognitive learning is comprehension. At this level the information that has been learned now makes sense to the students. Rather than just repeating the information, the students are asked to explain what the information means or to translate it into his or her own words. The "cognitive foolers" will have difficulty with such tasks, and when asked to explain a statement that they or others have made will repeat what was said, changing only a few words from those of the original statement. It is not just the cognitive fooler who experiences problems at this level. College students are often frustrated when they are asked to define a term without using the term in the definition. For instance, many students find it difficult to define the term "educational technology" without using "technology" in their definitions. Once they understand that technology is the systematic application of knowledge for practical ends and that it usually involves the use of tools, they are able to define it much more easily.

At the comprehension level, instructional time should be devoted to having students restate what they have learned and then to expand on the information by using their prior knowledge. Teachers can encourage learning at this level by asking open-ended questions. However, they must understand that students must be given time to formulate their answers, and if given enough time they will often improve upon their own definitions and come to a higher level of comprehension.

The third level of learning is application. At this level, the students are able to use their knowledge in a specific manner and can generalize from one application to another. Instructional tasks that require the students to demonstrate a skill or operate a piece of machinery are examples of learning at the application level. Achievement at this level means that the student can *demonstrate* how to do something as well as *explain* how to do it. At this level students are often following procedures in order to accomplish a given goal and will need to be given time to proceed through a series of trials and errors as they refine their own learning.

Instructional tasks that are at the analysis level require the student to separate the whole into its component parts. For instance, if students were asked to identify discipline problems that are occurring within the school and then to classify the problems by severity, frequency, and/or underlying cause of the problem they would be working at the analysis level because identifying, classifying, and organizing are all part of the analysis process.

When students are able to combine elements to come up with a new approach, they have learned to synthesize information and make use of their knowledge. In the discipline example just given, once the students have analyzed the information, they might be asked to develop a new school-wide discipline policy that would address the issues that they have just identified. In doing so, they would be working at the synthesis level.

Evaluation is the highest level of learning, according to Bloom. At this level the students learn to assess, judge, rate, measure and compare items based on some criterion that is either pre-established or that the students themselves develop. Rather than simply stating an opinion, the learner draws conclusions based on fact, evaluates why other solutions may or may not work, and provides a rationale for selecting one approach over another. In our discipline example, the students might be asked to develop a list of criteria for judging the policies that had been developed and then to use these criteria to evaluate their own work as well as the work of others.

When students are working at the lower learning level (i.e., knowledge, comprehension, and application), engagement rate is fairly easy to measure simply because one can observe a student practicing a task or applying a set of rules to a procedure. When students are working at the higher levels of learning, engagement rate becomes more difficult to measure, because much of the learning occurs at the cognitive level and students may appear, for instance, to be daydreaming when they are actually deep in thought.

Higher-level learning (analysis, synthesis, and evaluation) tends to be more dependent upon the student's style of learning. Some students may approach the task by drawing diagrams, others may choose to verbalize the key elements, and still others may reduce the problem to a formula or to written descriptions. In order to develop these skills, students normally need to spend more time working independently and/or in small groups. As a result, the teacher becomes more of a coach or mentor than a "dispenser of knowledge." In addition, the requirements for classroom management change (see Chapter 8), and if these changes are not implemented properly there is a real danger that the amount of academic time available in the classroom will be decreased because of increases in transitions, wait-time, and the number of discipline problems that are likely to arise.

The Psychomotor Domain

Heinich, Molenda, and Russell (1993) have identified four categories of psychomotor skills—imitation, manipulation, precision, and articulation. At the imitation level, the student mimics behavior that has been modeled. The model could be a teacher, a video, or even a printed model similar to those that physical therapists provide to their patients. At the manipulation level, students perform a skill independently, usually following a period of practice. When a student reaches the precision level it means that he or she is able to perform a skill with accuracy, and when students reach articulation they are able to perform a skill automatically without giving it much, if any, thought.

By way of example, consider the skill of driving a car. In the early stages of learning to drive a car, the instructor informs the student of each step he or she is to perform—"turn on the key," "lightly press the gas pedal," "turn on the turn signal," "apply the brake," and so on. After some practice, the student is allowed to drive the car with few directions from the instructor even though the instructor is still in the car with the student. Once the student has "learned to drive" and "proves it" by passing a driving test, he or she is allowed to drive by alone. Although the student may be nervous about driving without the instructor, he or she has learned to drive with enough precision to be considered competent to drive alone. At some point driving becomes "automatic" and at this point the driver has reached the articulation level of psychomotor skills.

The psychomotor taxonomy applies to the learning of any skill that involves a combination of motor and cognitive skills. It can be applied equally well to athletic feats, artistic endeavors, and word processing. When learning psychomotor skills, students must be given enough time to practice the skill, be given feedback on how well they are performing the skill, and then be given more time to master the skill.

Affective Domain

In the Taxonomy of Affective Learning developed by Krathwohl and his colleagues (1964), there are five levels of affective learning—receiving, responding, valuing, organizing, and characterizing. At the receiving level, the student listens to what is being said but does not respond. This is the student who "seems to hear but never reacts." At the next level, the student begins to respond or react to an event. This response may be either a positive or negative. The student listens and then reacts by making a face and refusing to do what is asked, or listens to the request and then does it. At the third level of affective learning, the student accepts or rejects ideas, concepts, and points of view. This is a higher level than simply responding because the student will, at this level, begin to "take a stand" or support or reject an idea, concept, or point of view based on his or her individual value system. Individuals have a number of different value systems. For instance, a student may value the opinion of his or her peers and at the same time respect the rules that have been established by his or her parents. As students begin to grow, it is not unusual for their value systems to occasionally come into conflict with one another. When students are able to determine which system holds the greater value for them and then react in a manner consistent with their determination, they have reached the organizing level of affective learning. In other words, the student is able to prioritize his or her values and react accordingly. "Organizing" is a higher level of affective behavior than "valuing" because the student is placed in a forced-choice position and has to make a conscious decision on how to react rather than simply reacting. At the highest level of affective learning, the value system becomes incorporated as part of the individual's personality or character. For instance, when given a choice, Connie prefers to go to an art gallery rather than to a football game. This behavior is so consistent that her friends no longer ask her to go to football games with them.

Affective learning incorporates the development of interests, attitudes and values. There is some argument as to how much emphasis the schools should place on affective education, especially at the valuing, organizing, and characterization levels. Issues dealing with the teaching of tolerance, values education, and character development become more complex as the learners within our schools become more diverse. Should time be allocated to affective learning, especially if such learning is considered non-academic? The reality is that we teach students and students have personalities, characteristics, and traits that influence their interests, attitudes, and values. The interest, attitudes, and values of the student help to determine, at least in part, their willingness to persevere, which in turn affects the amount of time they spend learning, which ultimately affects their level of academic achievement. Whether we teach the affective skills overtly through specific courses or covertly through the type of feedback we provide our students, the reality remains that we do teach within the affective domain every day that a child is in school, and the learning that occurs stays with the student as the child develops into adolescence and the adolescent develops into an adult.

Furthermore, some would argue, one of the primary purposes of public education is to transmit the societal values and cultural norms that are basic to the American way of life. They believe that by not devoting at least part of the instructional day to tasks that aid in this development, the schools are abdicating one of their basic responsibilities.

Still others would argue that there is more to being an educated person than simply being able to process information or to think at a critical level. They believe that the educated person is well-rounded, enjoys the aesthetic as well as the intellectual, accepts responsibility for his or her own actions, and behaves in an ethical and moral manner. When students are assigned tasks that are applicable only to academic learning, affective learning becomes incidental, unstructured, and left to chance. Many believe that, as a society, we cannot afford to let this happen, therefore, each teacher should assign at least some portion of the instructional tasks to those that fit within the affective domain.

Multiple Intelligences

The majority of the learning taxonomies grew out of behavioral research that defines learning as a change in the student's ability to perform. Cognitive psychologists, however, believe that learning results in more than a change in behavior—it also includes a change in the way a student "thinks." For instance, Howard Gardner, a cognitive psychologist, believes that there are at least seven different types of intelligences, or ways of thinking. The seven intelligences identified by Gardner are logical-mathematical, linguistic, musical, spatial, bodily-kinesthetic, interpersonal, and intrapersonal (see Table 9–1).

According to Gardner, "individuals may differ in the particular intelligence profiles with which they are born and that they certainly differ in the profiles they end up with" (Gardner, 1993, p. 9). He goes on to say that the purpose of school should be to develop the intelligences. Many educators agree with Gardner and they believe that, "intelligence should be viewed as a complex process that can be divided into subcomponents to be trained and improved in school" (Eggen and Kauchak, 1994, p. 4). If this is true, students need to be provided with opportunities to develop each of the intelligences—they need to be given tasks and activities that require them to use their multiple intelligences to complete the job.

TABLE 9–1   Gardner's Seven Intelligences

Intelligence	Core components
Logico-mathematical	Logical or numeric patterns, long chains of reasoning
Linguistic	Sounds, rhythms, meanings of words, different functions of language
Musical	Rhythms, pitch, timbre, forms of musical expression
Spatial	Visual-spatial relationships; transform perceptions
Bodily-kinesthetic	Control of body movements; object manipulation
Interpersonal	Moods, temperament, motivation, desires of others
Intrapersonal	Own feelings, strengths, weaknesses, desires, intelligences

Source: Adapted from Gardner, H. & Hatch, T. (1989). Multiple intelligences go to school: Educational implications of the Theory of Multiple Intelligences. *Educational Research, 18*(8), 4–10.

Level of Learning and Task Relevance

Whether taking a behavioral perspective, cognitive perspective, or eclectic perspective, the rule still holds—students will have a better chance of learning if they are given relevant tasks and the time needed to complete those tasks. What students learn, or what capabilities they acquire, will depend upon the domain(s), and at the level(s) within the domain(s), in which they are operating. It will also depend upon which of the seven intelligences are being employed, so when we say that academic learning time is dependent upon the relevance of the task, we must acknowledge that relevance goes beyond the subject matter content to incorporate the level and types of learning desired.

Instructional and Learner Needs

Task relevance also means that the task is appropriate for meeting the needs of the students. Students' needs are based on their individual characteristics such as perception, intelligence, temperament, motivation, biological equipment, rate of maturing, and social/cultural background. As we saw in the previous chapter, the characteristics of a student affect that student's level of perseverance (time student is willing to spend learning), which then has an impact on his or her level of learning. The amount of time that a student needs to meet a specific instructional goal is also affected by the student's ability and aptitude. Students will require less time if the instructional task is appropriate for their level of development, is consistent with their preferred learning style, and is motivating for them.

Developmental Level

Jean Piaget identified four main stages in cognitive development—sensori-motor (0–2 years), preoperational (2–7 years), concrete operational (7–11 years), and formal operational (11–15+). The stages are sequential, and each stage builds upon the one(s) that preceded it. The age ranges for the four stages, however, are normative rather than fixed—meaning that they represent an average age for development rather than an absolute age.

The school curriculum typically follows a developmental pattern similar to that outlined by Piaget and his colleagues. Doyle (1983) has noted that:

> As students progress through the grades, the emphasis gradually shifts from basic skills to the content and the methods of inquiry embodied in academic disciplines. Older students are expected to learn algebra, history, biology, and literature, rather than simply practice reading and computational skills. Also, in the middle school or junior high school years, students begin to develop the capacity for formal

operational thought, that is, the ability to think abstractly and use general strategies to analyze and solve problems (1983, p. 160).

If a student has not reached the level of development required by the curriculum or the instructional task, the student will be unable to successfully complete the task. For instance, high school freshmen who take Algebra I even though they have not reached the level of formal operational thought will have an extremely difficult, if not impossible, time mastering the concepts presented in the course. In other words, the learning expectations and requisite tasks would not be appropriate, or relevant, for these students because they have not reached the formal operational stage of cognitive thinking required by the task. For the task to be relevant, it must reflect the student's current developmental level. If it does not, the student will fall further and further behind and the time spent on the task will have been wasted.

The rate of development is dependent upon four main factors—maturation, equilibration, experience, and social interaction. Maturation means the act of maturing or developing over time. A junior high student who is interested in basketball may be able to explain how to "slam-dunk" a basketball but may be unable to do so because of his short stature. As his physical characteristics change and he grows, or matures physically, he may be able to complete a "slam-dunk," but right now he is simply too small. Just as the physical characteristics of children change over time, so do their cognitive structures. Schemata, or cognitive structures, adapt and change as children develop mentally, and this changing of the schemata is referred to as maturation in cognitive development.

Maturation in and of itself does not explain an individual's performance or lack of performance. There is no guarantee, for instance, that even if the junior high student grows to a height that would permit him to complete a slam dunk, that he would actually be able to do so. Other factors will come into play. Was the student able to interact with others who had perfected the shot? Was the child permitted to practice on a "real" basketball court using a regulation size ball? While he was practicing, was he able to determine what he was doing right and what he was doing wrong and make corrections as he went along? And just as there is no guarantee that the child, even though he matures physically, will be able to slam-dunk the ball, there is no guarantee that a student who is mentally developed will be able to do any and all tasks at the formal operational level. Which mental skills develop and the level to which they develop are greatly influenced by the other three factors mentioned earlier—equilibration, social interactions, and experience.

As a student encounters new information he or she will attempt to place the new information into his or her existing cognitive structure. If the process is successful, we say the student has assimilated the new information. If, however, the information cannot be integrated easily into an existing schema, the student will experience disequilibration and must create a new schema or modify an old one. In doing so, the student is accommodating the new information and achieves equilibration. The student strives for equilibration. The imbalance between equilibration and disequilibration is how Piaget defined motivation. If the student is unable to resolve the conflict between whether to accommodate or to assimilate, he or she will quickly reach a level of frustration. This is important, because when students are frustrated, this frustration tends to have a negative impact on their levels of perseverance, which in turn has a negative impact on their academic achievement.

Social interactions and experiences, the last two factors affecting cognitive development, are closely related. Social interactions relate to the social environment (e.g., culture and language) to which the child is exposed. Experience is defined as "the process or fact of personally observing, encountering, or undergoing something" (*Random House College Dictionary*). Because of limited social interactions and experiences within their environments, lower-socioeconomic students are frequently considered at-risk academically. The lack of social interactions and experiences represses the cognitive development process and causes many children to enter the formal education process already academically behind other students of the same age. If left untreated, some children may be expected to do tasks that are above their ability. In worst-case scenarios, these children may be labeled "slow," learning disabled, or below average or they may consistently be placed in learning environments that guarantee they will "always be behind." If the condition is recognized, steps can be taken to overcome the deficiencies and the students' rates of development may increase rapidly.

Personal experiences and social interactions can also help to explain why students who enter public school from a preschool environment are often considered advanced—the preschool environment provided them with learning experiences and social interactions that are different from those frequently found in the home. This can help to solve the mystery of why some children do very well in the beginning of their school career but then fail to live up to their "advance billing." The longer they are in school, the more their experiences and social interactions resemble those of the other students. This is especially true when placed in a classroom in which little is done to adjust for individual differences among children.

Repressed or advanced development does not explain all cases where children are considered "below average" or "learning disabled," but the developmental characteristics of the children will often provide the teacher with valuable insight into learning problems and their causes. A school curriculum or set of learning tasks that assumes that all children of the same age or in the same class are at the same level of development will almost certainly result in some children "breezing" through the content, some students struggling with the content, and some never mastering the concepts and skills necessary to reach the desired level of academic achievement. It also means that some children will have "time to waste" during the instructional day, some students will be given the time they need in order to learn, and still others will never have as much time as they need. As a consequence, the impact on total student achievement will be less than desirable.

A word of caution is necessary here. The value in understanding the cognitive development process is that it can aid in the diagnosis of learning problems. If students are being asked to perform tasks that are beyond their mental capabilities, they are doomed for failure. This does not mean that if we wait long enough they will develop the ability to perform the task. For instance, some individuals may never reach the highest level of cognitive development that is required by many high-school advanced placement courses (Gredler, 1992). It does mean that when prescribing relevant learning tasks, the teacher must take into consideration the developmental level of the student.

Learning Styles

"Learning styles" has been defined as the way students prefer to learn. "Learning styles" has also been defined as the way in which students learn best. The difference here is subtle, but important. When speaking of a student's preferences, the emphasis is on which instructional techniques the student favors. When defining learning style as the best method of learning, we are speaking of which methods are most effective in causing learning to occur. A student may prefer to learn in one way but actually learn best when a different type of intervention is used. For instance, a student may prefer to write a term paper, but actually learn best when studying for a test. Regardless of whether the term learning styles is being used to refer to "preferred" or "best" method, it is evident that learners do approach the task of learning from a variety of perspectives, or styles, and that these styles are affected by how the individual perceives and processes information.

Early learning style theories focused on differences in information processing and particularly on the effects of different types of perceptual stimuli (visual, auditory, and kinesthetic) on student learning. Today, the definition of learning style has extended to include at least 21 different variables that fall into five broad categories of stimuli—environmental, emotional, sociological, physiological, and psychological (Dunn & Dunn, 1993).

Environmental factors such as noise, amount of light, and room temperature affect students to varying degrees. At one time it was thought that students learned best in quiet environments. We now know that some students actually learn best when they have music playing in the background. We also know that some students work best when surrounded by bright light while others work best when the light is focused only on their work space. Some students are able to concentrate better if they sit in a straight-backed chair at a desk, but others can learn equally as well stretched out on the floor or reclining in an easy chair. And although most students will adjust to a temperature range of 70 to 74 degrees, some students work best when the temperature is slightly higher and some work best when it is slightly lower.

Emotional factors that affect the amount of time a student will need to master a task include the student's level of motivation and how persistent the student is when it comes to completing the task. Also included under the category of emotional stimuli is student responsibility. Responsibility for learning is included as an emotional factor because some students learn best (are most motivated and tend to persist longer) when they are required to take responsibility for their own learning. Other students learn best when someone is there to guide them through each element within the task and tend to focus on the learning task longer under such supervision.

Sociological style refers to with whether a student learns best when working independently or when working with others. Some students learn best when they are allowed to work by themselves and become distracted when they are forced to work with other students. The end result is that the amount of time they spend engaged in learning is decreased because of the distraction. There are other students, however, who spend more time engaged in learning when working with others. But even for students who prefer to work with others, the sociological preference may vary from working in a one-on-one situation, in a team environment, in pairs, or even in large-group environments.. For instance, some students who learn best when working with their peers are uncomfortable when working directly with an adult (even the teacher) and hence find it difficult to concentrate on the task at hand.

In numerous studies conducted in schools throughout the United States researchers found that students "achieved more, behaved better, and liked learning better when they were permitted to learn through their sociological preferences" (Dunn & Dunn, 1993, p. 15). The fact that students behaved better and liked learning more when allowed to work in their preferred sociological style strongly suggests that their engagement rate increased. This is important in terms of time and learning because, as we have seen, an increase in engagement rate often leads to an increase in achievement.

Physiological factors include perceptual preferences, time-of-day preferences, and preferred level of mobility. Research has demonstrated that students who succeed in school tend to be either auditory or visual learners while those who are less successful tend to be tactual or kinesthetic learners (learning by doing) (Dunn & Dunn, 1993). If a student has trouble remembering "what he or she heard," a learning task that is initiated through oral instruction may very well result in the student taking longer to complete the task. The same is true for a student who learns best kinesthetically (by doing) but is expected to learn by watching someone else perform. A student who learns best by listening may find it more difficult to learn if he or she is "forced" to take notes during a class discussion. Although students tend to be strong in one modality or another, most have learned to adapt to whatever format is presented. However, there has been some indication that when an instructional task fails to allow students to use their modality strengths it takes them longer to achieve the instructional objective.

Another physiological factor that can affect a student's performance is the time of day. This has only recently become an issue in the educational literature. Dunn and Dunn note that, "Time is one of the most crucial elements of learning style and demands attention—especially for underachievers (Gardiner, 1986; Gadwa & Griggs, 1985; Griggs & Dunn, 1988; Johnson, 1984; Thrasher, 1984), for whom learning at their energy high increases achievement" (Dunn & Dunn, 1992).

Mary Carskadon, a professor of psychiatry and human behavior at Brown University and Director of the sleep research laboratory at E. P. Bradley Hospital in Providence, Rhode Island, has found that sleep patterns change during adolescence, and this change is not merely a matter of choice but rather comes from what the researcher calls a "delayed phase preference." In an article in *Teacher Magazine* in which Millicent Lawton reported on the work of Carskadon, the author noted that Carskadon is convinced that the shift in sleep patterns "makes the transition from middle school to high school—where the day often begins an hour earlier—all the more troublesome. With their need for more sleep and their internal clocks increasingly set on a "go to sleep late, rise late" mode, adolescents are particularly hard hit by a 7:30 a.m. starting bell" (Lawton, 1995, p. 24). Carsksadon also noted that elementary schools often start an hour later than do high schools, but believes it would make sense to reverse the pattern and have elementary students start at 7:30 a.m. and the high school students start at 8:30 a.m. because such a schedule would more clearly match their biological states.

A third factor that Dunn and Dunn include under the physiological category is preferred level of modality. Some students prefer to sit quietly when they are concentrating, while other students may prefer to move about. The first group of students is analogous to adults who prefer to work complex problems sitting quietly at a desk or table. The second group of students is analogous to adults who prefer to pace when thinking about a complex problem. Forcing the student who is a "pacer," to sit at a desk for an extended period of time can affect that student's level of concentration, which in turn will affect the amount of time the student needs for learning. Teachers who are unaware of this aspect of the physiological learning style often have students stay in for recess because they "have been fidgeting all morning." Rather than staying in to finish their work, the students may need to recess because moving about helps to increase their levels of concentration.

Psychological learning style factors refer to the way the learner processes information. Often such processing is discussed under the topic of right-brain/

left-brain modality. When using this classification system, the right brain is considered to be more creative and to deal more with learning in the affective mode whereas "learning on the left side of the brain" tends to be more logical and structured. Schools have been accused of focusing on the left side to the detriment of developing right-side thinking because learning tasks in classrooms often call for students to respond to verbal instructions rather than to illustrated instructions, to read analytically rather than to synthesize information, to write rather than draw, to control their feelings rather than be free with their feelings, and to solve problems logically rather than intuitively. It may be that this is the case because the workplace in our society demands such skills. However, if students are to be successful with learning, they must be allowed to learn through tasks that stress their strengths rather than their weaknesses. When this is not the case, students will need more time to process the information, may exhibit a lower level of perseverance, and may experience a higher rate of error on the task. In other words, the amount of learning time needed will increase and it is likely that student achievement will decrease at the same time.

Learning Styles and Task Prescription

The previous discussion on learning styles is very cursory and only begins to touch on the complexity of the factors that define a student's learning style. As Dunn and Dunn have defined it:

> Learning style, then, is the way in which each learner begins to concentrate on, process, and retain new and difficult information. That interaction occurs differently for everyone. To identify a person's learning style pattern, it is necessary to examine each individual's multidimensional characteristics to determine what is most likely to trigger each student's concentration—maintain it—respond to his or her natural processing style—and cause long-term memory (Dunn & Dunn, 1992, p. 2).

For the classroom teacher with 25 to 30 students, each with their own learning style, the complexity of prescribing learning tasks that are relevant in terms of individual learning styles is overwhelming. Because of this complexity, it would be unreasonable to expect teachers, through the normal course of the teaching process, to assess all of the various elements of a student's learning style and then to develop lessons to meet this style. However, understanding the impact that a learning style has on a student's ability to learn under various conditions will go a long way toward helping teachers make more efficient use of classroom time. This is especially true when students appear to be having trouble learning material that should fall easily within their developmental level. In other words, understanding the various aspects of learning styles and their effects on individual learning can be important in diagnosing where a student may need help.

There are several other elements of learning style of which the teacher needs to be aware. First, the teacher should remember that the way students prefer to learn may not be the way they learn best. Students prefer tasks that call for them to operate in modes with which they are most comfortable. There are times, however, when they may learn better (may achieve more and retain the learning longer) if they are forced to operate in a style other than their preferred style. One reason for this is that it causes a high level of concentration to master the task. Placing students in such situations can be an effective strategy, but must be used with great caution and only used infrequently.

Although most students do have a preferred learning style, students who are considered average or above have learned to adopt a number of different styles. In other words, they have leaned a different style of learning. The weaker student may need to be "taught" how to learn using the various styles and even students who are average or above can often benefit from such instruction. In fact, it used to be common practice to teach students "how to study" or to teach them "study skills"—students were taught to use various types of learning styles. The trick in today's school is not to add to the curriculum by adding an additional course on study skills, but rather to integrate the improvement of study skills throughout all instruction. Often the teacher can do this by making certain that students are allowed to operate in their preferred learning style when learning new information or are building skills, especially if the skills are to be used in subsequent lessons. When students are learning to apply the skills and knowledge or are expected to transfer the skills and knowledge to new areas, they should be forced to occasionally operate in other modes or styles. The teacher, however, must help this to happen by pointing out sound techniques for learning in the various styles, focusing attention on key elements, demonstrating the process, and having students with different styles work together. Two excellent sources that can help the teacher design activities that will be compatible with the various learning styles are Rita and Kenneth Dunn's *Teaching Secondary Students Through Their Individual Learning Styles: Practical Approaches for Grades 7–12* (1993) and *Teaching Elementary Students Through Their Individual Learning Styles* (1992).

SUMMARY

The focus of this chapter has been on task relevance. Task relevance is one of the key elements that makes up academic learning time and separates time on-task from academic learning. Students may spend time working on a learning task assigned by the teacher and still fail to achieve at the expected level because the task is not relevant to (1) the subject matter or material to be learned, (2) the type of learning outcome desired, and/or (3) the specific learning needs of the student. If these three criteria are not met, the ratio between time spent and degree of achievement will be negatively affected, and merely adding more time to the instructional day, year, or class period will have little, if any, impact on this ratio.

At a rudimental level, it is rather easy to evaluate whether a task relates to the subject matter or material to be learned. If you walk into a math classroom and the students are all working on solving equations, the obvious conclusion is that they are working on tasks that are relevant in terms of the subject matter. However, if you walk into the same classroom and you see a student making a paper airplane, a large group of students completing the problems at the end of a chapter, and a smaller group of students discussing a track and field meet, you may be tempted to conclude that only one group of students is actually working on tasks related to the material to be learned—the group doing the problems at the end of the chapter. However, your conclusion may be inaccurate. The student who is making the paper airplane may actually be attempting to determine the effects of different angles on the flight pattern of the airplane and this may relate very closely to the content to be learned. The group discussing the track and field meet may also be working on a relevant task. The teacher may be using the track and field events as a way of showing students how algebraic formulas are created, so these students may also be working on a relevant task in terms of subject matter.

The second element that makes a task relevant is whether it relates to the desired learning outcome. Learning outcomes may be defined in terms of the taxonomies of learning (cognitive, psychomotor, or affective learning), in terms of the multiple intelligences (logical-mathematical, linguistic, musical, spatial, bodily-kinesthetic, interpersonal, or intrapersonal), or in terms of the benchmarks and standards that have been established by the various professional organizations and agencies. Task that are relevant in terms of content may not be relevant in terms of desired learning outcomes. For example, a group of students spends the majority of their arithmetic time on computations—problems that deal with the basic math facts or solving various types of mathematical equations. Their report cards show that, as a group, they do very well in math. However, they do very poorly on the state proficiency exam because the majority of the problems require skills in comprehension and application, rather than computation.

Another example comes from a composition class. The majority of the instructional time is spent on developing an outline that becomes the basis for the students' compositions. Among the tasks required of the students are the development of the outline, the production of a rough draft, revisions of the draft, and final composition. The students are evaluated on the quality (detail and cohesiveness) of the outline, on how well the composition matches the outline, and on the quality of the final composition, including punctuation and grammar. Within the unit, however, there were no activities or tasks that specifically addressed the use of proper punctuation or correct grammar. For this example, it would be easy to conclude that the teacher needs to incorporate punctuation and grammar into the unit if the students are to reach the desired outcome. This is not necessarily the case. It may be that the punctuation and grammar were covered in an earlier unit in which the students were taught basic rules and how to use punctuation and grammar guides available in the classroom, and the use of these guides has become part of the classroom routine.

The third factor that makes a task relevant is the degree to which the task relates to the specific learning needs of the student. The learning needs of a student are determined, at least in part, by the developmental level and the learning style of the student. Both learning styles and developmental levels can be affected by the experiences, social interactions, motivations, maturation, and intellectual profiles of the student. If, when assigning a task, the teacher fails to recognize the difference among students and how these differences alter the relevancy of the task, valuable instructional time will be lost, never to be regained. If students are assigned tasks and activities that are beyond their level of cognitive development, their degrees of success will be limited. In some cases, their success will be so limited as to be practically nonexistent. This is important to understand because success rate is one of the four components of academic learning time.

Learning styles, the way in which students learn best, can also impact both the amount of time that students need in order to learn and the degree of success that students will have in learning. Tasks and activities that call for students to operate outside of their preferred learning style will take more time than those that allow them to use the style with which they are most comfortable. This does not mean that students should never be asked to operate outside of their preferred learning style, but it should be understood that it will take them longer to complete the learning activity and there may be several false starts before they are actually able to complete the task effectively.

At this point, it may appear that the focus has shifted away from time and learning, but nothing could be further from the truth. The focus at this point is on the efficient use of student time. When students spend time on tasks and activities that are irrelevant (not directed toward a learning outcome, not related to the subject matter to be learned, or not directed toward their learning needs), they have given up the opportunity to use that time more efficiently. This does not mean that all classroom time should be so closely bound that each minute is spent on a task that has been narrowly defined. It does mean that if we are looking at time as either the solution or the source of the problem, we must explore the relationships between task relevancy, time spent, and learning outcomes.

REFERENCES

Bloom, B. S., Engelhard, M. D., Furst, E. J., Hill, W. H., & Krathwohl, D. R. (1956). *A taxonomy of educational objectives: Handbook I. The cognitive domain.* New York, McKay.

Borg, W. R., & Gall, M. D. (1983). *Educational research* (4th ed.) (pp. 5, 9). New York: Longman.

Carroll, J. B. (1963). A model of school learning. *Teachers College Record, 64*(8), 723–733.

DeHaan, R. F. (1963). *Accelerated learning programs.* Washington, DC: The Center for Applied Research in Education, Inc.

Doyle, W. (1983). Academic work. *Review of Educational Research, 53*(2), 159-199.

Dunn, R. & Dunn, K. (1992). *Teaching elementary students through their individual learning styles: Practical approaches for grades k-12.* Boston: Allyn and Bacon.

Dunn, R. & Dunn, K. (1993). *Teaching secondary students through their individual learning styles: Practical approaches for grades k-12.* Boston: Allyn and Bacon.

Eggen, P., & Kauchak, D. (1994). *Educational psychology: Classroom connection* (2nd ed.). New York: Macmillan College Publishing Company.

Gadwa, K., & Griggs, S. A. (1985). The school dropout: Implications for counselors. *The School Counselor, 33*, 9–17.

Gardiner, B. (1986). An experimental analysis of selected teaching strategies implemented at specific times of the school day and their effects on the social studies achievement test scores and attitudes of fourth grade, low achieving students in an urban school setting. *Dissertation Abstracts International, 47*, 3307A.

Gardner, H. (1993). Multiple intelligences: The theory in practice. New York: Basic Books.

Gardner, H. & Hatch, T. (1989). *Multiple intelligences go to school: Educational implications of the Theory of Multiple Intelligences. Educational Research, 18*(8), 4–10.

Gredler, M. (1992). *Learning and instruction: Theory into practice.* New York: Macmillan Publishing Company.

Griggs, S. A., & Dunn, R. (1988, September–October). High school dropouts: Doctoral dissertation, United States International University. *Dissertation Abstracts International, 45*, 2397A.

Heinich, R., Molenda, M., & Russell, J. (1993). *Instructional media and the new technologies of instruction.* New York: John Wiley & Sons.

Johnson, C. D. (1984). Identifying potential school dropouts: Doctoral dissertation, United States International University. *Dissertation Abstracts International, 45*, 2397A.

Krathwohl, D. R., Bloom, B. S., & Masia, B. B. (1964). *A taxonomy of educational objectives: Handbook II. The affective domain.* New York: McKay.

Lawton, M. (1995, November/December): Sleepy Heads: Does the high school day begin too early for many students? *Teacher Magazine*, 24–26.

Thrasher, R. (1984). *Analysis of the learning style preferences of at-risk sixth and ninth graders.* Pompano Beach: Florida Association of Alternative School Educators.

Walberg, H. J., Niemiec, R. P., & Frederick, W. C. (1994). Productive curriculum time. *Peabody Journal, 69*(3), 86–100.

▶ 10

Time and the Instructional Process

The quality of instruction that students receive will impact both their level of achievement and the amount of time they need to reach their learning goals. Carroll, in his Model of School Learning, defined quality of instruction in terms of the teacher's ability to deliver the instructional message in such a way that it would reduce the amount of time the students need to learn. This meant that the lesson was presented at the correct developmental level of the student, was presented in a manner that would assure that the student would attend to the message and persevere with the task, and that the lesson used language that was easily understood by the learner. The model made no attempt to define specific teaching processes but rather left room for individual teaching styles.

Bloom's Learning for Mastery model, on the other hand, is much more prescriptive. Quality instruction includes the defining of learning objectives that are broken into a sequential set of instructional tasks. The teacher, through a series of diagnostic procedures, determines which tasks are assigned to which students. How much time students spend on an instructional task will depend upon their levels of prior knowledge and the degree to which the task meets their instructional needs. Once a student has mastered one task he or she moves on to the next. The quality of instruction that a student receives relies heavily on accurately diagnosing the student's needs and on prescribing the right instructional treatment based on the task analysis.

The ALT model defined quality of instruction in terms of the teaching processes of diagnosis, prescription, presentation, monitoring, and feedback. According to this model of time and learning, quality of instruction is dependent upon how well the teacher is able to perfect the teaching processes of diagnosing student needs, prescribing instructional tasks that meet those needs, presenting the lessons, monitoring student behaviors, and providing feedback to the students on how well they are performing. The process was similar to that defined by Bloom, but relied less heavily on task analysis and much more heavily on the interaction of the teaching processes.

QUALITY OF INSTRUCTION: DIRECT VERSUS INDIRECT INSTRUCTION

A common criticism of the time and learning studies is that direct instruction is favored over indirect instruction in almost all of the models. Doyle (1983) provides us with a comparison of direct versus indirect approaches to teaching and instruction.

Direct Instruction
Direct instruction means that academic tasks are carefully structured for students, they are explicitly told how to accomplish these tasks, and they are systematically guided through a series of exercises leading to mastery. Opportunities for directed practice are frequent, as are assessments to determine how well students are progressing and whether corrective feedback is needed (pp. 173–174).

Indirect Instruction
Such instruction emphasizes the central role of self-discovery in fostering a sense of meaning and purpose for learning academic content. From this perspective, students must be given ample opportunities for direct experience with content in order to derive generalizations and invent algorithms on their own. Such opportunities are clearly structured on the basis of what is known about an academic discipline and about human information processing. However, the situations are only partially formed in advance. Gaps are left which students themselves must fill. In other words, the instructional program does only part of the work for students to open up opportunities for choice, decision-making, and discovery (pp. 176–177).

Many educators would argue that the problem with the direct approach to teaching (and hence with the time and learning studies) is that direct instruction leads to rote memorization and/or structured learning as opposed to critical thinking and/or creative learning. Certainly, this does tend to be the case. However, time and learning models do not preclude the use of indirect instruction or self-discovery learning. In fact, the models easily can be adapted to an indirect approach, but such an adaptation would be dependent upon the desired learning outcome and the students' prior levels of learning. Research on indirect instruction suggests that the effectiveness of such an approach is dependent upon the ability of the student and that the approach, in and of itself, does not guarantee that the students will become more critical, creative thinkers. Research has also shown that not all children can learn through indirect approaches and that "while increasing the opportunity for invention, indirect teaching also increases the chance for students to develop erroneous solution strategies and misconceptions of content" (Doyle, 1983, p. 177).

QUALITY OF INSTRUCTION: INDIVIDUALIZED VERSUS GROUP INSTRUCTION

Bloom's Learning for Mastery model builds upon the assumption that students vary in their rate of learning—it takes some students longer to master a learning task than it does other students. The implication is that, because learning is individualistic, instruction should be individualized, at least in terms of the pacing of the lesson. However, the implementation strategy for the learning for mastery model calls for individualized activities to be completed by the students on their own time (e.g., at recess or as part of their homework). Occasionally independent activities can be sprinkled in with whole-group or small-group instruction, but this is the exception rather than the rule. On the other hand, Keller's model of mastery learning was totally based on individualized instruction (hence the name Personalized System of Instruction). Under that model, the majority of instruction took the form of independent activities and group instruction was the exception rather than the rule.

ALT researchers found that when participating in whole group instruction, students experienced a higher rate of engagement than they did when they were working on independent activities. This would support Stevenson and Stigler's observation that:

> Working alone a large part of the time may also contribute to the American children's lower levels of academic achievement. Although children can learn without a teacher's direct attention, it seems unlikely that independent activity is the most effective means of instruction. One might argue that skill in a subject such as reading is highly dependent on practice and that children benefit from reading by themselves. It is more difficult to summon this argument for mathematics or science, where more information and demonstrations about definitions and operations may be necessary before children are ready to practice on their own. What appears to be a devotion to individuals and to small groups of children has the unintended effect of removing the American teacher from the remaining children and depriving those

children of valuable opportunities for instruction. We delude ourselves when we recommend individualizing instruction under the conditions that exist in American elementary schools. Teachers cannot possibly work individually and effectively during regular class periods with all of the children who need help (Stevenson & Stigler, 1992, pp. 69–70).

Much of the literature that is devoted to ways of increasing time on-task in the classroom also supports the position that direct, whole-group instruction increases time on-task. However, as was noted earlier, there is much more to the relationship between time and learning than simply having students engaged with a task assigned by the teacher. Not only must the task be relevant, as we saw in the previous chapter, but the students must experience a high level of success with the task. This means that the teacher must be prudent in allocating classroom time so that the time available for learning (opportunity time) is dispersed in such a way that it comes as close as possible to meeting the needs of every student.

Dispersing learning time so that it meets the needs of all students is not easy to accomplish in any setting, but is especially difficult in a large-group environment. First and Gray (1991) warn us that, "Any group of twenty-five to thirty-five elementary school students will vary widely in terms of learning speed and style, interest level, or aptitude" (p. 68).

Regardless of which type of instructional setting is being utilized—large group, small group, or individualized—for classroom time to be used in the most effective and efficient way possible the teacher must allocate time so that students spend as much time as possible engaged in relevant learning tasks with which they experience a high degree of success. In order to meet the criterion, the teacher must do the following: diagnosis the students' learning needs; prescribe instructional treatments to meet the needs; present the lessons in a format that will keep the children challenged, engaged, and actively working; monitor the students as they work to make certain that they are on-task and successful; and provide the feedback necessary to keep the students moving forward.

QUALITY OF INSTRUCTION:
THE INSTRUCTIONAL PROCESS OF DIAGNOSIS

"To diagnose" means to assess student learning to determine what is working and what is not working for the student. Bloom and his colleagues concluded that, "Diagnostic evaluation is an essential ingredient of good teaching, undertaken to adapt instruction to the needs and backgrounds of learners. 'Diagnosis' in education is not limited to the identification of deficiencies or problems. It is a broader concept that includes the identification of strengths and special talents" (Bloom et al., 1981, p. 116).

When diagnosing student learning, teachers may assess such things as the student's level of prior or background knowledge, the skills that they have attained or failed to attain, the interest and developmental level of the student, and any misconceptions that the student may have about the material to be learned. The purpose of the diagnosis is to assess how well the student is doing so that the teacher can then make decisions on how to improve the learning environment of that student, determine what type of intervention strategies may be necessary, and determine what the next steps in the learning sequence should be for a particular student. Without this information, the teacher is likely to use a method of instruction that is counter to the learning style of the student—reteach material that the students have already learned, use instructional examples that do little to clarify the students misconceptions, and/or use instructional materials that are inappropriate for the developmental level of the student. Any of these actions would result in both a loss of valuable instructional time and an increase in the amount of time a student would need in order to learn.

Unlike evaluation, which is an "end-of-process" measure, diagnosis is an ongoing "in-process" measure. In other words, evaluation tends to take place within a specific time period such as "mid-way through" or "at the end" of an instructional unit, "at the end" of a grading period, or "during" 10th grade. Conversely, diagnosis has virtually no time frame because it takes place *constantly* within the classroom. Diagnosis is not time bound but rather is time free; it is an ongoing, in-progress process, unlike evaluation that is a time-bound, summative process. In spite of the differences between evaluation and diagnosis, it is important to note that evaluation does not have to be done in isolation of the diagnostic process, but rather can, and should, be an inherent part of the student assessment process.

Methods of Diagnosis

According to Berliner (1987), teachers use informal, semiformal, and formal methods to assess or diagnose the needs of their students. Informal methods include "interpreting the cues emitted by students in the classroom, framing classroom questions and analyzing their answers, and some other relatively informal, usually unplanned, methods to decide if understanding has taken place" (Berliner, 1987, pp. 266). Madeline Hunter believes that "Informal diagnosis is the heart and core of diagnostic teaching. For each individual or situation, informal diagnosis yields bountiful information at the moment it is needed. The information may be less accurate than the result from formal diagnosis, but the information is reasonably reliable and immediately available" (Hunter, 1979, p. 45).

When informally diagnosing student learning, teachers will frequently stop to offer assistance to a student who is having trouble or struggling with a task. The type of assistance that is offered is based on the teacher's instantaneous diagnosis of the student's needs. The teacher may also use the knowledge gained during the informal assessment to change or alter future lesson plans for an individual student, a small group of students, or even for the entire class.

Not all diagnosis is informal, however. It can, and often does, take a more structured format, being either semiformal or formal. Among the semiformal methods are classroom practice, (e.g., seat work, group activities, or lab experiences) and homework assignments. Formal methods of assessment include both standardized and teacher-made tests. The teacher may give a test or quiz or prepare a special assignment, the results of which are used to determine where the students are in the learning process, what kind of additional help may be needed, and if it is time to move to the next instructional unit. In this case, the diagnosis is planned rather than instantaneous, and it takes place within a given time period.

Types of Instructional Problems

Through the process of diagnosis, teachers seek to understand and then resolve any instructional problems that may be faced by their students. It is important to note that we are talking about instructional problems rather than learning problems. Learning problems suggests that the student is having problems learning. Instructional problems, on the other hand, suggest that it is the teacher who is being challenged to improve the learning and teaching process so that the learning process is enhanced.

Three common types of instructional problems (or challenges) encountered within the classroom on a daily basis are problems associated with misconceptions or lack of understanding, problems associated with failing to remember, and attitude problems.

Misconceptions or Lack of Understanding
Errors that result as a natural part of the learning process and/or that arise from a limited understanding of the content fall into this category. The category includes trial and error mistakes, answers that are partially correct, and answers that the student can justify logically, but that are nonetheless incorrect.

An example of a problem that results from misconceptions is a student who is learning when to use "a" and when to use "an." The students have been "taught" the rule, "You use 'an' before nouns that begin with a vowel sound. If the word doesn't begin with a vowel sound, you use 'a'." On a practice exercise, one student places an "a" before each word beginning with a vowel and "an" before each word beginning with a consonant. The student misunderstood, and simply reversed the rule.

Diagnosing whether a deviation stems from lack of understanding or from a misconception is not always easy. For example, let's say the student placed an "a" before some words that begin with a vowel but not all of them. Likewise, the student placed an "a" before some words that begin with a consonant and an "an" in front of others. The teacher must now find out if the mistakes result from a lack of understanding, a misconception, or a partial understanding of the rule. If it comes from a total lack of understanding, it means the student is applying the rule in a haphazard fashion because he or she has no rule to guide him or her. If the student is able to give a reason for his or her answers that seems logical but is incorrect, then the mistakes most likely occur as a result of misunderstanding.

But what if the student is able to explain the rule, but unable to apply it? What then? It is most likely that he or she has a partial understanding of the content. The challenge for the teacher is to determine what part the student understands and what part the student doesn't understand. For instance, it may be that the student is unable to differentiate between vowels and consonants and, therefore, understands the rule but can't apply it. If the teacher misdiagnoses the situation, the teacher may spend additional class time attempting to reteach the rule, which would do little to improve the student's learning and would, in fact, be a waste of instructional time.

An example of a problem of deviation that results from trial-and-error learning would be a student who is learning to use a word processor and is told to "Use the pull-down menu to change from single spacing to double spacing." The student tries one menu and then another until he or she finally finds the correct menu. This is a normal approach to learning and to problem solving and therefore is not a learning problem. However, if the student continues to use this process, his or her proficiency in using the word processor will be less than desirable. Therefore, the teacher must help the student to move from a trial-and-error approach to a more systematic approach based on rules and concepts that have been taught.

Problems of Forgetting
Problems in this category are those that result from an inability to remember something that had been previously learned. These problems are most recognizable following an extended vacation. Such problems can also occur as a result of interference from other learning. Consider the following example:

> Jimmie was a normal second-grade student. Some concepts were easy for him and others were more difficult. The really delightful thing about Jimmie was that he loved learning. He almost preferred

the difficult tasks over the easy ones because he was so proud of himself when he was finally able to do what he set out to do. Imagine the teacher's surprise when Jimmie started having trouble in both reading and math. It started out simply enough, he couldn't do one of his assignments and it upset him. Within a very short time, however, Jimmie started crying at least twice a day—once during math and once during reading. The teacher talked to him, the counselor talked to him, and his parents came in for a conference and they talked to him. The teacher tried everything she could think of and nothing seemed to work. The most troublesome part was that Jimmie started to lose faith in himself. One day the teacher kept Jimmie in for recess under the pretense that she needed his help in filing some papers. The papers were copies of activities that Jimmie had already completed. The papers were piled in a random fashion and as Jimmie and the teacher filed, they talked about a number of things that were almost as random as the pile itself. All of a sudden Jimmie picked up two pieces of paper and said, "I just can't do these but I used to be able to do this one. Now I can't anymore." Trying to be causal, the teacher asked Jimmie why he couldn't do them anymore. His reply was very simple and held the key to all of his problem: "I can't remember if you go left or right." The teacher was puzzled until she looked at the papers he was holding. One was an arithmetic paper in which the student had to regroup. The other was a language arts paper with a list of words that the student was to alphabetize to the second letter. On the arithmetic paper Jimmie had to "go left" as he added his numbers and on the reading paper he had to "go right" as he alphabetized the words. He just couldn't remember which was which, and as a result the amount of time he needed for learning increased as the amount of time he was willing to spend decreased.

In the case of Jimmie, the instructional problem is one of renewal. Jimmie at one time understood the content and had developed the skills and knowledge necessary for double-digit addition. However, he became confused when another skill in a different area was introduced. The teacher must recognize that Jimmie has learned the material but that he needs help in knowing when to apply which rule. What Jimmie needs is instructional activities that call for him to apply one rule and then the other—to do a practice exercise on double-digit addition and then an activity where he must alphabetize to the second letter. The teacher should then help him to compare and contrast the two activities and to evaluate his own work. Teaching the two skills in different time periods (reading time and math time) will do little to ease his problems.

Attitudinal Problems

Problems in this category have to do with students' preconceived attitudes or notions about the instructional task in terms of subject matter, the nature of the instructional activity, their own ability to learn, or even the credibility of the teacher. It is not unusual for a student to develop the attitude of, "I do it this way," or "I want to do it my way," or "I don't think you know what you are doing." Although it may sound as if these phrases come from "problem students," the reality is that they are often attitudes held by some of our best students. They have learned to trust their own judgments and to question arbitrary ways of doing things. The teacher who attempts to help the student learn to "apply the best practice" may be frustrated by such attitudes. However, if time is spent helping the student compare and contrast the different approaches and then analyzing why one method is accepted as "best," the time spent generally will go a long way toward easing problems related to attitudes. If, however, the teacher fails to diagnose the problem as one of acceptance and instead decides to reteach the material, the problem will tend to worsen.

Problems of attitude also result from a student's sense of self-efficacy. When students believe that they are unable to accomplish a task, they will spend little time working on the task. In other words, their levels of perseverance will decrease and this in turn will have a direct impact on their academic achievements. In cases such as this, the teacher must take a proactive stance by helping the students understand that they would not be given tasks that the teacher thought they were incapable of doing, and helping the students to assess why they may have had trouble with the task in the past or why they may have trouble with the task in the future.

Diagnostic Skills

Regardless of the nature of the instructional problem, the earlier the problem is detected and the reason for the problem identified, the better for the student. In most cases, this process is facilitated when both the child and the teacher are concentrating on the skill in isolation, but is more difficult when the skill has been integrated with skills from other subjects.

To be good diagnosticians, teachers must have a high degree of subject matter knowledge—knowledge that relates directly to the content being taught. This is especially important in environments where the teacher takes on the role of facilitator. The teacher must understand the subject matter well enough to determine which concepts build upon one another, to recognize and anticipate typical misconceptions that students may have or problems they may encounter, and to be able to present concepts and generalizations in a number of different forms. This is true of the elementary teacher as well as the secondary teacher and is one of the reasons why all teacher preparation programs require that teachers complete a program of study that focuses on basic skills in math, science, language arts, and the social sciences.

In addition, teachers must develop the skills necessary to analyze the current knowledge, skill levels, strengths, and weaknesses of their students. Teachers must be able to interpret the signs and signals provided by their students' performances. They must be able to use historical data to analyze what has worked in the past with other students and what has worked in the past with this particular student. They must be able to identify sources of an instructional problem, be it achievement, behavior, social, language, task difficulty, or lack of prior knowledge. In other words, they must be able to assess in which of the domain(s) the problem falls and where on the learning taxonomy (or taxonomies) the student's performance falls. They must also understand what learning style the student prefers and under what learning conditions the student performs best.

A number of tools and techniques can be used to aid in the diagnostic process. Among these are work sampling, anecdotal records, portfolios, check sheets, interviews, time sampling, sociograms, and teacher-made tests. However, regardless of the method or technique used in diagnosis, there are three principles of good diagnosis that, when put into practice, will help every teacher improve his or her diagnostic skills. These are:

1. Diagnosis should be ongoing rather than episodic.
2. Diagnosis requires attention to outcomes, but equally important is attention to the experiences that lead to those outcomes.
3. Diagnosis is most effective when it reflects an understanding of learning as multidimensional, integrated, and revealed in performance over time (Banta et al., 1996, p. 2).

The Relationship between Classroom Time and Diagnosis

Margaret Gettinger has written that, "maximizing productive learning time involves assessing the current knowledge, skill level, and strengths and weaknesses of students to decide on appropriate instructional goals and activities, task difficulty, grouping, and scheduling" (Gettinger, 1990, p. 403). Examining Gettinger's statement closely reveals several elements of time and learning. "Maximizing productive learning time" is equivalent to maximizing academic learning time (or other types of learning time, including psychomotor or affective learning). "*Appropriate instructional goals and activities, task difficulty*" is tantamount to *task relevance* and *scheduling* corresponds to *time allocation*. "*Assessing the current knowledge, skill level, and strengths and weaknesses of students*" is at the heart of the current discussion on *diagnosis*.

Merely diagnosing student needs is not enough to ensure that learning time will increase. The teacher must go to the next step and prescribe the appropriate instructional treatment for the need that has been diagnosed. Otherwise, the teacher will be moving toward the point of "spending more time testing than teaching."

PRESCRIPTION

Once teachers have diagnosed the learning needs of their students, they must then determine the best way to go about meeting those needs. This often means that they will need to adapt, delete, or add instructional material to meet the needs of their students. It may also mean that they will need to reallocate time among and between the subjects. This does not mean that teachers will assign activities simply because they believe they will keep their students "busy and happy," but rather will attempt to make assignments that keep their students "busy, happy, and learning" or at the least "busy learning."

There is, however, a tendency for teachers to focus more on activities and subject matter rather than on the actual needs of their students. One reason for this is that the teacher is responsible for establishing the classroom agenda, and if the agenda doesn't call for students to be doing something almost constantly, there is a tendency for chaos to break out in the classroom. Then, when students don't do as well as expected on achievement tests, the teacher may be held accountable if the material wasn't covered, even if the students were ready for the material. The problem, however, is not new. Advice given to student teachers over four decades ago declared that:

One point that needs special emphasis is the importance of considering the time required to carry out projected activities. First of all, plan plenty of work so that purposeful learning will be going on throughout a given period. Second, provide adequate time to introduce the lesson so that it will be meaningful and purposeful to the group. Third, be sure to check the amount of time necessary for the group to carry out proposed experiences against the class schedule. This does not imply that up-to-date teachers are slaves to a time schedule. Rather, it means that they must give attention to the time needed to achieve the specific purposes that are of importance to a particular group of pupils (Michaelis & Grim, 1953, pp. 101–103).

If you examine the Michaelis and Grim passage closely, you will find that there are two facets to each of the points being made—one that has to do with time and one that has to do with student goals or learning outcomes. The trick for the classroom teacher is not to just fill the classroom time, but to fill it in such a way that it maximizes the amount of time students spend in productive learning. This means that the teacher must prescribe instructional treatments that are based on sound diagnostic processes and desired learning outcomes. The treatment itself takes the form of a relevant task that students are willing to spend time on and with which they experience a fair degree of success.

The teacher may begin planning the instructional treatment by outlining the content of the lesson or by identifying the specific learning needs of the student. It really makes no difference which way the teacher begins as long as the students' needs are paramount to the content in the treatment that is prescribed. The teacher's goal and purpose is not to cover content, but rather to teach students. However, teachers have specific learning goals in mind when they teach, and these goals include helping students to learn subject matter and content. This means that the teacher must be brave enough to vary from the prescribed curriculum if the curriculum does not meet the needs of the student but they don't vary from the curriculum capriciously, directed by whim or fancy. The teacher must be able to justify his or her decision by demonstrating an understanding of how the subject matter builds, how students' needs vary, and how specific instructional treatments and techniques can be used to address the students' learning needs.

Time and Prescription for Learning

Just as there are time elements in medical prescriptions—for example, take 3 times daily, take with food, take until prescription is gone, take for 30 days—there are also time elements associated with instructional prescriptions. These time elements include the pacing of the lesson, the sequencing of the lesson, the time duration or how long each segment of the lesson should last, and the time frame or amount of time that is allocated to specific content or subject-matter concerns. There are also developmental aspects of the treatment that have to do with introducing materials at the appropriate stage of learning.

When prescribing an instructional treatment, it is important and necessary to recognize and acknowledge the various roles that time plays within the instructional treatment because, as Walberg, Niemiec, and Frederick warn us, "Amount of time and concentration are the scarce resources, not the information available or the processing capacity of the mind—both of which, for practical purposes seem unlimited" (1994, p. 89). In other words, if we spend too much time on one area of learning, time will be lost to other areas. In addition, our students are only willing and able to expend a limited amount of their concentration in learning specific information or content. After this limited but often unidentifiable point, their level of perseverance will decrease and their aptitude, as defined by Carroll, in that area will be negatively affected. At the same time, the students must be given enough time to learn, otherwise they become frustrated, their work is incomplete, and their level of success and achievement drops. An analogy for this would be that of a teacher walking a time-line tightrope—it becomes a real balancing act. But just as tightrope walkers use a pole to help them maintain their balance, the teacher uses diagnostic techniques and analysis to maintain the balance between instructional obligations.

PRESENTATION

Once the teacher has prescribed the instructional treatment, or planned the lesson, the treatment must then be administered, or presented. The way in which the teacher presents learning materials to the student will affect the amount of learning time needed and the quality of the learning outcome.

According to John Carroll's Model of School Learning, one of the major factors that affects learning in school is whether a student is given the time needed for learning. Time needed is directly impacted by the quality of instruction that a student receives and quality of instruction is defined as "a measure of how clearly the task is *presented and explained*, and how appropriately it is placed in the sequence of graded tasks to be learned" (emphasis added).

The BTES researchers identified presentation as an interactive teaching process because, during the presentation phase, the student interacts directly with the teacher and/or the instructional material. For the purpose of their research, the BTES investigators went on to subdivide the presentation process into three subcategories: explanation-planned, explanation-needed, and structure/direct. Explanation-planned involves presenting the lesson as the teacher originally designs it. Explanation-needed is instruction that is provided as a response to students' questions or actions. Structure/direct refers to the portion of the instruction in which the teacher provides directions and establishes the structure for the lesson.

Obviously, a lesson is most effective when it is a direct output of the proper instructional diagnosis. However, simply designing a lesson based on students' needs is not enough. The presentation of the lesson must also be of quality. Factors that affect the quality of the presentation are the teacher's ability to clearly explain the content, to elaborate on the concepts being developed, to motivate the students, to adjust the lesson to meet the needs of the students, to show enthusiasm for the lesson, and to encourage student participation. The quality is also affected by the teacher's ability to ask questions and to respond to student questions. In addition, the teacher must establish a lesson structure that is easy to follow and is consistent with the instructional goal. This includes organizing material in a logical fashion, establishing a learning set, and helping students reach closure.

Research has shown that when the teachers have established routine lesson formats and classroom procedures they spend less time on correcting student behaviors, on directing and structuring lessons, and on providing additional explanation to the students beyond what was originally planned. Conversely, when the classroom routines are not as well established, more instructional classroom time is spent on reminding students to return to task, on repeating directions, and/or on going over the content a second, third, or fourth time. The same two statements also hold true when the lessons are not well planned or delivered as planned. In other words, valuable instructional time can be lost if lessons are not well planned, if the lessons do not build upon the instructional needs of the students, or if the students are not provided with directions that are clear and easy to follow and that involve logically organized and structured lessons.

There is a word of caution to be offered here. Few human endeavors go exactly as planned and consequently a teacher must be flexible enough to alter the lesson as needed. This is especially true when a new type of lesson, one that is different in format or subject-matter content, is being presented. The wise teacher will, therefore, allocate more time for establishing the learning set when changing the lesson format or introducing new subject matter or material to the students.

MONITORING

Michael Slavin has noted that, "Another important aspect of quality of instruction is the degree to which the teacher monitors how well students are learning and adapts the pace of instruction so that it is neither too fast nor too slow" (1994, p. 311). Gettinger states that, "Teachers monitor students' responses during engaged learning time to determine whether the instructional goals are appropriate and are being met" (1990, p. 403). Wyne and Stuck have written that, "It appears that, regardless of the instructional grouping pattern employed, (individual, small group, or whole class), the key to higher levels of time on task and achievement is the degree to which teachers monitor student learning" (1982, p. 72).

Teachers monitor students behavior to determine if they are on task, if they are having trouble with the task, if the task is too easy for them, and when it is time to slow down or speed up the instructional presentation. Regardless of the reason behind the monitoring, when teachers constantly monitor the learning behaviors of the students, the amount of quality learning time increases.

The ease with which a teacher is able to monitor students' progress and behaviors is enhanced if strong classroom management techniques are in place. Students should be seated in such a way that the teacher can maintain eye contact with each student the majority of time. When students are working independently, it should be the teacher who moves about the room, not the students. Rules of conduct should be well established early in the year, and the students should be informed of the teacher's expectations regarding the students' work habits. In addition, the teacher should work to develop his or her monitoring skills, building on strengths and working to overcome weaknesses. For instance, some teachers are very good at remembering which students have difficulties with which problems. Others may need to write notes to themselves for future reference. Some teachers had developed "eyes in the back of their heads" and seem to know intuitively which students need help and when. Other teachers need to remind themselves to periodically check on each student to see how they are doing.

FEEDBACK

Another important aspect of the teaching process is providing the students with appropriate feedback. Wyne and Stuck found that, "Feedback that has been found to be most positively related to increased time on task and achievement is characterized by its specificity and academic relevance" (1982, p. 72). Actually, there are two basic types of feedback that the teacher provides to the student—informational feedback and reinforcement feedback. Each has been shown to have an impact on time on-task, students' level of perseverance, and academic achievement. But Wyne and Stuck are correct in saying that feedback that is specific and academically relevant (i.e., informational feedback) will have the greatest impact on student engagement rate.

Informational Feedback

Informational feedback relates directly to the content or skill to be learned. Such feedback may be immediate or delayed. Immediate feedback is given during the directed portion of the instructional lesson. If there is a time lapse between the time of the lesson and the feedback (such as a written feedback provided on a homework assignment that is returned two days after the assignment is completed), then the feedback is considered to be delayed. All things being equal, the more immediate the feedback, the more effective it tends to be. However, delayed feedback may provide the teacher with more time to analyze the cause of the problem and to provide the student with more detailed and specific feedback. In such cases, delayed feedback is often superior to immediate feedback.

Whether it is immediate or delayed, for informational feedback to be effective it should indicate to a student whether a response is right or wrong, complete or incomplete, acceptable or unacceptable. The feedback may also provide specific suggestions for revisions and it should be linked to content and skills being taught or to the current behavior and study skills of the student. Feedback should be frequent, specific, and academically relevant.

In order for the feedback to be specific and academically relevant, it must relate to the student's needs, which often manifest themselves in the form of student responses. Rosenshine and Stevens (1984) reviewed the research on student responses and found that the responses typically fall into one of four categories: (1) correct, quick, and firm, (2) correct, but hesitant, (3) incorrect, but a "careless" error, and (4) incorrect, suggesting lack of knowledge of facts or a process. They further concluded that the feedback provided to students should be different depending on the type of response made by the student. If the student's answer is correct, quick, and firm, the teacher should acknowledge the correctness and may want to ask a follow-up question that requires deeper elaboration. If the student's answer is correct, but the student seems hesitant, the teacher should acknowledge the correctness of the answer and may then want to restate the student's response. When the student makes an incorrect response that results from "carelessness" on the part of the student, the teacher should simply correct the mistake and move on. If the response from the student is incorrect and suggests that the student lacks an understanding of the material, individual facts, or complete processes, the teacher may first offer hints or cues that prompt the student and, if this fails should then reteach the material.

Students may also receive corrective feedback from their peers. In math class one student may demonstrate how to do a particular problem while the other students check their work. In reading, one student may read aloud while the other students read silently, checking their own reading rate and skill.

Another way that students may receive informative feedback is by checking their work against an answer key or an instructional model. Teachers who are hoping to encourage the student to go from simply looking for a correct answer to being able to judge the quality of their own answers or to diagnose for themselves, will need to allocate at least some classroom time for demonstrating how to use the corrective materials.

Reinforcement Feedback

Reinforcement feedback relates to the general behavior of the students. Praising them for the quality of their work, for staying on task, or for cooperating with other students are all forms of reinforcement feedback.

The feedback that a teacher provides for students can serve to help the students monitor their own progress, help to correct problems as they are happening, and aid in keeping students on task. Feedback can also influence a student's level of perseverance and can affect the student's self-efficacy. The quality of the feedback a teacher provides to students plays an important role in academic learning time.

QUALITY OF INSTRUCTION: ACADEMIC VERSUS NONACADEMIC LEARNING

Time and learning studies have often been criticized because they focus so heavily on academic learning and ignore nonacademic learning. For purposes of definition, academic learning refers to the cognitive domain, the outcomes of which can often be measured through achievement tests. Nonacademic learning refers to all other types of learning, including affective, social, physical, and emotional. Most of the criticism of the time and learning studies is in direct reaction to the BTES research that focused strictly on reading and math. However, there have been a limited number of studies on time and learning in the nonacademic classroom and these were conducted both before and after the ALT study. (See, for instance, Kimbrough & Andres, 1969; Godbout et al., 1983; Lee & Poto, 1988; Beauchampt et al., 1990.)

Very few time-related studies have been conducted on nonacademic learning that is non-subject matter specific (e.g., social learning or attitudinal learning versus music or art education). One of the major reasons for the lack of studies appears to be the difficulty in structuring research studies in such a way that they can be repeated and the findings generalized from one setting, or one student, to another. Nonacademic learning of non-subject matter occurs over time and is influenced by so many factors outside of the school that it is difficult to measure the impact of time spent in school.

Practice, however, informs us that the affective side of classroom learning is often as important, if not more important, as the academic side. Teachers are becoming increasingly aware of the nonacademic needs of their students and are devoting more time to meeting these needs. The BTES researchers documented the trend in this direction through the description of one of the second-grade classrooms they observed.

> He (the male teacher) was a warm, easy-going, soft-spoken person. The classroom climate was "peaceful" ("even when he was angry"). In addition to the teacher, there was an aide who was "a warm, delightful teacher loved by the children." As the year went on, she was given increasing responsibility in the classroom.
>
> The emphasis in this classroom was on things other than achievement in basic skills. The field workers reported that the teacher placed heavy emphasis on teaching social values, was concerned with improving students' self-concept, and considered time spent on nonacademic activities very important. One-half hour was spent on music

almost every day. "On days when the classroom mood became tense, he spent a large part of the day doing artwork or singing." . . . There was little academic pressure in the class. It is worth noting that this class had high negative residual scores in attitude as well as achievement. Student attitudes would presumably be important to this teacher, and attitude toward reading and math as we measured it was not fostered in this classroom (Fisher et al., 1978, pp. 8–26).

The researchers stated that the teacher *placed heavy emphasis on teaching social values, was concerned with improving students' self-concept, and considered time spent on nonacademic activities very important.* We do not know how successful the teacher was in meeting these goals but there is some indication that, even when teachers value social learning, development of self-concept and spending time on nonacademic subjects, they are better prepared to deal with the academic lessons than they are with nonacademic lessons.

The results of a preliminary study conducted by this author supports the contention that the quality and amount of time spent in nonacademic (social learning) are as directly related to time and learning as they are to academic learning (Huyvaert, 1992). However, the researcher found that the quality of instruction in the nonacademic learning areas was often poorly defined and that teachers had a much more difficult time predicting the outcomes of instruction in the nonacademic areas than in the academic areas. The time spent in the nonacademic areas was less structured and often haphazard, occurring in response to a specific problem that arose in the classroom. The findings also support the conclusion that the influence of the teacher is much greater in nonacademic (social) learning than in academic learning.

In classrooms where teachers had a better understanding of how to diagnose a content problem, to prescribe the correct treatment, to present the material, to monitor the process of learning as it occurs, and to provide supportive feedback to the students, the academic achievement of the students was higher. This was not always the case in nonacademic (social skills) teaching. However, when teachers who attempted to teach social skills were more adept in the teaching processes, their students appeared to learn more and were more receptive to applying their skills outside of the classroom.

SUMMARY

Quality of instruction impacts learning time in one of three ways. It can reduce the amount of time a student needs to learn (Carroll), it can reduce the gap between the amount of time needed by faster and slower students (Bloom), and it can result in an increase in learning without a similar increase in instructional time (ALT). Quality of instruction is achieved through the dynamic interactions of the teaching process variables of diagnosis, prescription, presentation, monitoring, and feedback.

Based on an evaluation of the learners needs and the desired learning outcome, the teacher prescribes or plans an instructional treatment. This portion of the teaching process is often compared to the doctor who first diagnoses the cause of the illness and then determines how to treat the illness. A more appropriate analogy would be a doctor who encompasses the philosophy of holistic medicine and who is concerned with keeping the entire body healthy rather than just treating illnesses and ailments. Just as there may be a variety of treatments available to doctors, so too do teachers have a variety of approaches that they may use. Just as in the case of the doctor where the success of the treatment depends upon the quality of diagnosis, the success of the instructional approach will depend on the quality of the learner analysis.

Simply making the correct diagnosis and prescribing the correct treatment does not guarantee that the student will learn or that the amount of time that the student will need to learn will be reduced. The treatment must be presented in such a way that a student is willing and/or able to accept or receive it. For instance, students may need to improve their keyboarding skills in order to reduce the amount of time it takes for them to complete the tasks assigned in a computer class. The teacher may decide to have the student work on keyboarding exercises that are similar to those that were originally developed for teaching typing. Or the teacher may decide to use a game format that disguises the repetitive actions necessary for skill building. The typing-like exercises are a more direct approach and therefore it should take less time to accomplish the improvement that is needed. However, if the student is bored with the exercises and consequently only does them haphazardly, the teacher may find that it is better to use the game-like format.

Quality of instruction is also affected by the teachers' ability to monitor learning as it is occurring and to provide students with feedback that helps them to correct or improve their performance or that encourages them to remain on task. The teacher monitors instruction to make certain that students are on task and that the instructional treatment is effective. When the teacher discovers that students are off task or that the instructional treatment is not working, quality instruction demands that the teacher immediately take the steps necessary to correct the situation. If this does not occur, the amount of time students spend on tasks that are instructionally relevant and with which they experience a high degree of success will be decreased and the amount of time they will need to learn will be increased.

The amount of quality instructional time varies from school to school, classroom-to-classroom, and day to day, and an overwhelming portion of this variation can be traced to the individual teacher. The teacher makes the decisions about how to allocate time within the instructional period, assigns the instructional tasks, and monitors the students' performances. The teacher performs the learning diagnosis, interprets the diagnosis, and then prescribes the instructional treatment. These actions and decisions make up the instructional process, and the teacher's implementation of the instructional processes has the greatest impact on time and learning in the classroom. Accordingly, any discussion of time and learning in schools would be incomplete without at least a portion of the discussion being devoted to how the teacher impacts, and is impacted by, the restraints of time. In the next chapter we will examine a number of the issues related to time and the teacher.

REFERENCES

Banta, T. W., Lund, J. P., Black, K. E., & Oblander, F. W. (1996). *Assessment in practice: Putting principles to work on college campuses.* San Francisco: Jossey-Bass.

Beauchamp, L., et al. (1990). Academic learning time as an indicator of quality high school physical education. *Journal of Physical Education, Recreation, and Dance, 61*(1), 92–95.

Berliner, D. C. (1987). But do they understand? In Richardson-Koehler, V. (Ed.), *Educator's Handbook: A Research Perspective.* New York: Longman.

Bloom, B. S. (1974). Time and learning. *American Psychologist, 29*(9), 682–688.

Bloom, B. S., Madaus, G. F., & Hasting, J. T. (1981). *Evaluation to improve learning.* New York: McGraw-Hill.

Carroll, J. B. (1963). A model of school learning. *Teachers College Record, 64*(8), 723–733.

Doyle, W. (1983). Academic work. *Review of Educational Research, 53*(2), 159–199.

First, J. & Gray, R. (1991). *The common school.* Boston: National Coalition of Advocates for Students.

Fisher, C., et al. (1978, June). *Teaching behaviors, academic learning time and student achievement: Final report of phase III-B, beginning teacher evaluation study* (Technical Report V-1.) San Francisco, CA: Far West Laboratory for Educational Research and Development.

Gettinger, M. (1990). Best practices in increasing academic learning time. In Thomas, A., & Grimes, J. (Eds.), *Best Practices in School Psychology—II* (pp. 393–404). Washington, DC: The National Association of School Psychologists.

Godbout, P., et al. (1983). Academic learning time in elementary and secondary physical education classes. *Research Quarterly for Exercise and Sport, (54)*1, 11–19.

Hunter, M. (1979, September) Diagnostic teaching. *Elementary School Journal,* 45.

Huyvaert, S. (1992). *Refinement of a computer simulation model developed to student time-on-task in the educational environment.* Unpublished sabbatical report, Eastern Michigan University, Ypsilanti, MI.

Keller, F. S. (1968). "Good-bye, teacher . . .". *Applied Behavior Analysis, 1,* 78–89.

Kimbrough, R. B., & Andres, J. O. (1969). *Project ideals: Administrative organization (Area J).* Gainesville, FL: Florida Educational Research and Development Council.

Lee, A., & Poto, C. (1988). Instructional time and research in physical education: Contribution and current issues. *Quest, (40)*1, 63–73.

Michaelis, J. U., & Grim, P. R. (1953). *The student teacher in the elementary school.* New York: Prentice-Hall.

Rosenshine, B., & Stevens, R. (1984). Classroom instruction in reading. In P. D. Peason (Ed.), *Handbook of Reading Research*. New York: Longman.

Slavin, R. E. (1994) *Educational psychology: Theory and practice*. Boston: Allyn and Bacon.

Stevenson, H. W., & Stigler, J. W. (1992). *The learning gap*. New York: Summit Books.

Walberg, H. J., Niemiec, R. P., & Frederick, W. C. (1994). Productive curriculum time. *Peabody Journal, 69*(3), 86–100.

Wyne, M. D., & Stuck, G. B. (1982). Time and learning: Implications for the classroom teacher. The *Elementary School Journal, 83*(1), 67–75.

▶ 11

Time and the Teacher

Time is, in the words of the National Education Association (NEA), "the basic dimension through which the teachers' work is constructed and interpreted. Time often defines the possibilities and limitations of teachers' professional performance" (NEA, 1994, p. 2). Because teachers are being asked to accept more and more responsibilities without being given the requisite time demanded by these additional responsibilities, many believe that time is now presenting more limitations than possibilities. The NEA acknowledged this concern stating that:

> Educators are besieged by a multiplicity of demands which preclude adequate time for planning, reflecting, collaborating, researching, and assessing. *The shortage of time is a problem in all schools and is one of the most complex and challenging problems teachers face every day* [emphasis added] (NEA, 1994, p. 1).

The recognition of how important time is to the teacher is not a new. As early as 1939, Henry Otto recognized the impact of time on the teacher and wrote:

> The schedule under which a school operates is of vital concern to the teacher. The teaching load; the length of the teacher's time on duty; the sequence of subjects or classes taught; the amount of daily or weekly teacher-pupil contact; the opportunities for providing for individual differences of pupils; the utilization of the teacher's best talents; the mental and physical health of the teacher; the ease with which the curriculum can be enriched by such activities as trips, excursions, clubs, school paper, play days, assemblies, and library and auditorium experiences; and the degree to which fundamental

principles of psychology of learning are applied are all factors which are influenced and partially controlled by the schedule or program of operation and management of the school (Otto, 1939, p. 83–84).

This quote from Otto supports the contention that time is a powerful influence in our schools. It directs the curriculum, limits the teacher's course of action, and builds boundaries around learning. Lack of time has been identified as one of the major causes of teacher stress and has been blamed for poor student achievement. When discussing the power of time in schools, it is common practice to focus on the way in which students' spend their time. However, the way in which teachers use their professional time can serve as a catalyst or as a retardant in the time and learning process. Professional time includes not only the time teachers spend with students in the classroom but also includes time spent on other responsibilities such as preparing lesson plans, grading papers, participating in-service and professional development activities, and working with parents and other educational professionals. In order to understand the relationship between teacher's time and student learning we must first examine how teachers spend their time.

THE USE OF TEACHERS' TIME

Every five years since 1961, the U. S. Department of Education has sponsored a national school and staffing survey. Data collected from these surveys include information related to teachers' time. The results of the 1961 through 1991 surveys are summarized in Table 11–1. The data reveal that the amount of time teachers spent on their professional duties changed very little from 1961 to 1991.

The latest survey (conducted in 1993–94 and reported in the 1996 edition of *Conditions in Education*) was based on a sample of 52,000 public school teachers. According to this latest survey, the average public school teacher worked 45.2 hours per week. Teachers with less than four years of experience worked an average of 48.3 hours. The hours were further broken down into average number of hours required to be in school (33.2 hours) and average number of hours spent before and after school and on weekends (12.1 hours). (See Table 11–2).

The Department of Education also reported that elementary teachers spent an average of 21 hours per week teaching the core subjects of language arts/reading, arithmetic/math, science, and social studies. The same data were not reported for secondary teachers because teachers are assigned by subject matter and an averaging of the data would hold very little meaning.

Other than the data on how much time elementary teachers spent on teaching the core subjects, there is little or no data on how teachers actually

TABLE 11–1 Average amount of time teachers spent on professional duties—1961 through 1991

	1961	1966	1971	1976	1981	1986	1991
Average number of hours in required school day	7.4	7.3	7.3	7.3	7.3	7.3	7.2
Average number of hours per week spent in all teaching duties (all teachers)	47	47	47	46	46	49	47
Elementary teachers	49	47	46	44	44	47	44
Secondary teachers	46	48	48	48	48	51	50
Average number of days of classroom teaching in school year	—	181	181	180	180	180	180
Average number of non-teaching days in school year	—	5	4	5	6	5	5

Data Source: U. S. Department of Education. National Center for Education Statistics. *The Conditions of Education 1996*, NCES 96-304, by Thomas Smith. Washington, DC: U. S. Government Printing Office, 1996.

TABLE 11–2   Average hours per week teachers spent at school and in school-related activities

Level of school and teacher characteristics	Average hours worked per week	Average hours required at school	Average hours spent before and after school and on weekends		
			Total	Activities involving students	Other related activities
Total	45.2	33.2	12.1	3.3	8.7
Elementary	44.0	33.0	11.0	1.7	9.2
Secondary	46.5	33.3	13.2	5.0	8.2
Years of teaching experience					
Less than 4 years	48.3	34.4	14.0	4.2	9.8
4 years or more	44.8	33.0	11.8	3.2	8.6

Data Source: U. S. Department of Education. National Center for Education Statistics. *The Conditions of Education 1996*, NCES 96-304, by Thomas Smith. Washington, DC: U. S. Government Printing Office, 1996.

allocate and use their professional time. However, a study conducted by Horn and Chaikind between 1984 and 1986 does provides some insight into teachers' use of professional time. Based on the data collected during their study, Horn and Chaikind concluded that the amount of time teachers' spent on professional duties tended to be evenly divided between classroom instruction and non-classroom school-related activities (e.g., lesson planning, parent/teacher conferences, grading papers).

The Horn and Chaikind study was conducted over a decade ago, and since that time schools there have been increases in professional development activities for teachers, the use of portfolios and authentic assessment methodologies has increased, teachers are being encouraged to spend more time communicating with parents, and site-based/collaborative management is on the increase. All of these activities require additional time commitments from the teacher and suggest that the scale will soon be tipped so that teachers will be devoting as much, if not more, of their professional time to school-related non-student-directed activities as they are to activities that directly involve their students. But, even as the scale tips, the number one concern is how the use of teachers' time affects the quality of instruction that takes place in our classrooms each day, every day.

TABLE 11–3   Average number of hours teachers spent per week by category

Activity	Elementary Teachers		Secondary Teachers	
	Public	Private	Public	Private
Classroom teaching	26.0	27.1	24.4	21.8
Planning and evaluation (total)	15.1	14.4	15.4	16.7
Reviewing & grading	6.4	6.1	6.7	6.9
Class preparation	6.1	5.9	6.2	6.7
Administrative activities	1.7	1.7	1.9	2.6
Parent conferences	0.9	0.7	0.6	0.4
Extracurricular supervision (total)	1.4	1.5	4.4	4.3
Transporting students	0.1	0.3	0.3	0.3
Coaching athletics	0.6	0.5	2.4	2.4
Field trips	0.4	0.4	0.5	0.2
Advising school clubs	0.4	0.4	1.2	1.3
Other direct-student contact	3.8	3.9	5.4	6.3
Activities (total)				
Tutoring	1.0	0.9	1.8	1.9
Counseling & guidance	0.7	0.6	1.2	1.4
Monitoring	2.2	2.5	2.4	3.0
Other activities	2.3	2.2	2.7	3.2
Lunch and free time				
Absent	0.3	0.2	0.3	0.1

Source: Horn, R., & Chaikind, S. (1989). *Time allocation patterns of teachers in public and private schools; 1984–1986.* Washington, DC: National Center for Education Statistics.

TEACHERS' TIME AND THE QUALITY OF INSTRUCTION

We know that quality of instruction varies from school to school, from teacher to teacher, and from classroom to classroom. We also know that time acts as both a catalyst and as an inhibitor in the instructional process. Teachers need time to accomplish instructional goals just as students need time to learn. But just as students are hampered in their learning when they are provided with less time than needed, so are teachers limited in what they can accomplish when time restraints are placed on them. This often becomes very frustrating for the teacher. By way of illustration, consider the following 1993 excerpts from a student teacher's journal. (The author of the journal remains unidentified at her request.)

October 3
I'm not too pleased at how today's health lesson went. I had it planned out to include K-W-L, a direct lesson, and hands-on discovery in combination. I originally had a 45 minute time slot. Because the spelling pre-test took longer than expected, I only had 20 minutes for the entire lesson. I began with group brainstorming for the K-W-L and then did the directed lesson with demonstration in place of hands-on. I really think this is a *poor* substitute. In truth, I feel the whole thing went so badly that I doubt the children learned anything about the muscular/skeleton system.

October 5
Once again, it's back to TIME. There doesn't seem to be any! Spelling seems to comprise the majority of the whole language lesson time this week. One hour for introducing the words and for the pretest on Monday, 35–45 minutes of seatwork writing sentences on Tuesday, 30 minutes seatwork on alphabetizing on Wednesday, word search and dictation took 40 minutes on Thursday, and then we had the test on Friday. Four to four-and-a-half hours spent on 15 spelling words! Somehow this seems really ridiculous to me! Reading groups are 30 to 40 minutes a day—one hour if you include seatwork, so only five hours are spent on reading. In math we spend 5 to 10 minutes a day on Mad Minutes pages. (third graders and they still don't know their addition facts? What did they do in second grade?) and then we give them 30 minute whole class lesson. Mrs. M. [the cooperating teacher] wants to have at least two 30 minute sessions a week for handwriting lessons. So this leaves one-and-a-half to two hours total for two science lessons and one multicultural lesson per week—and the Chapter 1 teacher has seven of our kids during this time! The type of lessons I've been encouraged to do by the [University] and by my Montessori background are hands-on science, cooperative group social studies, discovery lessons, etc.—all of which take more than 30 minutes to do a thorough job! Boy, am I frustrated.

October 14
Once again rushed through a science lesson, but not as bad this time. I did have to give up the paragraph writing at the end of the lesson, which I think will impact negatively on the learning. It had to be assigned as part of their seatwork time for tomorrow. I don't think they will retain as much as they could because of the delay in transference.

October 20
I was trying to do a demo of the pumping action of the heart using water in a balloon. It burst all over me! Ordinarily this wouldn't have

phased me—I would just have let the kids have a good laugh and gradually lead them back to the lesson. But because I was so aware of time I was anxious to move on and had to struggle to get the kids back on track.

November 1
Went to two seminars this morning. You could tell the speakers felt pressed for time as though they felt their topics were too immense to be covered in one or two hours. They're right! Both presenters were well prepared and good speakers, but the result of the seminars did support another of my tenets—one-shot lessons do not have lasting effects no matter how well formatted and presented.

November 12
I have been teaching two health lessons and 1 social studies lesson (45 minute average) a week. I don't think much is being learned by the average student. The more able students are able to absorb quite a bit, but not the majority of the kids. I think a second exposure to the same lesson would increase the number of students achieving an adequate level of understanding, but there just isn't time for this!

These excerpts provide insight into the sometimes subtle, and sometimes not so subtle, relationships between classroom time, the teaching process, and student learning. Through her journal entries, the student teacher shares her concerns over how classroom time is allocated, discusses ways in which time places restrictions on the type of instructional techniques that can be used throughout the day, explains how she thinks the gap between the more able students and the "average" students is widening because of lack of time to review previously taught lessons, and shares her frustration over having to take instructional time to review concepts that students should have mastered at an earlier grade level. She also shares how her feelings of time pressure alter her reaction to the students and their behaviors.

Although these concerns are expressed by a "teacher-in-training," it would be a mistake to dismiss the concerns as arising from lack of experience. Teachers at all levels of experience and from all across the nation have shared similar concerns regarding the ways in which time influences and often controls the quality of instruction that takes place in their classrooms. Articles in professional journals, informal discussions during in-service and professional development workshops, conferences between teachers and administrators, and even private conversations with friends and colleagues often bear witness to the teachers' frustrations.

The relationship between time and quality of instruction becomes even more complex when the concept of time-on-task is added to the formula of classroom learning time. The comments of one teacher provide insight into the complexity of the relationship.

> This is a hideously complex issue for me. It is something I think about a lot because I have to juggle so many conflicting interests. I have to try and know every child so well in order to say it's okay for that child to carry a task off into other directions, and to know all that requires so much of me that I feel very pressured. I'm responsible for moving kids onward and upward, emotionally, socially and all those other good things. . . . I have had some students who can seem to be off-task and still know everything for a test. This raises important questions. For the casual observer coming into my class, the traditional quiet, busy behavior generally is thought to be synonymous with learning. I'm not so sure. I have 'quiet' seemingly 'on-task' students who do not seem to be learning. I think it is much more difficult to determine on-task behavior and learning than it would at first seem (Johnson, 1985, pp. 19–20).

The comments of this teacher confirm that the teaching/learning process is a multifaceted process that takes place in a very complex environment. Teachers strive to make the best use possible of limited time available in this complex environment so that quality instruction becomes the rule rather than the exception. If they are to do so, however, they must devote a great deal of time to diagnosing the instructional needs of their students and, based on this diagnosis, select and prepare the proper instructional treatment. This takes time. It takes time to evaluate the students' work, it takes time to consult with other professionals and with parents, and it takes time to design the lesson, develop materials, and prepare the instructional environment. This is just the time that must be spent on a routine, day-in, day-out basis. To be truly prepared, teachers must also spend time in professional development activities that keep them abreast of the latest information regarding best practices in education. They must also spend time developing the skills required by the new methods. This includes developing the skills necessary for the appropriate use of technology in the classroom and/or making the best use of newer curriculum materials and methods.

The time available for these professional activities, however, is just as limited as the time available for classroom instruction. Teachers are constantly on the go from the time they first arrive at school until they leave the building at the end of the day. The following scenario, developed by Linda Darling-Hammond of the Rand Corporation, provides additional insight into the time-pressured nature of the teacher's professional universe.

> Imagine that you are a high-school English teacher . . . you would like to impart to your students the joys of great literature and the

skills of effective communication. You have at your disposal a set of 100 textbooks for your 140 students. You cannot order additional books so you make copies of some plays and short stories, at your own expense, and you jockey with the 50 other teachers in your school for access to one of the two available typewriters so that you can produce other materials for your class. You stand in line after school to use the secretary's telephone to call parents of students who have been absent or are behind in their work.

You spend roughly 12 hours each week correcting papers, because you believe your students should write a theme each week. You feel guilty that this allows you to spend only 5 minutes per paper. You spend another 6 hours each week preparing for your five different sections, most writing up the behavioral objectives required by the system's curriculum guide, which you find meaningless and even counterproductive to your goals for your students. You do all of this after school hours, because your one preparation period is devoted to preparing attendance forms, doing other administrative paperwork, and meeting with students who need extra help. Between classes, you monitor hallways and restrooms, supervise the lunch room, and track down truants (Darling-Hammond, 1984, p. 174).

The situation has changed little since the scenario was written over a decade ago. Perhaps the biggest change, other than standing in line waiting for a computer rather than a typewriter, is that, on the average, the amount of time the teachers spend writing behavioral objectives has decreased. However, the time that was once spent preparing objectives is now used for more contemporary instructional initiatives such as the organization and evaluation of portfolios and the development of individual educational plans.

What *has* changed in the last decade is that we now have more children at risk of school failure, more children living in poverty, and the academic demands being placed on our students are on the increase. These changes threaten to overwhelm our educational system, especially if teachers are not given the time they need to meet these changing conditions. In the words of the NEA:

Profound changes that are occurring in society, the home environment, and the workplace have invaded schools, increasing exponentially the number and kinds of interactions teachers must conduct with children on a daily basis. The time burden looms large as schools are forced to extend their custodial responsibilities for children to include performing social services previously assigned to human services agencies, as well as confronting the myriad problems concerning health, safety, and well-being inherent in today's very needy school populations. These time demands must be factored with the increased time pressures teachers face as they address the burgeoning amount of knowledge and skills today's students are required to master (NEA, 1994, p. 6).

The increase in the number and types of interactions that are essential for quality of instruction demands that teachers be given the requisite time needed for the diagnosis and treatment of the instructional needs of their students. If teachers are to address the unique needs of children at-risk while at the same time challenging all children academically, they must be given time for planning and evaluation, for collaborating with their colleagues, for professional development, and for interactions with parents.

But in such a complex environment where actions are often controlled by the clock, how do teachers find the time to diagnose the needs of each individual child and then design and develop lessons that meet these needs? How are they able to present lessons that utilize the knowledge they have regarding sound instructional practices when the clock keeps such a tight reign their actions? How do they find the time to monitor the instructional performance of each student and provide the individual feedback that is an essential part of the teaching process? Many schools are currently struggling with these issues, and a number of different strategies have been developed in an attempt to ease the problems associated with insufficient professional time.

STRATEGIES FOR RELIEVING PROFESSIONAL TIME PRESSURES

Among the more common strategies used for reducing the time pressure faced by teachers are: (1) releasing the teacher from classroom duties and thus freeing up some of the teacher's time, (2) restructuring or rescheduling professional time, (3) making better use of the time available, and (4) buying more of the teachers' time (Watts and Castle, 1992).

Release Time

The strategy of *release time* calls for teachers to be "freed" from classroom duties so that they have more time for other professional responsibilities. This occurs routinely at the high-school level through the use of planning periods. During certain periods of the day or week, teachers are assigned to a prep period, as opposed to an instructional period. At the elementary level, teachers are provided with release time when their students attend "special classes" such as music, art, gym, library, and computer lab. During this time, the classroom teacher is "free" to perform professional obligations that do not involve direct contact with the children. The routine scheduling of release time is analogous to the study hall where students spend the equivalent of one class period reviewing material that has been taught in their classes and preparing for upcoming classes. Teachers perform similar tasks during their prep periods or routinely scheduled release time. This time is used to work on lesson plans, grade papers, prepare for parent teacher conferences, fill in reports, and so on. The time is also used as a break in a very hectic schedule and provides time for the teacher to "catch his or her breath."

Freed-up time that is scheduled and occurs on a routine basis is often considered by teachers to be almost sacrosanct, so much so that they tend to become very upset if something occurs that deprives them of this time. This is understandable, because teachers depend heavily on planning time and often have this time scheduled extremely tightly. When the time is taken away, and especially when it is taken away without notice, it can cause great havoc in the classroom, particularly if the teacher had planned on using the time to review the lesson plan, prepare instructional materials, or arrange the instructional environment for the next class period.

At both the elementary and secondary level, the teacher's time may be "freed-up" by having teaching assistants or volunteers take over responsibilities that have in the past been assigned to the teacher. Teaching assistants or aids may be used to "free" the teacher from routine task that require little, if any, professional skills. These include tasks such as taking attendance, collecting lunch money, monitoring halls, bus and lunchroom duty, and recess. Although none of these activities take an exorbitant amount of time, being freed from such tasks does provide the teacher with extra minutes that can make the difference between a successful instructional day and a less-than-successful day. Once teachers have been provided with this kind of support, they will be extremely reluctant to give it up.

Occasionally a substitute teacher or even an administrator may relieve the teacher of his or her classroom duties for a short period of time. Such solutions tend to be temporary and ad hoc and are most often used when teachers need time for a one-time-only type of activity. Teachers are less protective of the ad hoc time because it is not provided on a routine basis and often occurs in an almost random fashion.

A strategy that is employed more frequently is the use of substitutes to release teachers from their classroom duties. Schools often provide time for teachers so that they may participate in nonclassroom directed professional activities. In the 1993–94 School and Staffing Survey, 48.2 percent of the public school teachers reported that they were provided with release time in order to participate in in-service or professional development activities.

Even though teachers report that they appreciate efforts to provide them with the much-needed additional time, they often are less than enthusiastic about release time strategies that, rather than relieve their time pressure, frequently increase it. As one teacher put it: "First I have to plan for the substitute. That takes time. Next I have to find out what the sub did while I was out of the class. That takes time. And then, nine times out of ten, I have to go back over the material just to make certain the students really understood it. In the end, I use more time to prepare for the sub than I gain by being released. The only way to avoid all this extra time is to have the sub do some kind of activity that it makes no difference if the kids' do it or not. But then this really becomes a waste of everybody's time—the kids time, my time and the substitute's time. It's a no-win situation."

In many instances, as the teacher's comments illustrate, rather than "freeing-up" their time, teachers find that they must spend *more* time preparing for the time that they are to be away from the classroom than they would if they stayed with their class. Not only must they plan for their own activities, they also have to plan the activities for whomever is taking over the class. In addition, teachers often find that quality instructional time is sacrificed because it is more practical to assign "busy work" or tasks that keep the students occupied and out of trouble. In addition, teachers often report that they "feel guilty" when nonroutine release time strategies are used, because they feel their primary obligation is to their students and when someone else is in the classroom they are not always sure that the obligation is being met.

Restructuring of Professional Time

A second set of strategies that has been recommend as a way of relieving or reducing the time pressure felt by teachers is to *restructure or reschedule* teachers' time. For instance, a district may decide to increase the amount of time that students spend in school four days a week. On the fifth day, students would be released early and teachers would use this time for planning. Prior to the implementation of the new schedule, the students' school day runs from 8:45 A.M.. to 2:45 P.M. This means that the students are in school six hours a day, five days a week. Once the new plan is implemented, the students' day would run from 8:30 to 3:15 on Monday, Tuesday, Thursday, and Friday. For these four days, the school day would have been increased by 45 minutes. On Wednesday, however, the students are in school for only three hours, from 12:45 to 3:15. As a result, the students would spend the same amount of time under both the old and new schedule—a total of 30 hours per week.

The total amount of time that teachers spend in school would also remain unchanged. Under the old schedule teachers were required to be in school from 8:30 to 3:30, Monday through Friday. With the new schedule, the teacher's day begins at 8:15 on Monday, Tuesday, Thursday, and Friday. As a result, teachers are in school 15 minutes longer each day, for a total of one hour for the four days. On Wednesday, however, they would not be required to report until 9:30, so the total amount of time that teachers are required to be in school each week remains the same under both schedules.

The advantage of the new schedule is that it allows for a longer block of planning time in which teachers can plan together. The block comes from shaving 15 minutes off the beginning of planning time and an additional 45 minutes at the end of the day. The restructured schedule *does not* provide for additional professional time, just a reallocation of the time available. In fact, many teachers may feel that they still need at least a half hour of planning time before school to prepare for the teaching day, and that 15 minutes at the end of the day is not long enough to straighten the room, let alone meet with students who need extra help, grade papers, consult with colleagues, and do all of the other things that must be done. As a result, the restructured schedule may actually increase the amount of time that teachers spend at school and/or on school work during the evening hours, ultimately adding to the time pressure on the teacher rather than relieving it.

Another approach that can be used to restructure the professional day calls for the "banking" of time. The amount of time spent in one activity is reduced and then "banked" for later use as professional time. For instance, the lunch hour might be reduced from 45 to 35 minutes. This saves ten minutes a day, or 50 minutes a week. The time saved is added to end of the day, one day a week. This allows students to be released 50 minutes early one day each week without losing any school time. Theoretically, time can be shaved from study halls, recesses, and/or time between classes.

Often strategies that call for a restructuring of the professional day also call for the instructional day to be increased during at least part of the week. One argument that is often presented in opposition to strategies of this type is that the longer instructional day is both mentally and physically taxing, and therefore it is more difficult for the teacher to complete the tasks that are normally completed after the school day is over—activities such as grading papers, writing lesson plans, preparing materials for the next day's instruction, and meeting with parents and/or other teachers. This is not a new argument. In a booklet published by the American Association of School Administrators in 1970, it was observed that:

> During the regular school year teachers are appropriately and rightfully devoting almost all of their time and energies to working directly with pupils. In the hours immediately after school closes, teachers are too tired to be very imaginative and creative; in the evenings they have homework to do such as correcting papers and making last-minute preparations for the next day's teaching assignments (American Association of School Administrators, 1970, p. 7).

For some this argument may seem rather far-fetched, because the average work day in this country is eight hours (nine if you include a lunch hour) and yet teachers spend approximately seven hours a days at school, including the lunch hour. However, it is important to understand that not all of the teacher's work is completed on the school premises or within the confines of the school day. According to the 1996 School and Staffing Survey conducted by the U. S. Department of Education, the typical teacher spends an average of 45.2 hours per week on professional duties even though they are required to be on the school premises only 33.3 hours a week. Also, teachers get very few breaks during the school day, and they spend most of their day with students in a time-pressured environment. Such conditions contribute to teachers being physically drained and mentally exhausted at the conclusion of the instructional day.

The restructuring of the school schedule does not necessarily require that the students spend less time in school, but it often appears to the casual observer that the students aren't spending as much time in school when they are released from school an hour early one day a week. This frequently leads to confusion among the general public regarding the impact of the restructured schedule on the amount of time students spend in school. As one rather irate parent put it: "You're telling us there isn't enough time in the school day to do what needs to be done, and then ask us to give you some of this limited time so you can decide what to do with the even smaller amount of time that is left. It just doesn't make sense." One way to reduce this criticism is to initiate a public relations campaign prior to the start of the new schedule. To be effective, the campaign must go beyond informing parents and inform the general public as well. After all, there are many "empty nesters" who help to pay the tax bill and they too have a right to be informed about what is happening in their schools. Also be aware that even though a public relations campaign may reduce some of the criticism of a restructured program, it is unlikely that it will eliminate it altogether.

Even when parents understand that the amount of time students spend remains relatively stable, they may still be upset with the restructured schedule, especially if it interferes with arrangements they have made for child care. This is especially true if the elementary and secondary schools go on different schedules, which is often the case. One way to reduce this concern is to offer a program similar to the before- and after-school programs that were discussed earlier. This will not, however, completely reduce the criticism, especially if there is any kind of a fee associated with the program. Parents may interpret this to mean that they are now having to pay for services that were once free, and this is likely to result in even greater dissatisfaction with the program.

Although restructuring school time to allow for longer blocks of planning time may appear to be a recent innovation, the strategy was used as early as

1935 in Winchester, Massachusetts. Elementary students were released from school just before lunch on Wednesday afternoons. The teachers stayed at school and used the afternoon for planning and other professional activities. Students who needed extra help because they had been sick or because they were having trouble with a subject could (and often were required to) return to school so that they could receive the special help they needed. Teachers then took turns working with these students. Parents were very supportive of the program because they felt that the teachers were going out of their way to help the children who needed it most (Meggary, 1996). Of course, things were a little different in 1935 than they are today. Most of the mothers stayed at home and child care was not a problem. The majority of students walked to school and transportation was not an issue. Also, teachers commanded a degree of respect and their opinions were highly regarded by most parents. But even though some things have changed, others have not. Parents still appreciate when teachers go out of their way to help their child, and they support schools when they believe that what the school is doing is for the good of their child. If parents believe that the school day is truly being restructured to meet the needs of their children, they will support it regardless of whatever arguments are set forth against it.

Making Better Use of Teachers' Time

A third set of strategies that is often used to solve the professional time dilemma revolves around finding ways to *make better use of the teacher's time*. The process begins by attempting to answer two basic questions: "What are teachers doing that they don't need to be doing?" and "Are there any tasks, duties, or responsibilities that could be organized differently so that they require less time?" The focus is on using time more efficiently.

Most teachers find ways to save time on their other professional duties. Some teachers become very good at doing two things at once (e.g., grading papers while attending a faculty meeting) or at finding ways to shortcut the grading process. They may develop strategies that call for them to use the same material year after year and thus reduce the amount of time they spend on lesson planning, preparing classroom materials, and designing bulletin boards.

Because of the time-pressured nature of the teaching job, developing shortcuts for routine tasks becomes almost a matter of survival. But the problem with many of these strategies is that, although they are effective in reducing the amount of time the teacher spends on the respective tasks, they do not actually make better use of the teacher's time. Grading papers during a faculty meeting may mean that the teacher is doing neither task very well. Last year's lesson plans may not be appropriate for this year's students, so using the plans may be a waste of both the teacher's and the students' instructional time. This is not to say that all such strategies are not necessarily ineffective or unsatisfactory, but when teachers are truly time pressured they find ways of relieving the pressure, and not all of these ways are good. And, as might be expected, some teachers are better at developing time-saving strategies than are others.

Members of the school community need to work together to identify and create strategies that will work for their specific environments. Some schools have found that they can reduce the amount of time that teachers spend in faculty meetings by having teachers use e-mail to communicate with one another and/or by providing announcements of upcoming events through written updates. Some schools have selected a group of teachers to handle administrative tasks for all the other teachers (e.g., calculating average daily attendance, setting up appointments with parents, filling out forms required by central administration). This is a strategy that should be used only with extreme caution. Teachers are not administrators—they are not paid to be administrators and most have not been trained to handle such responsibilities. Neither are teachers' clerks. Advanced training and education are not required to make appointments or to fill out most forms. When teachers' time is used in this way it does not make the best use of their time. Implementing a strategy where one or two teachers take over many of the "administrivia" tasks for the other teachers can serve a useful function—it can help to highlight just how much time teachers spend doing such jobs and what the nature of these jobs are. Once this is understood, steps can be taken to reduce and even eliminate the time teachers spend on these tasks.

Unfortunately, strategies that are designed to make better use of the teacher's time are seldom created as a result of a careful analysis of what has caused the problem originally. Instead, they often to fall into the category of "fire-fighting" and thus they may not always be as effective as they should be or need to be. One notable exception is the concept of differentiated staffing.

Differentiated Staffing

One strategy that is often proposed as a way of making the best use of professional time is differentiated staffing. The roles and responsibilities of the school staff are differentiated based on the skills and abilities of the individual staff members. Differentiated staffing is the rule rather than the exception in our schools and has been since we left the one room/one teacher schoolhouse. Many different types of workers are needed to run a school—principals, teachers, secretaries, custodians, bus drivers, cafeteria workers, to name a few. However, when differentiated staffing is used as a strategy for making better use of the teachers' time, teachers' roles are modified and different levels of teaching responsibilities are identified and assigned based on the modified roles. In a typical model, teachers are divided into instructional teams and each team is composed of a senior teacher, staff teachers, beginning teachers, student teachers or interns, and teaching assistants.

Senior teachers are full-year employees who have a minimum of five years of teaching experience and hold at least one advanced degree in education. Senior teachers assume the major responsibility for curriculum design, are expected to participate in professional activities at the local, state, and national level, and to become active members of the wider professional community. Although they do undertake some instructional tasks, the majority of the time that senior teachers spend working with students is spent in diagnosing students' needs and working with students who need special attention. Senior teachers are also responsible for the evaluation of team members, both individually and collectively. And even though most decisions are made in a collaborative environment, whenever there is disagreement over assignments, the senior teacher must make the final determination.

Staff teachers make up the largest portion of the professional staff and carry the bulk of the instructional load. To be considered a staff teacher, a teacher must have at least one year of teaching experience and most staff teachers have at least some professional training beyond the bachelor's degree. A staff teacher may have training and experience comparable to the senior teacher. Whereas the senior teacher spends a great deal of time in curriculum development, attending professional meetings, evaluating staff, and so on, the bulk of the staff teacher's time is spent in the classroom working directly with students. This is not to say that all of their time and effort is not spent on classroom activities; staff teachers are also responsible for course design and often serve as mentors for beginning teachers.

Beginning teachers are usually first-year teachers with very limited teaching experience. Although their responsibilities resemble those of a staff teacher, beginning teachers are usually assigned students with fewer problems. Beginning teachers work very closely with mentors. The mentor's job is to review and evaluate the teaching processes being used by the beginning teacher and to offer suggestions for improvement while providing encouragement and support.

In addition to their instructional duties, beginning teachers are often assigned the "administrative" duties of the classroom. These duties may include such things as calculating average daily attendance, scheduling appointments with parents, and so on. Although not responsible for curriculum or course development, beginning teachers will assist in both of these tasks as well.

Student teachers are considered to be members of the professional team. Their assignments vary throughout the course of their student teaching experience, but they do participate in the designing of courses, the development of curriculum, and the teaching of classes. They also participate in all staff meetings and in parent-teacher conferences.

Other members of the school's instructional staff are professional and non-professional team members, including librarians, special teachers (e.g., art, music, and physical education), counselors, teaching assistants, clerks, and technical assistants (e.g., computer technologists). The nonprofessional staff are under the direct supervision of the senior teacher and the members of this staff are assigned duties based on their skill and knowledge. The professional staff works with the senior teacher in a collaborative relationship to determine the best way to assign professional responsibilities and allocate professional time.

Before employing differentiated staffing as a strategy for making better use of professional time, one should be aware of some of the potential obstacles and drawbacks to such a strategy. A major drawback is that variable staffing programs tend to increase the instructional budget, for a couple of reasons. First, senior teachers are more expensive than regular teachers because they are paid for 12 months rather than for the customary nine months, and because the salary rate for senior teachers is usually higher than the salary rate of the regular teaching staff. A second reason for an increase in the budget is that aids are hired to perform tasks that are normally done by the teacher at no extra cost to the district. Of course, some would argue that when school districts use trained professionals to do lower-level tasks they are not getting "the most bang for the buck," so even though the budget may be lower, the actual cost of services is higher.

A common obstacle to the successful implementation of differentiated staffing is the potential for professional jealousy among the teaching staff. The jealousy grows out of the recognition that being appointed a senior teacher is a way of acknowledging one's professional accomplishments. Faculty members may become resentful if they believe the professional accomplishments of one teacher have been acknowledged while the others have been ignored. Professional jealousy may also present itself when the teachers believe that one teacher has been given more power than the others. The likelihood that professional jealousy will become an issue appears to be strongest when the members of a team have taught together before, several teachers have the same level of training and expertise as the senior teacher, or more than one teacher expresses an interest in the senior teacher position. Frequently, this problem can be alleviated by having team members select their own senior teacher or by having the teachers alternate the position from year to year. At the very least, all teachers should be informed about the process used for selecting the senior teacher and each teacher's strengths should be acknowledged as an integral part of the process.

Another obstacle to the successful implementation of differentiated staffing is one that is almost the complete opposite of the one just mentioned. The teachers in a particular building may be unwilling to accept the role of senior teacher. When teachers are placed in the role of senior teacher against their will, they often become resentful and take their resentment out on other members of the team. In many instances, the senior teacher is not even cognizant of what he or she is doing. When this happens, soon everyone on the team becomes dissatisfied with the arrangement. Building a strong support system for senior teachers can go a long way toward reducing the negative effects of this obstacle.

One additional obstacle that must be overcome if differentiated staffing is to be successful is the proper training of the senior teacher as well as other team members. When they first begin in their new role, many senior teachers do not possess the skills and knowledge that are required by the job. They may have no training on how to evaluate team members, on how to design curriculum for other teachers, and/or on how to maintain a balance between their teaching and administrative duties. Lack of skills in each of these areas can quickly lead to disaster for the team. The senior teacher may be unable to provide corrective feedback to a fellow teacher or may become "power hungry" and attempt to dictate approaches and instructional techniques that must be used by the team. The staff teachers may feel that the senior teacher is being given release time to take care of administrative duties and therefore refuse to do routine instructional bookkeeping. Of course, the danger always exists that the role of senior teacher will turn into junior administrator, with the senior teacher taking on fewer and fewer instructional tasks and more and more managerial tasks.

Differentiated staffing is more common than is generally recognized and has become even more popular in the last few years. Department chairs are common in the high school and the role and responsibilities of the chair are often similar to those of some of the senior teachers. Teams of teachers are now working together in the classroom in an attempt to better serve the student with special needs. First-year teachers are being placed in mentoring programs, and the use of teacher aids is on the increase. The most common problem associated with such approaches, from a time-related perspective, is the failure to recognize that the teaming of teachers and the differentiation of roles demands that teachers time be used in different ways. Until the changing time demands are recognized, acknowledged, and factored into the formula, differentiated staffing will not only fail as a strategy for making better use of teachers' time, but it will actually add to the problems of the time-pressured teacher.

Purchasing of Teachers' Time

The fourth set of strategies that is used to reduce the time dilemma faced by teachers involves *purchasing additional time* for professional duties. Extending the length of the teachers' school day or year would fall into this category, if the teachers are paid for this additional time. Also included in this set of strategies would be compensating teachers for the time spent on any additional work they do after school, on the weekend, or during summer vacation.

Paying teachers for the time they spend on school-related activities that go beyond the expected or contractual responsibilities is not a new or unusual strategy. In the 1993–94 School and Staffing Survey, 34.9 percent of the public school teachers surveyed reported that they received "additional compensation from their school or school district for additional responsibilities such as coaching, student activity sponsorship, or teaching evening classes." In the same survey, 17.2 percent of the teachers reported that they received additional compensation for school related work during the summer (see Table 11–4).

TABLE 11–4   Percentage of full-time public school teachers who received various types of compensation in addition to their regular salary, by state: 1993–94

	Other school-year compensation[1]	Summer supplemental salary[2]	Non-school income[3]	Other earned income[4]
TOTAL	34.9	17.2	24.8	13.9
Alabama	15.6	11.6	24.8	3.4
Alaska	41.3	11.2	30.0	16.5
Arizona	36.1	19.8	27.0	14.9
Arkansas	19.9	13.8	25.6	4.1
California	34.1	21.9	20.6	8.9
Colorado	37.4	11.9	25.5	5.5
Connecticut	27.7	15.2	22.4	4.9
Delaware	34.2	19.0	24.9	6.3
DC	29.9	26.9	25.7	4.9
Florida	32.5	30.1	22.1	6.9
Georgia	24.4	11.9	22.6	14.4
Hawaii	23.0	21.9	23.1	5.4
Idaho	35.2	15.5	33.2	9.8
Illinois	44.0	19.8	25.9	6.1
Indiana	39.7	23.3	23.4	7.4
Iowa	41.1	19.9	29.0	34.8
Kansas	53.2	18.6	32.7	5.7
Kentucky	40.9	17.8	19.6	4.9
Louisiana	20.9	11.0	20.8	13.7
Maine	36.0	12.6	32.0	7.6
Maryland	34.3	20.1	31.9	6.3
Massachusetts	28.3	14.8	31.6	9.9
Michigan	35.1	11.1	20.6	6.7

TABLE 11–4   *Continued*

	Other school-year compensation[1]	Summer supplemental salary[2]	Non-school income[3]	Other earned income[4]
Minnesota	40.3	18.8	30.5	3.9
Mississippi	14.6	12.5	22.7	3.0
Missouri	43.7	22.2	29.0	18.4
Montana	42.4	13.0	37.3	5.3
Nebraska	52.2	13.6	31.1	50.1
Nevada	33.2	13.7	23.1	12.1
New Hampshire	29.6	14.5	36.4	5.7
New Jersey	37.5	19.6	27.3	6.1
New Mexico	34.3	13.7	26.7	5.1
New York	35.3	20.9	23.5	12.4
North Carolina	31.4	17.1	25.6	59.4
North Dakota	46.0	18.5	35.9	3.4
Ohio	43.1	11.1	23.8	5.2
Oklahoma	42.5	15.0	27.3	6.7
Oregon	36.3	9.1	25.4	4.4
Pennsylvania	35.2	9.2	24.1	4.9
Rhode Island	23.3	9.6	24.9	9.3
South Carolina	22.0	10.5	22.5	38.2
South Dakota	45.1	14.0	35.5	9.1
Tennessee	23.6	19.7	26.4	42.6
Texas	32.8	15.2	22.8	34.6
Utah	46.5	15.7	30.3	37.3
Vermont	25.9	17.8	32.4	3.0
Virginia	28.8	23.1	22.4	6.7
Washington	55.1	12.2	23.3	13.3
West Virginia	26.1	9.7	20.9	8.0
Wisconsin	45.2	20.9	31.1	3.5
Wyoming	46.6	16.5	27.5	5.4

[1]Includes additional compensation from their school o school system for additional responsibilities such as coaching, student activity sponsorship, or teaching evening classes.
[2] Includes teaching summer school or working in a nonteaching job at their own or any other school.
[3]Includes nonschool summer jobs and school-year jobs outside their school system.
[4]Includes all other earned income, such as a merit pay bonus or state supplement.

Source: U.S. Department of Education. National Center for Education Statistics. *School and Staffing in the United States: A Statistical Profile, 1993–94.* NCES 96-124, by Robin R. Henke, Susan P. Choy, Sonya Geis, and Stephen P. Broughman. Washington, DC: 1996.

Among the more common types of activities for which teachers receive extra compensation are coaching, sponsorship of student activities, teaching evening classes, teaching summer school, and working on revision of the school curriculum. It is unusual for teachers to receive additional compensation for routine instructional responsibilities such as grading papers, developing lesson plans, and/or preparing instructional materials. This is true even though these activities are essential for quality instruction and currently limited time is provided for performing these activities during the school day. Some would argue that because these activities have always been the teacher's responsibility they do not warrant extra compensation. On the other hand, as has been noted earlier in this chapter, teachers are now accepting more and more responsibilities and, in many cases, they are doing so without being provided the requisite time needed. As a result, much of the work spills over into the evening and weekend hours, and many believe that teachers should be compensated for this time.

In reality, compensating teachers for the extra time they spend outside of the classroom does little to address the problem of limited time. One teacher was rather adamant about this when she stated:

True, many teachers are underpaid. . . . But the problem is more than money. What the experts have missed is time . . . how it is being spent now and how teachers can spend more of it in teaching.

And she goes on to say:

The only way your child ever might get more from me is if someone— school boards, superintendents, principals, parent groups—helps me reorganize my day and reorder my priorities so I can save the time that now is being lost (Graham, 1985, p. 35).

Teachers are already spending an average of 12 hours per week outside of the school day working on school-related activities. Even if additional compensation were available, many would be unable to find time for the additional tasks that they are being asked to perform. The NEA is concerned that strategies that call for teachers to be compensated for time spent beyond the required school day contain an inherent danger because of the assumption that the time needed can be deducted from the teacher's personal time. What is really needed, according to the NEA, is "a reconceptualization of professional time for teachers with a professional salary commensurate with their responsibilities" (NEA, 1994, p. 14). Therefore, the NEA has strongly recommended that standard professional calendars be changed from 9 months to 12 months.

The idea that teachers need to be on a 12-month contract is not new. In 1970, the editors of the magazine *Compact* argued:

> Society has a considerable investment in every trained professional teacher. When there are thousands of students in desperate need of more and better education, society loses in many ways when they permit professionally trained people to clerk at the store, or work part time to keep the wolf from the door. The time has come when we should get away from assuming that public education is a part-time profession. It is a full-time job (Jensen, 1970, p. 8).

The authors of this quote argued that the 9-month contract was unfair to both society and to the teacher. The calendar is unfair to society because the return on its investment (trained teachers) is not as great as it could or should be. The calendar is unfair to teachers because it guarantees them a lower salary than other professions with comparable training and education and forces many teachers to seek part-time employment to supplement their incomes.

It is true that some teachers do supplement their school income by working at "other," nonschool-related jobs during the school year and/or throughout the summer (see Table 11–4). It may be that these teachers would prefer to work year round, but no one has actually surveyed these teachers to see how many of them would want to, or be willing to, forfeit these "other" jobs in order to spend more time on schoolwork. Neither has anyone surveyed the teachers who do not hold extra jobs to see if they would be willing to work the extra months in school.

Teachers' willingness or unwillingness to work a 12-month schedule is only a minor obstacle when compared to the obstacle presented by the large dollar tag that goes with the lengthened professional year. In 1993–94 approximately 2.6 million teachers worked in public schools and the average teacher earned a base salary of $34,153 for nine months (see Table 11–5). This means that on the average a teacher earned approximately $3,800 per month.

If you multiply this figure by the additional three months needed to make up the 12-month calendar, the average teacher would make an additional $11,400, resulting in a base salary of $46,500 a year. This calculation is only used for the purpose of illustration and the cost would vary from state to state and district to district. In addition, because averages of averages are being used, the figures appear to be more precise than they actually are. However, in terms of salary dollars only, they do provide a sense of just how costly it would be to extend the professional calendar.

Some would argue that teachers already are working approximately a 12-month year. If you multiply the hours the average teacher works each week

TABLE 11-5   Average base salary for public school teachers by state, 1993–94

State	Average teacher base salary ($34,153)	State	Average teacher base salary
Alabama	27,334	Montana	26,452
Alaska	45,754	Nebraska	25,582
Arizona	31,440	Nevada	33,692
Arkansas	26,290	New Hampshire	33,485
California	39,649	New Jersey	45,370
Colorado	32,310	New Mexico	26,737
Connecticut	48,142	New York	45,487
Delaware	37,329	North Carolina	27,348
DC	42,022	North Dakota	23,491
Florida	30,892	Ohio	33,754
Georgia	29,035	Oklahoma	26,371
Hawaii	35,059	Oregon	33,953
Idaho	26,233	Pennsylvania	41,065
Illinois	36,347	Rhode Island	40,212
Indiana	35,356	South Carolina	28,614
Iowa	27,213	South Dakota	23,405
Kansas	28,861	Tennessee	28,171
Kentucky	30,399	Texas	28,330
Louisiana	24,422	Utah	27,661
Maine	29,950	Vermont	33,326
Maryland	38,431	Virginia	31,000
Massachusetts	37,510	Washington	35,299
Michigan	43,018	West Virginia	29,872
Minnesota	34,682	Wisconsin	35,231
Mississippi	24,485	Wyoming	28,706
Missouri	27,946		

Note: The averages were computed using only teachers with that type of compensation; consequently, the average in total earnings does not equal the sum of the averages for the various types of compensation.

Source: Henke, R. P., Choy, S. P. Geis, S., & Broughman, S. P. (1996). *School and staffing in the United States: A statistical profile, 1993–94.* NCES 96–124. Washington, DC: U.S. Department of Education. National Center for Education Statistics.

(45.2) by the number of weeks in the school year (36), and then divide this number by 40 hours (average work week), you will find that teachers work an average of 10 to 10.5 months. Add the 4-week vacation that many salaried employees receive in other occupations and you find that the teacher is working the equivalent of 11 to 11.5 months per year. This argument can be used by two very divergent groups. The first group would extend the argument by saying that because teachers are working an 11- to 11.5-month year, their salaries should be increased to reflect the work that is actually being done. The second group would extend the argument by asking, "Why would we want to change the professional calendar to 12 months when this means that we will have to pay teachers extra for work they are already doing?"

Of course, one could argue that the second group has missed the point. The NEA is arguing that the extended professional calendar is necessary because of *new* expectations and demands that are being placed on the teacher's time. But wait! Is it possible that the NEA has missed the point also? How many new responsibilities can we expect teachers to accept when they don't have enough time for their current responsibilities? Would not the 12-month contract, accompanied by its increased demands, add to the time pressure that teachers already feel? It may be possible to relieve the day-to-day time pressure by moving the majority of the nonclassroom activities, such as curriculum design and professional development, to the summer months. But is it possible to compartmentalize the teacher's job? Can curriculum design, professional development, and school restructuring be accomplished in just three months each year, or will it be expected that activities begun in the summer will continue during the other nine months? Can activities designed to improve our schools be done in isolation of the students, or does the 12-month contract make it inevitable that students will also go to school year round? And perhaps the most important question of all: "Is it the assumption that the additional time provided for in the new calendar will relieve the time pressure felt by the teacher, or is it that the teacher will now have time to take on added responsibilities?"

Even as educators struggle with these questions, state departments of education have taken steps to address at least one facet of the problem—providing time for professional development activities. By the end of 1996, 39 states had made recommendations or mandates regarding the minimum number of days to be set aside for professional development (see Table 11–6). It appears that while full-year employment may be a concern for some time to come, the movement toward an extended professional calendar has already begun.

Problems Inherent in All the Time Strategies

The strategies presented in this section—release time, restructured time, better use of time, and the purchase of additional time—are not new or unique.

TABLE 11–6   Number of in-service training/staff development days recognized by individual states

State	Teacher in-service training/staff development requirements (Unless otherwise indicated, days/hours are minimum pupil/teacher contact days/hours)
Alabama	5 days[1]
Alaska	Up to 10 days (Included in 180 instructional days)
Arizona	LEA option
Arkansas	5–7 days
California	Up to 8 days (Included in 175 instructional days)
Colorado	Up to 24 hrs. (Included in minimum instructional hours)
Connecticut	18 hrs.
Delaware	5 days
DC	3 days (Included in 180 instructional days)
Florida	LEA option
Georgia	Up to 10 days
Hawaii	Up to 5 days
Idaho	Up 11 hrs.—kindergarten Up to 22 hrs.—grades 1–12 (Included in minimum instructional hours)
Illinois	Up to 4 days[2]
Indiana	LEA option[3]
Iowa	1 day
Kansas	LEA option
Kentucky	4 days
Louisiana	Up to 5 days
Maine	Up to 5 days
Maryland	LEA option
Massachusetts	LEA option
Michigan	1 day, 97–98; 2 days, 98–99; 3 days, 99–00; 4 days, 00–01; 5 days, 01–02 and each succeeding year[4]
Minnesota	No noninstructional day or hour requirements as of 96–97 school year
Mississippi	Up to 7 days
Missouri	LEA option[5]
Montana	3–7 days
Nebraska	10 hrs.
Nevada	Up to 5 days (Included in 180 instructional days)
New Hampshire	Up to 10 days
New Jersey	LEA option
New Mexico	Up to 3 days

TABLE 11–6   *Continued*

State	Teacher in-service training/staff development requirements (Unless otherwise indicated, days/hours are minimum pupil/teacher contact days/hours)
New York	Up to 4 days (Included in 180 instructional days)
North Carolina	Up to 20 days
North Dakota	2 days[6]
Ohio	Up to 2 days (included in 182 instructional days)
Oklahoma	Up to 5 days
Oregon	Up to 30 hrs. (Included in minimum instructional hours)
Pennsylvania	Up to 5 days
Rhode Island	LEA option
South Carolina	Up to 10 days
South Dakota	LEA option
Tennessee	5 days
Texas	5 days, 96–97[7]
Utah	LEA option
Vermont	5 days
Virginia	Up to 20 days
Washington	LEA option
West Virginia	3–5 days (2 days must be scheduled prior to January 1)
Wisconsin	LEA option
Wyoming	Up to 5 days

[1]In 1995, Alabama repealed legislation enacted in 1994 which would have phased in 180 days of instruction and 10 professional development days by the 2004–2005 school year.

[2]In Illinois, days not used for staff development must be added to the 176 instructional days.

[3]In Indiana, upon approval of the Indiana Department of Education, schools may accumulate student release time to use for staff development, performance-based accreditation, or program development activities. Schools must have a base 105% of the required minimum instructional time before they can accumulate release time (at least 945 hrs. per year, elementary; 1,134 hrs. per year, secondary). Students must be released on 6 occasions for a minimum of 30 minutes and a maximum of 2.5 hours a day. Release time may not exceed 15 hours per school year, even if a school accumulates more than 15 hours.

[4]In Michigan, the scheduled increase in days/yours will not go into effect if the percentage of growth in the basic foundation allowance in a state fiscal year, as compared to the preceding year, is less than the percentage increase in the average consumer price index. MICH. COMP. LAWS ANN. 380.11284 (West 1996 Supp.)

[5]In Missouri, the length of the school day may vary for 3–7 hours, giving districts the flexibility to schedule release time for in-service training.

[6] North Dakota schedules two days for a teachers' convention. According to the state's Department of Public Instruction, department policies promote in-service training by acknowledging schools that have extended their school year for in-service training and by recommending that some time be set aside for in-service training, which may require the shortening of some days.

[7]In Texas, for the 1997–98 school year, the teacher in-service training days will be determined by a formula. The results will be at least 5 days of in-service training. TEX. EDUCATION CODE ANN 21.401 (b) (West 1996 Special Pamphlet).

Source: Used with permission of the Education Commission of States, 1996.

Many have a long history of attempts and failures. The strategies tend to be temporary, ad hoc, and/or expensive (e.g., hiring of substitutes or purchasing additional teacher time). More importantly, strategies that increase the amount of time available for nonclassroom duties are almost always accompanied by increased demands upon the teachers' professional time and thus usurps the time that has been gained.

The problem of providing additional time for nonclassroom duties is further complicated by the manner in which the role of the teacher is viewed. According to Watts and Castle:

> The traditional view of the teacher's work is governed by the idea that time with students is of singular value. This view rests on the instructional premise that teachers are deliverers of content and that curricular and pedagogical planning and decision making rest at higher levels of authority, and that professional development is somehow not related to improving instruction (Watts and Castle, 1992, p. 3).

In other words, strategies that take the teacher out of the classroom often compete with the teacher's sense of professional obligation. A teacher is, according to the definition given by *The Random House College Dictionary*, "a person who instructs." This then is the fundamental role of the teacher, yet how can a teacher instruct when he or she is away from his or her students? Of course, the teacher is also a highly trained professional whose job is to facilitate learning. This requires that teachers spend time away from their students planning lessons, developing instructional materials, reviewing student's progress, communicating with parents, and making improvements to the learning environment. It also requires teachers to spend time updating their professional skills and knowledge. Although teachers understand the importance of these different roles, many, if not all, teachers still feel that time spent with their students is the most important time spent on professional duties. Would we have it any other way?

SHORTAGE OF TEACHER TIME: IS IT GETTING WORSE?

Even though there are numerous indications that teachers have taken on additional roles and responsibilities, the amount of time they spend each week on school-related activities has changed very little since at least 1961 (see Table 11–1). Three possible explanations for this are: (1) the responsibilities of today's teacher are no different than they were in 1961, (2) the teacher's schedule and/or workload has been restructured so that more time is available for professional nonclassroom responsibilities, or (3) the teacher's time was already being used to the maximum in 1961 and there is no more time to give to the additional responsibilities.

Responsibilities Unchanged?

Many of the "new" roles and responsibilities are ones that the teachers of yesterday accepted as being an integral part of their jobs. The difference is that the these roles and responsibilities have become more complex. For example, consider the task of planning a lesson to teach the concept of family. In 1961, the typical school was part of a neighborhood school system in which most children spent eight years of their lives, so it was not unusual for teachers to have children and even grandchildren of former students in their classrooms. Today, children are bused from many different neighborhoods, and classrooms are composed of children from different cultural backgrounds. Some may live in homes with extended families, some may live with a single parent or with a grandparent, and some may live in homes with single-sex parents. There may be children from three different marriages in the same household. Some children will have been born out of wedlock and others will have been conceived through artificial insemination. How then does a teacher prepare a lesson to teach the concept of family that will build on the personal knowledge of the students and at the same time not offend at least one group of parents in the process? At the very least, the teacher will need to take the time to find out how the curriculum defines family and then analyze how this definition melds with the cultural realities within the classroom. As a result of the analysis, the teacher may find it necessary to develop new instructional aids that are less offensive to a particular group of students, or to find out from other teachers how they have taught the concept. In all likelihood, none of these time-consuming steps would have been required by the teacher in 1961. This is just one example of the time required to teach one rather "simple" concept!

Another example of how the teacher's responsibilities, although referred to in the same terms, have actually become more complex is also from the area of lesson planning. In the 1960s and early 70s, "teacher proof" textbooks were the rule. Teachers of reading, for instance, were provided with a teacher's guide in which each lesson was planned out in great detail—in such detail, in fact, that teachers were actually given the words they were to use when presenting the lesson. Today, many schools have moved to a literature-based reading program that provides general guidelines for instruction but allows for a great deal of discretion on the part of teachers. This not only permits but requires the teachers to use their professional expertise, which is what many would say they are being paid for. The problem is that it takes longer to prepare the lessons under the new approach and the process is much more laborious than it was 30 to 40 years ago.

Numerous other examples could be provided of how the responsibilities of the teacher have become more complex and more time consuming. The increase in the number of children considered at-risk, the movement toward school reform and site-based/collaborative management, providing education in the least restrictive environment, and the ever-increasing number of reports that must be completed in order to comply with state and federal laws all add to the ever-increasing complexity of the teacher's job. The net result of the increased complexity is that it now takes longer to do the tasks that were once considered a routine part of the teacher's job.

Teachers' Time Restructured?

It is possible that even though the job became more complex, teachers weren't required to spend more time on professional duties because their schedules and/or workloads had been restructured and, as a result, they had more time during the school day to do tasks that they normally reserved for after school or weekends. The data necessary to confirm whether teachers were allocated more time for nonclassroom professional duties is difficult, if not impossible, to obtain because the amount of time provided for nonclassroom professional duties has been left to the discretion of the individual school districts. Data collected by the U. S. Department of Education do indicate that the average number of nonteaching days provided during the school year remained fairly consistent from 1966 through 1991 (see Table 11–1). However, the data tell us nothing about how the time during the work days is actually spent. It may be that the teacher's instructional load was reduced, thus allowing more time for planning within the framework of the instructional day. This seems likely, because teachers' unions have become much more influential in the last 25 years and one of their major objectives has been to improve the working conditions of teachers. As part of this initiative, the unions have pushed for contracts that included additional planning time for teachers. In 1991, the director of labor relations for the Michigan Association of School Boards noted that, "virtually every round of teacher contract talks brings a call for more planning time" (Wilkins, 1991, D4).

Time Exhausted?

It is possible that teachers had expended all of their time in 1961 and therefore had no more time to give in 1991. You may recall the earlier quote in which the American Association of School Administrators (AASA) asserted that, " immediately after school closes, teachers are too tired to be very imaginative and creative; in the evenings they have homework to do such as correcting papers and making last-minute preparations for the next day's teaching assignments" (AASA, 1970). This implies that teachers were already spending all of the time they could afford, both physically and mentally, on schoolwork. They were using the time before and after school and on weekends in order to meet their professional obligations and there was simply no more time available. This contention is supported by the work done by James Stigler and Harold Stevenson (1991) who, based on extensive field research, found that teachers in Taiwan spent an average of 9.1 hours per day or 45.5 hours per week at school. Teachers in Japan spent and average of 9.5 per day or 47.5 hours per week. During this same time period, the American teacher was working an average of 47 hours per week. Because there is such a small variation among the three countries in the amount of time teachers work, there is support for the claim that teachers in 1961 were already working to their full time-potential and had no more time to give.

Without the data to support one view or the other, it is difficult to determine whether the current shortage of teacher time is worse than it was 30 or 40 years ago. Unlike the extensive research that has been conducted on how teachers spend their classroom time, very little data have been collected on how teachers spend the remainder of their professional time. The shortage of data in this area will become more critical as the teacher's take on additional nonclassroom duties and unions push for additional time compensations that ultimately result in additional cost. Justifying these costs to the general public will be difficult if the public continues to perceive the teacher's role as unchanged from when they were in school. Until schools are able to provide the data that clearly delineate how professional time is being used and its impact on student achievement, we can expect this to be a hotly contested issue for some time to come. But even as the argument continues, we must remember, it is the teacher's implementation of the instructional processes that has the greatest impact on time and learning in the classroom, and all of the time and learning issues and concerns are crystallized in the actions and reactions of the teacher. It is the teacher who makes the decisions about how to allocate time within the instructional period, who assigns the instructional tasks, and who monitors the students' performance. It is the teacher who performs the learning diagnosis, interprets the diagnosis, and then prescribes the instructional treatment. All of this takes time.

REFERENCES

American Association of School Administrators. (1970). *9+: The year-round school*. Washington, DC: Author.

Darling-Hammond, L. (1984). *Beyond the commission reports: The coming crisis in teaching*. Santa Monica, CA: The Rand Corporation.

Graham, J. B. (1985). Serious about keeping good teachers? Help them reclaim lost teaching time. *American School Board Journal, 172*(1), 35–36.

Henke, R. P., Choy, S. P., Geis, S., & Broughman, S. P. (1996). *School and staffing in the United States: A statistical profile*, 1993–94. NCES 96-124. Washington, DC: U. S. Department of Education. National Center for Education Statistics.

Horn, R., & Chaikind, S. (1989). *Time allocation patterns of teachers in public and private schools: 1984–1986*. Washington, DC: National Center for Education Statistics.

Jensen, G. (1970). Does year-round education make sense? *Compact* 4(6), p. 4–6.

Johnson, M. (1985). How elementary teachers understand the concept of "on-task": A developmental critique. *Journal of Classroom Interactions, 21*(1), 15–24.

Meggary, G. (1996, March 6). Conversation with author. Cape Coral, FL.

National Education Association. (1994). *It's about time!!* Washington, DC: Author.

Otto, H. J. (1939). The organization of schools and classes. Chapter 4 in *The Implications of Research for the Classroom Teacher: Joint Yearbook American Educational Research Association and the Department of Classroom Teachers* (pp. 83–98). Washington, DC: National Education Association.

Smith, T. M., Young, B. A., Choy, S. Perie, M., Alsalam, N., Rollefson, M. R., & Bae, Y. (1996). *The Conditions of Education 1996, NCES 96-304*. U. S. Department of Education. National Center for Education Statistics. Washington, DC: U. S. Government Printing Office.

Stigler, J. W., & Stevenson, H. W. (1991, Spring). How Asian teachers polish each lesson to perfection. *American Educator*, 12–18, 43–47.

Watts, G. D., & Castle, S. (1992, April). *The time dilemma in school restructuring*. Paper presented at the meeting of the American Educational Research Association, San Francisco, CA.

Wilkins, D. (1991, July 21). Time for teachers: Uproar over planning time reflects an old argument. *Ann Arbor News*, p. D-4.

▶ 12

Time Is of the Essence

Time is a necessity inherent in all types of learning. If one hopes to learn, one must spend time in learning. This is a commonsense notion that is supported by research including that of Carroll, Bloom, and the BTES researchers. But in order to spend time learning, you must have time for learning. As a nation, we provide children with time for learning through the structure of formalized education, that is, through the school calendar and the allocation of time within that calendar. But simply providing students with time is not enough. Students must be willing to spend the time they are provided on the task of learning and to persevere with the task until they have mastered it. The degree to which students are willing to persevere will depend upon a number of factors, including their prior knowledge, their motivations, and their attitudes toward learning. These in turn will be affected by the degree to which the students feel safe and secure and, more importantly, the degree to which their basic needs of food and shelter have been met.

Even when students are willing to spend their allocated time on the task of learning, they still may not learn to the degree that is expected or desired. When students spend time on inappropriate tasks—tasks that are irrelevant to the learning goal—the time spent will fail to yield the degree of learning sought. For a task to be relevant, it must relate to the material to be learned, the type of learning outcome desired, and the specific learning needs of the student. When students spend time working on relevant tasks at their appropriate level of learning, they will experience success in learning and this often translates into "the joy of learning." Their successes provide the building blocks for the next level of learning and help to develop the students' self-confidence, which results in their willingness to persevere with a learning task for a longer amount of time.

In the formal processing of schooling, it is most often the teachers who make the decisions about the types of activities and learning tasks that are to be undertaken by the students. Before making such decisions, the teacher must first diagnose the needs of the students and then prescribe the instructional treatment based on the diagnosis. As important as these two processes are, it is not enough to simply diagnose and prescribe; the teacher must also present the lessons in such a way that the students comprehend what is expected of them and are motivated to stay on-task. The teacher must monitor the students' progress in case the prescribed treatment needs to be adjusted in any way. In addition, the teacher must provide the students with feedback that will ensure that they develop the ability to monitor their own learning. When these tasks are performed at their highest levels, quality instruction is guaranteed, but these instructional processes take time. If teachers do not have the time required, one or more of the processes get shortchanged, the quality of instruction suffers, and academic goals and expectations are not met.

Time alone is not enough to ensure quality instruction. Teachers must be highly skilled in the process of teaching and extremely knowledgeable about the content to be taught. Teachers must be forever learning, because the general knowledge base and our understanding of the teaching/learning process are constantly changing and expanding, and the teacher's knowledge and skills must keep pace with these advances. Just as the student in school must be provided with the opportunity to learn and be willing to spend the time needed to learn, so must teachers be provided with time to meet their professional responsibilities.

Learning in school is a function of the amount of time a student is willing to persevere with a relevant learning task that results in a high degree of success. The amount of time that a student spends is limited by the amount of time that is made available to the student through the school calendar and the allocation of that time within the classroom. The amount of time that the student needs and the amount of time the student is willing to spend are both affected by the quality of instruction that is received. The quality of instruction is dependent, at least in part, on how the teacher has used his or her professional time, both in terms of instructional processes and professional development. Time, therefore, is an essential, key element of school learning.

ELEMENTS OF SCHOOL TIME

There are many facets to school time, but most fit into one of the six major categories presented in Figure 12–1. The top of the diagram depicts the time elements related to the school. The bottom half represents elements related to the classroom. The first two categories in both the top and bottom of the diagram focus primarily on student time. The last category in each division focuses on teacher time. Teacher time is included in both the top (school time)

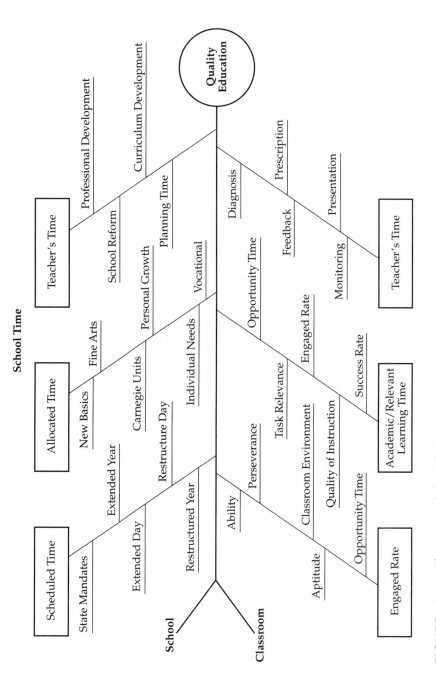

School Time

FIGURE 12–1   Elements of school time

and bottom (classroom time), because teachers spend almost as much of their professional time outside of the classroom as they do within it.

Figure 12–1 provides a global view of the aspects of school time but does not portray the depth of any one category. To depict the depths of the categories more accurately, each category would need to be divided even further. For instance, one of the subcategories under scheduled time is "restructured time." This category could be further divided into "year-round school," "block scheduling," and so on. Year-round school could be divided into "45-15," "Concept 6," "Quarter Plan," and so on. In addition, each of the other subcategories could be similarly divided, resulting in an almost infinite number of subcategories. The categories presented in Figure 12–1 are the major ones discussed in this book and were chosen because they are generally relevant in the educational arena of today, at least in a global sense.

The diagram also fails to depict the complexity of time issues. In fact, it would be next to impossible to actually capture the complexity of time-related issues in a diagram because categories within and across categories are linked. This means that a change in one element can be expected to create a concomitant change in another. For instance, if one of the states makes a change in the number of mandated days, it is almost certain that the change will have an effect on all of the other categories. In some instances, the effect may be very direct and easy to measure, and less direct and harder to measure in others. For instance, if the length of the school day were to be increased, it would be easy to show the impact of that change on the way in which time is allocated within the school day. What impact the additional minutes would have on students' learning could not be measured as easily.

When focusing on time as an agent of school improvement and/or reform, it is important to consider the depth and breadth of the issues. When considering the depth of the issues, the focus is on one category at a time. The degree to which each of the categories is subdivided will depend on site-specific conditions, the educational goals that are to be accomplished, and the decisions that must be made. When considering the breadth of the issues, the focus is on the "world view" of time issues, with the goal of understanding the relationship between each of the categories.

FACTORS THAT INFLUENCE SCHOOL TIME

On the surface, time appears to be a variable that is easy to measure and relatively simple to manipulate. When the school day or year is lengthened, there is no room for debate on how much time has been added. High school students can be required to take four years of math, and it can be rather quickly calculated whether a student has spent the required time in math. Teachers can alter the way time is used in their own classroom and then compare the use of students' time under the different methods. However, it can be difficult, it not impossible, to measure the direct impact of time on learning, because time is so intertwined with other aspects of schooling.

This intertwining of elements is further complicated because the total environment in which formal education exists is itself so complex. Economic constraints, social trends, political concerns, historical legacies, philosophical dispositions, the school curriculum, school policies, the characteristics of the students, and the expertise of the teacher all work together to shape the school environment and influence the impact of school time on student achievement. These zones of influence are presented in the diagram in Figure 12–2.

In the diagram, the levels of school time—scheduled time, allocated time, engaged time, and academic/relevant learning time—are represented by the lines of the circle, and the width of the circle represents the amount of time enclosed within each of the levels. It should be noted at this point that "Academic/relevant learning time" is being substituted for what previously had been referred to as "academic learning time." The reason for this rather subtle change is that the responsibilities of schools go beyond academic learn-

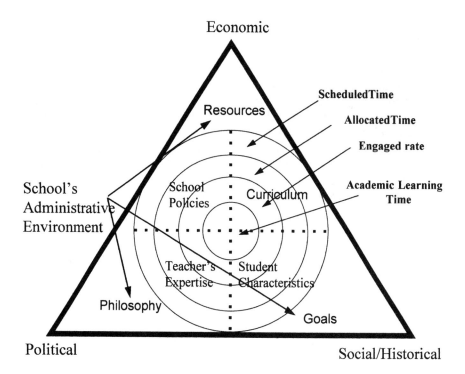

FIGURE 12–2   Factors affecting school time

ing and encompass other types of learning as well. The term "relevant" implies that time is spent on activities that are relevant to the type of learning that is expected, even if the learning outcome does not fall within the scope of academic learning.

Theoretically, it would be possible to have one large circle that represents all four levels. This would happen when all the scheduled time was allocated to relevant learning tasks and students spent the entire time working on these tasks with a high degree of success. In the reality of the classroom, however, it is virtually impossible to reach this educational utopia. However, it is almost always possible to increase the size of the inner circles so that academic/relevant learning time expands to the degree that it commands more of the time that is available.

Environmental factors within the classroom will determine the degree to which the inner circles can be expanded. Factors within the classroom environment—including school policies, the curriculum, the characteristics of the students, and the expertise of the teacher—work together to shape and direct the ways in which classroom time is used. Classroom factors can have both positive and negative impacts on the sizes of the circles. Positive effects push the circle(s) outward. Negative impacts have the opposite effect, making the circle(s) smaller. For instance, a school policy that allows for no extraneous disruptions during the instructional day would tend to have a positive effect on engagement time, meaning that the students would spend more time engaged in learning. A policy that allows parents free access to the classroom would tend to have a negative effect on the students' engagement rates.

In most cases, the impacts from classroom environmental factors are not as straightforward as the one just given. Take the case of teacher expertise, and consider by way of example two teachers who teach in different schools and have been assigned to teach classes in the computer labs at their schools. The teachers are good at motivating students and as a result their students spend the majority of their computer lab time on-task. However, neither teacher feels comfortable teaching the computer class because both lack basic computer skills. Because they do not feel confident with the subject matter, they often choose "easy, fun activities" rather than trying to teach the more difficult computer concepts and skills. One school recognizes the problem and decides to send its computer teacher to a week-long computer class. Because there is no one else who can teach the class, the students are sent to study hall during this week. The other school, faced with the identical situation, decides that it can't afford to waste a week of the students' time and the teacher is told to "just do the best job you can."

Which is the better decision in terms of academic/relevant learning time? To answer this question, consider the data presented in Table 12–1. Both teachers were allocated 50 minutes per day to teach computer skills and concepts. Prior to the workshop, the engagement rate of the students in both

TABLE 12–1   Time spent on-task in a fictional computer lab

	Week Prior to Workshop		During Week of Workshop		Week After Workshop	
	Class 1	Class 2	Class 1	Class 2	Class 1	Class 2
Length of class period						
Day	50	50	50	0	50	50
Week	250	250	250	0	250	250
Average time spent on-task						
Day	10	10	10	0	10	35
Week	200	200	200	0	200	200
Average time spent on relevant task						
Day	10	10	10	0	10	35
Week	50	50	50	0	50	175

Total time for the Three weeks

	Class 1	Class 2
Length of class period	750	500
Average time spent on-taks	600	400
Average time spent on relevant task	150	225

classes was high (approximately 80 percent of the allocated time). The time spent on academic/relevant learning was very low (only 20 percent of the allocated time). During the week of the workshop, the students in the Class 2 lost 250 minutes of allocated time but only 50 minutes of academic/relevant learning time. During the third week, however, their academic/relevant learning time increased by 250 percent. As a result, when total times are calculated for all three weeks we find that, even though Class 2 lost an entire week of class time, the total time they spent in academic/relevant learning was 1.5 times greater than the amount spent by the students in Class 1.

The answer to the question, "Which school made the better decision?" has become much easier to answer. Based on the figures provided, clearly the school that allowed the teacher to go to the workshop made the better decision. In this case, both school policy and teacher expertise impacted the students' academic/relevant learning time.

Many time-related strategies that are designed to improve the achievement of students have very little impact when actually implemented. Often this occurs because the strategies are based on only one aspect of the classroom environment or one level of school time and ignore the relationship with other aspects within the environment. In the example just given, one school focused only on student engaged rate and ignored all other aspects of the time and learning equation. At the end of three weeks, the students in this school did spend more time on "the task of using the computer" than did the students in the second school, but the students in the second school spent more time on "the task of learning computer skills." A subtle but critical difference!

In a similar fashion, strategies that call for increasing the school day by 15 minutes may add an hour each week, or approximately one week per year, and thus increase one level of school time—scheduled time. But if the strategy fails to take into consideration how to make the best use of this time so that academic/relevant learning time is increased, the increased time will have little impact on student learning.

Because of the complicated interactions of elements within the system two schools that are equal in all respects and share identical school calendars and allocate time within those calendars in exactly the same way still end up with extremely different levels of student achievements. This complicated interaction makes it impossible to determine what impact changing the school calendar would actually have on student achievement. Does this mean we should never increase the length of the school year or change the calendar in some other way? The answer is a resounding "NO!" But any strategy that uses time as a way of increasing student achievement must be made in light of the impact that the strategy will have on academic/relevant learning time.

The more we are able to increase time at the center of the diagram, (i.e., academic/relevant learning time), the greater and more positive will be the impact on student learning. Understanding the relationships between and among these elements is not always easy, but the better they are understood, the easier it becomes to shape and modify the impact of time on learning.

But how does one go about doing this? If the system is so complex, how is it possible to identify the essential elements that are worthy of treatment? How will you know if the strategy you are planning to implement will have an impact on learning? As you attempt to answer these questions, you may want to study the dilemma of a certain "Mr. Centipede."

The Story of Mr. Centipede

One day Mr. Centipede realized that it was taking him longer to make the trip from work to home than it did previously. This frustrated Mr. C. because he hated wasting time and so when he happened to run into Ms. Spider he asked if she were experiencing the same problem. "No," said Ms. Spider, "but maybe I can help. Let me watch you walk. You never know, there may be something wrong with one of your legs." And so Mr. Centipede began to walk back and forth. "Stop!" yelled Ms. Spider. "It's impossible for me to tell which of your legs you moved first and I must know that if I'm to help you." "Gee, I don't know," said Mr. C. "I don't think about it, I just do it." Ms. Spider shook her head and replied, "Well, until you know that, I'm afraid I can't help, but I do wish you luck." After the encounter with Ms. Spider, it took Mr. C. even longer to make the trip because he always had to stop and think, "Which leg should I move first?"

One day, Mr. Bee noticed the troubled look on Mr. C.'s face and asked if he could help. "Oh, I wish you would," said Mr. C. "It seems to take me so long to get anywhere these days." "Well, let's see," said Mr. Bee, "Which leg do you move first?" Of course Mr. C. had no trouble answering that question, after all he thought about it a lot. However, the next question threw him for a loop. "Why do you move that leg first?" asked Mr. Bee. Mr. C. intuitively knew the answer, but how could he explain it to a bee who flew from place to place? The only way he could think to respond was, "Because I've always done it that way. That's the way all centipedes do it." "Well," says Mr. Bee, "it doesn't make sense to me, there has to be a better way." And with that he left. Now the situation was worse for Mr. C. Not only did he have to think about which leg to move first, but he also worried that he might be moving his legs in the wrong sequence.

Mr. C. finally decided to ask some other centipedes how they went about moving their legs and he called a conference of all the eminent centipedes. At the conference, it became very clear that no two centipedes moved their legs in exactly the same way and it was not long until the other centipedes became just as concerned as Mr. C. After many hours of discussion, several of the centipedes got together and decided to call in a consultant, Mrs. Bug. Mrs. Bug spent many hours studying the problem before rendering her opinion that the reason that the centipedes were having so much trouble was that their legs were pulling against one another. According to Mrs. Bug, what the centipedes needed to do was to move the legs on the front half of their bodies and then move the legs on the back half. Mrs. Bug then left, leaving the centipedes with a bill for her services.

The centipedes had a heated discussion about Mrs. Bug's recommendation and finally half of the centipedes decided to try her suggestion. It wasn't long before everyone realized that the recommendation simply wasn't working and the centipedes sought the advice of other locomotion consultants. One consultant said that Mrs. Bug had been correct in her analysis, but the centipedes first needed to move the legs on the back half of their body before they moved the legs on the front half. Another consultant also agreed with Mrs. Bug, but said the that centipedes should move all of the legs on one side of the body and then move all of the legs on the other side. Unfortunately, these recommendations were no more effective than Mrs. Bug's had been and by this time the centipedes had spent a great deal of money on consultants. However, at this point they decided that they had no options but to bring in the most respected (and most expensive) of all of the locomotion consulting firms—the firm of Snake and Worm.

Mr. Snake and Ms. Worm took one look at the centipedes and nodded their heads very wisely. "The problem is quite obvious," said Mr. Snake. "You simply have too many legs. Get rid of some of them. Look at Ms. Worm and me. Or look at Mrs. Bug, or Mr. Ant, or even Ms. Spider. None of us have as many legs as you and we get around quite well. With that many legs you are unnecessarily burdened." The centipedes were astonished. This had to be the answer. Snake and Worm were right—no one else in the community had as many legs as the centipedes. And besides, Snake and Worm were well respected and it had cost the centipedes a fortune to seek their advice. They would be foolish not to accept it.

When it came time to cut off legs, no one could decide which leg to cut off first or how many legs they actually needed to cut off. After many hours of discussion, one centipede spoke up. "It seems to me that we don't have enough legs. Think about it. Mr. Bee doesn't need as many legs as us because he flies everywhere. Mrs. Bug, Mr. Ant, and Ms. Spider all have smaller bodies to carry around. Mr. Snake and Ms. Worm aren't expected to get into the tight places that we have to go. That's why they don't have as many legs as we do. We don't need fewer legs, we need more!" Slowly the other centipedes began to nod in agreement and said, "Yes, that is just what we need." They weren't sure how they were going to go about getting more legs, but they all agreed that more legs was what they really needed.

The centipedes agreed to form a committee that would develop a strategy for obtaining more legs. It was at this point that Grandfather Centipede arrived on the scene. He asked them what they were doing and when they told him he began to laugh. "Do you know why we have so many legs? Every two or three thousand years or so, a centipede decides that he isn't moving as well as he should, and before long he convinces the other centipedes that it's because they don't have enough legs. The wisest of the centipedes then finds some way for everyone to get more legs. This has gone on for thousands and thousands of years and if it continues we will eventually be known as millipedes! How did it start this time?"

Mr. C. explained that it was taking him longer to get to work and no one else seemed to be having that problem. Grandfather then looked at Mr. C. with total disdain and asked, "Do you realize that someone moved a large rock across your usual path to work. Mrs. Bee flies over the rock and Mr. Spider and Mr. Ant both go under the rock. Mrs. Bug doesn't even go near the rock. The rock doesn't change their paths to work at all. But for you, the rock presents a barrier and keeps you from getting to work as quickly as you did before. It has nothing to do with how many legs you do or do not have. If it really bothers you, just find a different way to go work!"

School time is analogous to the legs of the centipede. Obviously, the centipede must use its legs if it hopes to get anywhere. How quickly the centipede arrives at its destination will depend upon how its legs were used. Similarly, how far and how fast our students progress along the achievement continuum will depend to a great extent on how we use school time.

Continuing with our analogy, we find that the solutions that were offered to the centipede's problem are similar to those that are recommended as answers to the time dilemma faced by our schools. In the case of the centipedes, most of consultants suggested that he make better use of the legs he already had. This is similar to suggestions that call for a restructuring of the school calendar, reallocating school time, and/or developing strategies that reduce time off-task. Snake and Worm suggested that Mr. C. was unnecessarily burdened by all the extra legs. This suggestion parallels those of educational reformers who suggest that the schools have taken on too much and need to shed some of their nonacademic responsibilities. The last centipede to speak up in the meeting suggested that what the centipedes needed was more legs. This is comparable to suggestions of those who argue for a longer school year or day because they believe students need more time in school. Grandfather Centipede, in all his wisdom, brought a historical perspective to the problem that suggested that the legs weren't the problem at all, but rather it was the changing environment that affected the progress of the centipedes. So is it with those who suggest that time really isn't the cause of the school dilemma but rather a symptom of the problems that are caused by being unresponsive to the changing needs of the larger environment.

The trouble with blindly following the suggestions offered by "friends and experts" is that these suggestions can lead to unexpected and sometimes disastrous results. In the centipede story, Mr. C. was slowed down by the suggestions of his friends. However, the recommendations of the consultants led to the centipedes having difficulty even moving. If they had followed the recommendations of Snake and Worm, the results would have been disastrous because they would no longer have been centipedes. A rock in the road, a rather minor inconvenience that caused Mr. C. to take longer to get to and from work, came very close to creating a catastrophe because the centipedes failed to take into consideration the larger view and thus failed to recognize the real cause of the problem. What was even more threatening to the centipedes' progress was that everyone had failed to take into consideration what was working—their legs.

As we deal with the issue of school time, we must be careful to not repeat the mistakes of the centipedes. Seeking the advice of friends and experts can be helpful, but the advice should only be followed if we are able to evaluate the suggestions and recommendations and apply them in light of site-specific concerns and definable educational goals.

AVOIDING THE MISTAKES OF THE CENTIPEDES

How do you avoid the mistakes of the centipedes? By following one very critical rule: Never lose sight of the fact that learning, not time, is what is important. Any problem resolution or school improvement recommendation that focuses on time, and time alone, is doomed to failure or, even worse, to false successes. In the case of school time, when a strategy results in failure it simply means that it made no noticeable difference. When a strategy results in false success, it precludes us from seeking other alternatives and may even lead others to try out the "wonder cure." Therefore, in our attempt to follow our critical rule, we must be guided by ten basic principles.

1. Build your analysis on relevant data.
2. Look for connections among the various aspects of student learning, including time.
3. Seek out alternative solutions that go beyond a focus on time alone.
4. Set realistic expectations.
5. Be committed but don't be afraid to change.
6. Remember that seemingly simple solutions are often the most elegant.
7. Be wary of simple solutions.
8. Think in terms of interconnectedness.
9. Keep what is working.
10. Use time not only as an agent of change but also as a measure of success.

Principle 1: Build your analysis on relevant data.

Collect data that both support and refute the basic premise that is being set forth. Seek input from experts, but also rely heavily on the knowledge and opinions of those who know your system best and look for data that both support and refute any claims that are being made. Ask such questions as:

- Why are we focusing on school time? (Possible answers are: a problem has been identified and time is considered to be part of the problem and/or as a possible solution to the problem, a school improvement plan is being developed and a portion of the plan focuses on school time, or a change in school time has already been implemented and now needs to be evaluated.)

- What are the indicators that we need to focus on school time? (Look for existing data that can be objectively analyzed, such as test scores, the majority of teachers having difficult covering all of the content, or an upcoming change in state mandates)
- Who says there is a problem? (For instance, a cry for more planning time may be coming from the union leadership or from teachers and administrators.)
- How widespread does the problem appear to be? (A teacher who wants to improve the quality of instructional time may find that certain routines disturb certain students but not others. The degree of the effect may determine whether to change the routine.)

Principle 2: Look for connections among the various aspects of student learning, including time.

If you fail to heed this principle, you will be focusing on time and time alone, and as a result will violate the "critical" rule. Among the connections you may want to look at are those between:

- the way teachers are spending their time and the way students spend theirs,
- a student's past achievement in reading and the type of learning tasks the student is expected to perform, and
- student characteristics and how they impact the classroom environment and how the interactions of these two impact time usage.

Of course, the number of connections that you could consider are almost limitless. Which connections you focus on will depend upon the analysis that resulted from Principle 1.

Principle 3: Seek alternative solutions that go beyond a focus on time alone.

Manipulating school time is often an expensive proposition and is not always the best alternative for increasing student achievement. Therefore, you must ask the question, "Are there other ways of increasing their academic/relevant learning time that are less expensive?" For instance, the use of teacher aids might provide the teacher with more time to focus on instructional processes and thereby improve the quality of instruction that the students receive. Improvement in the quality of instruction will have a greater impact on the student achievement than will adding additional time—unless the problem is solely one of time, and that is seldom, if ever, the case.

If teachers don't have enough time to do all that is expected of them, one solution might be to provide them with additional time by using one of the strategies discussed in Chapter 11. But it may be that we are expecting too much of the teachers, and rather than providing them with more time, we need to restructure the job. The same is true for students. If the school year is not long enough to provide them with the time they need to achieve the level of learning we expect, then increasing the amount of time they spend in school may be the answer. An alternative, however, may be to reevaluate what we expect. This does not mean that we lower standards, it simply means that we evaluate which standards the students are required to meet and which ones are merely encouraged, but optional. By examining alternative approaches to problem resolution, we become more confident of our final decision.

Principle 4: Set realistic expectations.

Don't expect that adding ten minutes to the school day or one day to the school year will result in all of our students meeting and exceeding world standards. It won't happen! Don't give teachers more time for planning and then give them more to do and expect them to stop complaining about not having enough time. It won't happen! And don't expect that because you decrease the number of interruptions during the school day that students will spend more time on-task on relevant learning activities. It may happen, but there are no guarantees.

In some cases, unrealistic expectations are set because those who support a change exaggerate the expected outcomes from the change. They do so to convince "the powers that be" that the new approach is worth the disruptions it will cause. In other cases, exceptions are not clearly delineated at the beginning of the change process and, as the strategy is implemented, expectations develop that have little to do with the original goal. The most frequent reason for expectations not being met, however, is that as the time and learning strategies are being implemented, other changes are occurring simultaneously and these alter the effectiveness of the strategy.

Principle 5: Be committed but don't be afraid to change.

If you believe that some strategies for improving the time and learning ratio are betters than others, don't be afraid to say so. Back you opinion up with data and professional insights, and once you make a decision to try a new strategy, don't implement it with the idea that "if this doesn't work, we'll go back to the old way." If you're not convinced that a certain strategy is a good idea with sound merits, then don't attempt it.

No approach to improving the time and learning ratio is without drawbacks and none is perfect. The idea is to apply the best of strategies in our schools. But even the best have room for improvement and you should be willing to adapt and change the strategy as needed. Make certain, however, that you really have given it "the old college try" and that you are not simply giving up in the face of adversity.

Principle 6: Remember that sometimes simple solutions are the most elegant.

Sometimes a simple change can result in extraordinary results. Setting classroom routines that reduce the number of interruptions and making certain that the learning tasks that the students are engaged in are relevant to their learning needs are two rather simple solutions that can have great payoff in terms of academic/relevant learning. Simple solutions work best when they are implemented in direct response to an individual need, rather than in response to a global condition. The further out from the academic/relevant learning time circle, the more complicated the solution will become because of the number of people involved. Therefore, under normal circumstances, a simple solution will only work within the school building, and the further removed from the classroom, the less likely it is that the solution will have a major impact on student's learning time.

Principle 7: Be wary of simple solutions.

This principle appears to be in conflict with Principle 7, but is not. The principle simply says you must be cautious of any solution that seems to be too simple, because it probably is. This is especially true if the recommendation for change is coming from someone who doesn't know the system or if the recommendation comes with no hints at possible barriers to implementation.

Principle 8: Think in terms of interconnectedness.

Do all that you can to understand the interconnectedness of the various components of school time but act to change those elements that are within your sphere of influence. For instance, classroom teachers may have input into the way in which the school calendar is structured, but their greatest level of influence is within the classroom. Therefore, they should do all within their power to make certain that this time is used effectively and efficiently. In other words, they should micromanage the students' time. State Departments of Education, on the other hand, should avoid micromanaging. They should certainly understand the different levels of school time, the factors that influence the effective use of this time, and how time impacts student learning. However, to attempt to make rules and regulations that are directed toward individual classrooms and their use of time would be an ineffective strategy. They should, instead, develop policies and procedures at the macrolevel. Their focus should be on recurring problems that are more or less universal throughout their individual states, because that is where their spheres of influence lie.

Principle 9: Keep What Is Working.

This principle needs very little explanation. It simply says, in the rush to improve the use of school time, don't "throw the baby out with the bathwater." The trick, however, is not in understanding the principle, but rather in applying it. How do you know what is working and what isn't? You don't rush to judgment and you proceed directly to Principle 1!

Principle 10: Use time not only as an agent of change but also as a measure of success.

We know that there is a direct relationship between time and learning, and many of the strategies that are designed to improve this relationship focus on the manipulation of time. However, time can also be a measure of what is working and what isn't in terms of the other aspects of school learning. By examining how long it takes students to master a unit, we can gain insight into which instructional methods work best. By investigating how teachers spend their professional time, we can decide if the teacher's job needs to be restructured.

WHY EVEN CONSIDER SCHOOL TIME?

If learning, not time, is what is important, why do we focus on time at all? The answer should be obvious—time is essential if learning is to occur. Time has become an easy target for school reform because it is a concept all can understand. Number of days in a year and number of hours in a day are standardized quantities that are easily measured and communicated, and most adults can relate and sympathize with educators when they say, "There simply is not enough time to do all that is expected."

In addition, as Nancy Karweit has noted, the way in which time is used is one of the features of school learning than can be altered and, in her words, "how time is spent is not only an alterable feature of schools, it is alterable by the personnel who are accountable for its use" (Karweit, 1988, p. 32). Other educational writers have also provided us with insight into why school time is so important. Consider the following quotes:

> What emerges from the current calendar controversy may or may not involve calendar changes, but if the great debate can be the occasion for fruitful internal analysis and heightened public understanding it will have served well the continuing evolution of American education and American society (Schoenfield and Schmitz, 1964, p. 99)

> Bells divide the school day into standard segments of time for most (in some schools, all) school subjects. These look-alike periods get in the way of varying time with the purposes and activities of instruction and prevent the school from dealing effectively with individual differences among students and teachers (Swenson, Keys, & Trump, 1966, p. 5)

> If schools can improve the use of time, school workers can improve student learning (Bailey, 1992, p. 78)

> There has been a lot of talk about the importance of time in the determination of educational outcomes. . . . Certainly we should take a look at how time is being used and misused in our schools. It may indeed be the culprit that critics claim. As we test this possibility, however, we must keep in mind that time itself is valueless. It acquires value chiefly because it marks the expenditure of a precious commodity—human life. . . . Let us not seize too quickly remedies for our educational ailments that call for little more than adding days or hours to our present efforts (Anderson, 1984, p. 128)

> There are those that argue that the instructional time variables may have their use but that they can never capture any of the really important aspects of instruction. This is not true. Both a person's philosophy of education and commonsense understandings about the meaning of "quality instruction: can be examined using time variables (Berliner, 1990, p. 30)

> Before we know it, the superintendent will dictate we spend 30 minutes more a day on math and expect our achievement to skyrocket (Johnson, 1985, p. 15)

An important conclusion from the time-and-learning research suggests that balanced attention should be given to the quality as well as the quantity of time on task. It appears that increasing the amount (proportion or percentage) or time students spend on task is a necessary condition for improved academic performance. However, time alone may not be sufficient to influence achievement optimally (Wyne & Stuck, 1982, pp. 73–74)

The issues that revolve around school time are not new—most have been present since the beginning of the American educational system. The issues are so interwoven within the educational system that the accumulation of the attempted resolutions of the issues has become the very fabric of our schools. At times the fabric appears as a poorly designed patchwork quilt, with each patch having meaning in and of itself but little relationship to the other patches. At other times, the fabric resembles a child's favorite blanket. And just as the child carries the blanket as a form of security, so schools find security in allocating time in ways that produce the least resistance from the community as a whole. At still other times, the fabric of school time has the quality of a stadium blanket, rich in tradition, but of little substance. And at still other times, the fabric is comparable to a baseball tarp, attempting to cover all bases at once! The substance of the fabric may be similar to linsey-woolsey—harsh, coarse, and unpleasant to live with. Or it may be more analogous to cotton—practical, relatively inexpensive, and familiar to all. Of course, there are those who dream of a school schedule in which the allocation of time is as rich as silk—luxurious, elegant, and pleasurable to live with. But just as the typical household is unable to afford the luxury of a closet full of silk garments, so is the public school unable to afford the luxury of a silk-stocking approach to education. Choices must be made, and these choices are limited and shaped by economic constraints, social trends, political concerns, historical legacies, and philosophical dispositions. Within the classroom, the choices are shaped by the nature of the school curriculum, the characteristics of the students, school policies, and the expertise of the teacher. Taken together, these then make up the fabric of school time.

REFERENCES

Anderson, L. W. (Ed.). (1984). *Time and school learning: Theory, research and Practice.* NY: St. Martin's Press.

Bailey, W. J. (1992). *Power to the schools: School leader's guide to restructuring.* Newbury Park, CA: Corwin Press, Inc.

Berliner, D. C. (1990). What's all the fuss about instructional time? In Ben-Peretz, M. & Bromme, R. (Eds.), *The nature of time in schools: Theoretical concepts, practitioner perceptions.* New York: Teachers College Press.

Johnson, M. (1985). How elementary teachers understand the concept of "on-task": A developmental critique. *Journal of Classroom Interactions, 21*(1), 15–24.

Karweit, N. (1988). Time-on-task: The second time around. *NASSP Bulletin,* (February, 1988), 31–39.

Schoenfeld, C. A., & Schmitz, N. (1964). *Year-round education*. Madison, WI: Dembar Educational Research Services, Inc.

Swenson, G., Keys, D., & Trump, J. L. (1966). *Providing for flexibility in scheduling and instruction*. Englewood Cliffs, NJ: Prentice-Hall, Inc.

Wyne, M. D., & Stuck, G. B. (1982). Time and learning: Implications for the classroom teacher. *The Elementary School Journal, 83*(1), 67–75.

Name Index

Subject Index